THE DAILY STUDY BIBLE

THE LETTER TO THE ROMANS

H—I

THE LETTER TO THE ROMANS

The Rev. WILLIAM BARCLAY, D.D.

Lecturer in New Testament Language and Literature and in Hellenistic Greek in the University of Glasgow

THE SAINT ANDREW PRESS

EDINBURGH

Published by The Saint Andrew Press
121 George Street, Edinburgh 2
and printed in Scotland by
McCorquodale & Co., Ltd., Glasgow

First Edition	-	March, 1955
Second Edition	-	April, 1957
Second Impression	-	January, 1958
Third Impression	-	August, 1960
Fourth Impression	-	August, 1962
Fifth Impression	-	April, 1963

To
G. H. C. M.
WHOM IT IS MY HONOUR
TO CALL MY CHIEF
AND MY PRIVILEGE
TO CALL MY FRIEND.

GENERAL INTRODUCTION

IT may truly be said that this series of Daily Bible Studies began almost accidently. A series which the Church of Scotland was using came to an end, and another series was immediately required. I was asked to write a volume on *Acts*, and, at the moment, had no intention beyond that. But one volume followed another, until the demand for one volume became a plan to write on the whole New Testament.

The translation which is given in each volume claims no special merit. It was included in order that the reader might be able to carry both the text of the New Testament and the comments on it wherever he went, and that he might be able to read it anywhere. While I was making the translation, the translations of Moffatt, Weymouth, and Knox were ever beside me. *The American Revised Standard Version, The Twentieth Century New Testament,* and *The New Testament in Plain English,* by Charles Kingsley Williams, have been in constant use. Since its publication, I have consistently consulted *The Authentic New Testament,* translated by Hugh J. Schonfield.

I cannot see another edition of these books going out to the public without expressing my very deep and sincere gratitude to the Church of Scotland Publications Committee for allowing me the privilege of first beginning, and then continuing, this series. And in particular I wish to express my very great gratitude to the convener, Rev. R. G. Macdonald, O.B.E., M.A., D.D., and to the committee's secretary and manager, Rev. Andrew McCosh, M.A., S.T.M., for constant encouragement and never-failing sympathy and help.

As these volumes went on, the idea of the whole series developed. The aim is to make the results of modern scholarship available to the non-technical reader in a form that it does not require a theological education to understand; and then to seek to make the teaching of the New Testament books relevant to life and work to-day. The whole aim of these books is summed up in Richard of Chichester's famous prayer; they are meant to enable men and women to know Jesus Christ more clearly, to love Him more dearly, and to follow Him more nearly. It is my prayer that they may do something to make that possible.

FOREWORD

THERE are many people who would hold that the *Letter to the Romans* is the greatest book in the New Testament. Certain it is that no book has had a greater influence on the theology of the Protestant Church, and no book contains more of the quintessence of the mind of Paul. It is not an easy book to understand, for Paul is leading men in it into the deep things of the Christian faith, and he is often writing at such white-heat that the threads of his words are difficult to disentangle. But, difficult as it may be to study and understand, the rewards of studying it are very precious. And it is my hope that there will be many who will be willing to make the mental effort of the journey through this tremendous book.

Romans is fortunate in its commentators. The volume in the International Critical Commentary by W. Sanday and A. C. Headlam is one of the great commentaries. The volume in the Moffatt Commentary by C. H. Dodd is one of the two finest volumes in that series. There is not a line in it which is without illumination. The volume by E. H. Gifford in the Speaker's Commentary is full of help. The little volume by K. E. Kirk in the Clarendon Bible is excellent in every way. The work of James Denney in the Expositor's Greek Testament is one of the best things Denney every wrote. The commentary by Karl Barth marked the beginning of an epoch. And the commentary by Anders Nygren, translated into English very recently, is one of the greatest of all modern commentaries. All these books have been continually by my side, and my debts to Dodd, and Sanday and Headlam are too numerous to mention.

The translation of *Romans* is especially difficult. Moffatt, and the American Revised Standard Version, and J. B. Phillips have been constantly used; but, in order to make

ix

the meaning clear, I have been compelled not seldom to resort to paraphrase rather than translation.

It has been a great experience to live with Paul throughout the months I was writing this book, and it is my prayer that something of Paul's great mind may shine through these pages for the reader of to-day who seeks to reach the heart of Paul's gospel.

WILLIAM BARCLAY.

CONTENTS

THE LETTER TO THE ROMANS

CONTENTS

THE LETTER TO THE ROMANS

CONTENTS

A GENERAL INTRODUCTION TO THE LETTERS
OF PAUL

The Letters of Paul

There is no more interesting body of documents in the
New Testament than the letters of Paul. That is so because
of all forms of literature a letter is most personal. Demetrius,
one of the old Greek literary critics, once wrote, " Every
one reveals his own soul in his letters. In every other
form of composition it is possible to discern the writer's
character, but in none so clearly as the epistolary." (Demetrius, *On Style*, 227). It is just because he left us so many
letters that we feel we know Paul so well. In these letters
he opened his mind and heart to the folk he loved so much;
and in them, to this day, we can see that great mind
grappling with the problems of the Early Church, and
we can feel that great heart throbbing with love for men,
even when they were misguided and mistaken.

The Difficulty of Letters

And yet, at the same time, it remains true that there
is often nothing so difficult to understand as a letter.
Demetrius (*On Style*, 233) quotes a saying of Artemon,
who edited the letters of Aristotle. Artemon said that
a letter ought to be written in the same manner as a
dialogue, because he regarded a letter as one of the two
sides of a dialogue. To put it in a more modern way, to
read a letter is like listening to one side of a telephone
conversation. So when we read the letters of Paul we
are often in a difficulty. We do not possess the letter which
he was answering; we do not fully know the circumstances
with which he was dealing; it is only from the letter
that we can deduce the situation which prompted the

letter. Always, in reading these letters, we are presented with a double problem. There is the problem of understanding the letter, and there is the prior problem that we will not fully understand the letter itself unless we understand the situation which was the moving cause for the sake of which the letter was written. We have continuously to seek to reconstruct the situation against which the letter is to be read.

The Ancient Letters

It is a great pity that Paul's letters were ever called *epistles*. They are in the most literal sense *letters*. One of the great lights on the interpretation of the New Testament has been the discovery and the publication of the *papyri*. In the ancient world, *papyrus* was the substance on which most documents were written. It was composed of strips of the pith of a certain bulrush that grew on the banks of the Nile. These strips were laid one on the top of the other to form a substance very like brown paper. The sands of the Egyptian desert were ideal for the preservation of these papyri, for papyrus, although it is very brittle, will last forever so long as moisture does not get at it. So from the Egyptian rubbish heaps archaeologists have rescued literally hundreds of documents, marriage contracts, legal agreements, government forms, and, most interesting of all, hundreds of private letters. When we read these private letters we find that there was a pattern to which nearly all letters conformed; and we find that the letters of Paul reproduce exactly and precisely the pattern of the letters which people in the ancient world wrote to each other every day. Here is one of these ancient letters. It is from a soldier, called Apion, to his father Epimachus. He was writing from Misenum to tell his father that he had arrived safely after a stormy passage.

" Apion sends heartiest greetings to his father and lord
Epimachus. I pray above all that you are well and
fit; and that things are going well with you and my
sister and her daughter and my brother. I thank
my Lord Serapis (his god) that he kept me safe when
I was in peril on the sea. As soon as I got to Misenum
I got my journey money from Caesar—three gold
pieces. And things are going fine with me. So I
beg you, my dear father, send me a line, first to let
me know how you are, and then about my brothers,
and thirdly, that I may kiss your hand, because
you brought me up well, and because of that, I hope,
God willing, soon to be promoted. Give Capito my
heartiest greetings, and my brothers and Serenilla
and my friends. I sent you a little picture of myself
painted by Euctemon. My military name is Antonius
Maximus. I pray for your good health. Serenus
sends good wishes, Agathos Daimon's boy, and
Turbo, Gallonius' son." (G. Milligan, *Selections from
the Greek Papyri*, 36).

Little did Apion think that we would be reading his letter
to his father 1800 years after he had written it. It shows
how little human nature changes. The lad is hoping for
promotion quickly. Who will Serenilla be but the girl
he left behind him? He sends the ancient equivalent of
a photograph to the folk at home. Now that letter falls
into certain sections. (i) There is a greeting. (ii) There is
a prayer for the health of the recipients. (iii) There is
a thanksgiving to the gods. (iv) There are the special
contents. (v) Finally, there are the special salutations
and the personal greetings. Practically every one of Paul's
letters shows exactly the same sections. Let us apply
these sections to Paul's letters.

(i) *The Greeting:* Romans I: I; I Corinthians I: I;
2 Corinthians I: I; Galatians I: I; Ephesians I: I;
Philippians I: I; Colossians I: I, 2; I Thessalonians
I: I; 2 Thessalonians I: I.

(ii) *The Prayer:* in every case Paul prays for the grace of God on the people to whom he writes: Romans I: 7; I Corinthians I: 3; 2 Corinthians I: 2; Galatians I: 3; Ephesians I: 2; Philippians I: 3; Colossians I: 2; I Thessalonians I: 1; 2 Thessalonians I: 2.

(iii) *The Thanksgiving:* Romans I: 8; I Corinthians I: 4; 2 Corinthians I: 3; Ephesians I: 3; Philippians I: 3; I Thessalonians I: 3; 2 Thessalonians I: 3.

(iv) *The Special Contents:* the main body of the letter contains the special contents.

(v) *Special Salutations and Personal Greetings:* Romans 16; I Corinthians 16: 19; 2 Corinthians 13: 13; Philippians 4: 21, 22; Colossians 4: 12-15; I Thessalonians 5: 26.

It is clear that when Paul wrote letters he wrote them on the pattern which everyone used. Deissmann, the great scholar, says of the letters of Paul, " They differ from the messages of the homely papyrus leaves of Egypt, not as letters but only as the letters of Paul." When we read Paul's letters we are not reading things which were meant to be academic exercises and theological treatises, but things which are human documents written by a friend to his friends.

The Immediate Situation

With a very few exceptions all Paul's letters were written to meet an immediate situation. They are not treatises which Paul sat down to write in the peace and the silence of his study. There was some threatening situation in Corinth, or Galatia, or Philippi, or Thessalonica, and it was to meet that immediate situation that he wrote. He was not in the least thinking of us when he wrote; he was thinking solely of the people to whom he was writing. Deissmann writes, " Paul had no thought of adding a few fresh compositions to the already extant Jewish epistles; still less of enriching the sacred literature of his nation. . . . . He had no presentiment of the place his words would occupy in universal history; not so much that they would be in existence in the next generation, far less that one day people would look at them as Holy Scripture." We must always remember that a thing need not be a transient thing because it was written to meet an immediate situation. All the great love songs of the world were written for one person, but all the world loves them. It is just because Paul's letters were written to meet a threatening danger or a clamant need that they still throb with life. And it is because human need and the human situation do not change that God speaks to us through them to-day.

The Spoken Word

One other thing we must note about these letters of Paul. Paul did what most people did in his day. He did not normally pen his own letters; he dictated them to a secretary; and then after he had dictated them he added his own authenticating signature. We actually know the name of one of these people who did the writing for Paul. In Romans 16: 22 Tertius, the secretary, slips in his own greeting before the letter draws to an end. In I Corinthians 16: 21 Paul says, " This is my own signature, my autograph, so that you can be sure this letter comes from me." (cp. Colossians 4: 18; 2 Thessalonians 3: 17). This explains a great deal. Sometimes Paul is hard to understand, because his sentences begin and never finish; his grammar breaks down and his sentences become involved. We must not think of Paul sitting quietly at a desk, carefully polishing each sentence as he wrote. We must think of him striding up and down some little room, pouring out a torrent of words, while his secretary raced to get them down. When Paul composed his letters, he had in his mind's eye a vision of the folk to whom he was writing.

and he was pouring out his heart to them in words that fell over each other in his eagerness to help. Paul's letters are not careful, academic products written in the seclusion of a scholar's study; they are living, vital, torrents of words poured straight from his heart to the heart of the friends for whom he wrote them.

AN INTRODUCTION TO THE LETTER TO
THE ROMANS

The Epistle that is Different

There is an obvious difference between Paul's *Letter to the Romans* and any other of his letters. Anyone coming, say, from a reading of the *Letters to the Corinthians*, will immediately feel that difference. There is a difference both of atmosphere and of method. A very great part of that difference is due to one basic fact—when Paul wrote to the Church at Rome he was writing to a Church with the founding of which he had had nothing whatever to do, and with which he had had no personal contact at all. That explains why in *Romans* there are so few of the details of practical problems which fill the other letters. That is why *Romans*, at first sight, seems so much more impersonal. As Dibelius put it, " It is of all Paul's letters the least conditioned by the momentary situation."

We may put that in another way. *Romans*, of all Paul's letters, comes nearest to being a theological treatise. In almost all his other letters he is dealing with some immediate trouble, some pressing situation, some current error, some threatening danger, which at the moment was menacing the Church to which he was writing. But *Romans* is the nearest approach to a systematic exposition of Paul's own theological position, independent of any immediate set of circumstances.

Testamentary and Prophylactic

Because of that, two very great scholars have applied two very illuminating adjectives to *Romans*. Sanday called *Romans* "*testamentary*." It is as if Paul was writing his theological last will and testament, as if into *Romans* he was distilling the very essence of the last word of his faith and belief. Rome was the greatest city in the world, the capital of the greatest Empire the world had ever seen. Paul had never been there, and he did not know if he

ever would be there. But, in writing to such a Church
in such a city, it was fitting that he should set down for
them the very centre and core of his belief, that by which
he was prepared to stand or fall at any time. Burton called
Romans "*prophylactic*." A prophylactic is something which
guards against infection. Paul had seen too often what
harm and trouble can be caused by wrong ideas, twisted
notions, misguided conceptions of Christian faith and belief.
He therefore wished to send to the Church in the city
which was the centre of the world a letter which would
so build up the structure of their faith that, if infections
should ever come to them, they might have in the true
word of Christian doctrine a powerful and effective defence.
He felt that the best protection against the infection of
false teaching was the antiseptic of the truth.

The Occasion of Paul's writing to Rome

All his life Paul had been haunted by the thought of
Rome. It had always been one of his dreams to visit
Rome and to preach there. When he was in Ephesus he
was planning to go through Achaea and Macedonia again,
and then comes the sentence obviously dropped straight
from the heart, " After I have been there, I *must also see
Rome* " (Acts 19: 21). When he was up against things in
Jerusalem, and the situation looked threatening and the
end seemed near, he had one of those visions which always
lifted up his heart. In that vision the Lord stood by him
and said, " Be of good cheer, Paul. For as thou hast
testified of me in Jerusalem, *so must thou bear witness
also at Rome* " (Acts 23: 11). In the very first chapter of
the letter Paul's desire to see Rome breathes out. " I
long to see you that I may impart unto you some spiritual
gift to the end ye may be established " (Romans 1: 11).
" So, then, as much as in me is, I am ready to preach
the gospel to you that are in Rome also " (Romans 1: 15)
It might well be said that the name *Rome* was written on
Paul's heart.

When Paul actually wrote the *Letter to the Romans* the date was sometime in the year A.D. 58, and he was in Corinth. He was just about to bring to its completion a scheme that was very dear to his heart. The Church at Jerusalem was the mother Church of them all, but it was a poor Church, and Paul had organized a collection throughout the younger Churches for the Jerusalem Church (1 Corinthians 16: 1ff, 2 Corinthians 9: 1ff). That collection was two things. It was an opportunity for his younger converts to put Christian charity into Christian action, and it was a most practical way of impressing on all Christians the unity of the Christian Church, of teaching them that they were not members of isolated and independent congregations, but of one great Church, each part of which had a responsibility to all the rest. When Paul wrote *Romans* he was just about to set out to Jerusalem with that gift for the Jerusalem Church. " But now I go unto Jerusalem to minister unto the saints " (Romans 15: 25).

The Object of Paul's Writing

Why, then, at such a moment should he write? (*a*) Paul knew that the journey to Jerusalem was not without its peril. He knew that he had enemies there, and to go to Jerusalem was to take his life and liberty in his hands. He desired the prayers of the Roman Church before he set out on this expedition. " Now I beseech you brethren, for the Lord Jesus Christ's sake, and for the love of the Spirit, that ye strive together with me in your prayers to God for me, that I may be delivered from them that do not believe in Judaea " (Romans 15: 30, 31). Paul was mobilizing the prayers of the Church before he embarked on this perilous undertaking. (*b*) But Paul had great schemes simmering in his mind. It has been said of Paul that he was " always haunted by the regions beyond." He never saw a ship at anchor but he wished to board her, and to carry the message of the good news to the men across the sea. He never saw a range of mountains, blue in the distance, but he wished to cross them, and to bring the story of the Cross to the men who had never heard it. Now, at this time, Paul was haunted by the thought of Spain. " Whensoever I take my journey into Spain I will come to you " (Romans 15: 25). " When I have done this (that is, when he had delivered the collection to the Church in Jerusalem) I will come by you into Spain " (Romans 15: 28). Why this great desire to go to Spain? Rome had opened up Spain. Some of the great Roman roads and buildings still stand in Spain to this day. And it so happened that, just at this time, there was a blaze of greatness in Spain. It so happened that many of the great figures who were writing their names on Roman history and literature at this time were Spaniards. There was Martial, the master of the epigram. There was Lucan, the epic poet. There were Columella and Pomponius Mela, great figures in Roman literature. There was Quintilian, the master of Roman oratory. And, above all, there was Seneca, the greatest of the Roman Stoic philosophers, the tutor of the Emperor Nero, and the Prime Minister of the Roman Empire. It was most natural that Paul's thoughts should go out to this land which was producing such a scintillating galaxy of greatness. What might happen if men like that could be touched for Christ? Spain was the inevitable target for the Christian faith. As far as we know Paul never got there. On the visit to Jerusalem he was arrested and he was never freed again. But, when Paul was writing Romans, that was his dream.

Now, Paul was a master strategist. He had an eye for the lay-out of territory like a great commander. He felt that by this time he could move on from Asia Minor, that he could for the time being leave Greece behind. He saw the whole west lying in front of him, virgin territory to be won for Christ. But, if he was to launch a campaign in the west, he needed one thing—*he needed a base of*

operations. He needed a headquarters. He needed somewhere from which his lines of communication could go out,
There was only one such base possible—*and that base was
Rome.* That was why Paul wrote this letter to Rome.
He had this great dream in his heart, and this great plan
in his mind. He needed Rome for a base for this new
campaign. He knew that the Church in Rome must know
his name. But he also knew, for Paul was a realist, that the
reports which reached Rome would be mixed. His opponents were not above spreading their slanders and their
false accusation against him. So he wrote this letter to
set out for the Church at Rome an account of the very
centre and essence of his belief, so that, when the time
came for action, he would find in Rome a sympathetic
Church, from which the lines of communication might
go out to Spain and the west. It was with such a plan,
and such an intention, that in A.D. 58 Paul sat down in
Corinth to write his letter to the Church at Rome.

The Lay-out of the Letter

Romans is at once a very complicated and a very carefully
constructed letter. It will therefore help us to find our
way through it if we have in our minds an idea of the
scheme and frame-work round which it is written. It
falls into four definite divisions.

(i) Chapters 1-8, which deal with the problem of
righteousness.
(ii) Chapters 9-11, which deal with the problem of
the Jews, the Chosen People.
(iii) Chapters 12-15, which deal with practical questions
of life and living.
(iv) Chapter 16, which is a letter of introduction
for Phoebe, and a list of final personal greetings.

(i) When Paul uses the word *righteousness*, he means
a right relationship with God. The man who is righteous
is the man who is in a right relationship with God, and
whose life shows it. Paul begins with a survey of the Gentile

world. We have only to look at the decadence and corruption of that Gentile world to know that it had not solved the problem of righteousness. He looks at the Jewish world. The Jews had sought to solve the problem of righteousness by meticulous obedience to the law. Paul had tried that way himself, and it had issued in frustration and defeat, because no man on earth can ever fully obey the law, and, therefore, every man must have the continual consciousness of being in debt to God and under God's condemnation. So Paul finds the way to righteousness in the way of utter trust, and utter yieldedness. The only way to a right relationship with God is to take God at His word, and to cast oneself, just as one is, on the mercy and the love of God. It is the way of faith. It is to know that the important thing is, not what we can do for God, but what God has done for us. For Paul the centre of the Christian faith was that we can never earn or deserve the favour of God, nor do we need to. The whole matter is a matter of grace, and all that we can do is to accept in wondering love and gratitude and trust what God has done for us. But that does not free us from obligations or entitle us to do as we like; it means that for ever and for ever we must try to be worthy of the love which does so much for us. But there is a change in life. We are no longer trying to fulfil the demands of stern and austere and condemnatory law; we are not like criminals before a judge any more; we are lovers who have given all life in love to the one who first loved us.

(ii) The problem of the Jews was a torturing problem. In a real sense they were God's Chosen People, and yet, when God's Son had come into the world, they had rejected Him. What possible explanation could there be for this heart-breaking fact? The only explanation that Paul could find was that, in the end, it was all God's doing. Somehow the hearts of the Jews had been hardened; but it was not all failure, for there had always been a faithful remnant. Nor was it for nothing, for the very fact that the Jews had rejected Christ opened the door to the Gentiles. Nor was it the end of the matter, for in the end the Gentiles would bring the Jews in and all men would be saved. But Paul goes further than that. The Jew had always claimed that he was a member of the Chosen People in virtue of the fact that he was a Jew. It was solely a matter of lineage, of blood, of pure racial descent from Abraham. But Paul insists that the real Jew is not the man whose flesh and blood descent can be traced to Abraham. The real Jew is the man who has made the same decision of utter yieldedness to God in loving faith which Abraham made. Therefore, Paul argued, there are many pure-blooded Jews who are not Jews in the real sense of the term at all; and there are many people who come from all nations who are really Jews in the true sense of that word. The new Israel was not a racial thing at all; it was composed of those who had the same faith and the same attitude to God as Abraham had. To be a member of the Chosen People was not to be a racially pure Jew, but to have had the same faith in God as Abraham had.

(iii) The twelfth chapter of Romans is so great an ethical statement that it must always be set alongside the Sermon on the Mount. There Paul lays down the ethical character of the Christian faith. The fourteenth and fifteenth chapters deal with an ever-recurring problem. In the Church there was a narrower party who believed that they must abstain from certain foods and drinks, and who counted special days and ceremonies as of great importance. Paul thinks of them as the weaker brethren, because their faith was dependent on these external things. There was a wider and more liberal party, who had liberated themselves from these external rules and regulations and observances. Paul thinks of them as the brethren who are stronger in the faith. Paul makes it quite clear that his sympathies are with the more liberal party; but he lays down the great principle that no man must ever do anything to hurt the conscience of a weaker brother or to put a stumbling block in his way. His whole point of view is that we must never do anything which makes it harder for someone else to be a Christian; and that that may well mean the giving up of something, which is right and safe for us, for the sake of the weaker brother. Christian liberty must never be used in such a way that it injures another's life or conscience.

(iv) The fourth section, with which the letter closes, is a letter of recommendation from Phoebe, a member of the Church at Cenchreae, who is coming to Rome. The letter ends with a list of greetings and a final bene-diction.

Two Problems

The sixteenth chapter of Romans has always presented scholars with a problem. Many scholars have felt that it does not really form part of the *Letter to the Romans* at all; and that it is really a letter to some other Church which became attached to *Romans* when Paul's letters were collected. What are the grounds on which these scholars come to that conclusion? First and foremost, in this chapter Paul sends greetings to twenty-six different people, twenty-four of whom he mentions by name, and all of whom he seems to know very intimately. So intimate is his knowledge in some cases that he can, for instance, say that the mother of Rufus has also been a mother to him. Now, is it likely that Paul knew intimately twenty-six people in *a Church which he had never visited*, which he had not founded and in which he had never in his life been? He, in fact, greets far more people in this chapter than he does in any letter, and yet he had never set foot in Rome. There is something there that needs explanation.

But, if this chapter was not written to Rome, to where was it originally written? It is here that Prisca and Aquila come into the argument. We know that they had left Rome in A.D. 52 when Claudius had issued his edict banishing the Jews (Acts 18: 2). We know that they went with Paul to *Ephesus* (Acts 18: 18). We know that they were in *Ephesus* when Paul wrote his letter to Corinth, less than two years before he wrote *Romans* (I Corinthians 16: 19). And we know that they were still in *Ephesus* when the Pastoral Epistles were written (2 Timothy 4: 19). It is certainly true that if we had come across a letter sending greeting to Prisca and Aquila we should certainly have assumed that that letter was sent to Ephesus, if no other address was given. Is there any other evidence to make us think that chapter sixteen may have been sent to Ephesus in the first place? There is the perfectly general reason that Paul spent longer in Ephesus than anywhere else, and it would be very natural for him to send greetings to many people there. Paul speaks of Epaenetus, *the firstfruits of Asia*. Ephesus is in Asia, and such a reference would be very natural in a letter to Ephesus, but not so natural in a letter to Rome. Romans 16: 17 speaks about *offences against the doctrine which you have learned*, which sounds as if Paul was speaking about possible disobedience to his own teaching, and he had never taught in Rome.

It could be argued that the sixteenth chapter was originally addressed to Ephesus, but the argument is not as strong as it looks. For one thing, there is no evidence that the chapter was ever attached anywhere except to the *Letter to the Romans*. For another thing, the odd thing is that Paul does *not* send personal greetings to Churches which he knew well. There are no personal greetings in *Thessalonians*, *Corinthians*, *Galations*, and *Philippians*, all of which were Churches he knew well; whereas there *are* personal greetings in Colossians, another Church where Paul had never set foot. The reason is really quite simple. If Paul had sent personal greetings to Churches he knew well, jealousies might well have arisen; on the other hand, when he was writing to Churches he had never visited, he liked to establish as many personal links as possible. The very fact that Paul had never been in Rome makes it likely that he *would* try to establish as many personal connections as possible. Again, it is to be remembered that Prisca and Aquila *were banished by edict* from Rome. What is more likely than that, after the trouble was over, six or seven years later, they would return to Rome and pick up the threads of their business after their stay in other towns? And is it not most likely that many of the other names are names of people who shared in this banishment, who took up temporary residence in other cities, who met Paul there, and who then, when the coast was clear, returned to Rome to their old homes? Paul would be delighted to have so many personal contacts in Rome and to seize hold of them. And further, as we shall see, when we come to study chapter 16 in detail, many of the names—the households of Aristobulus and Narcissus, Amplias, Nereus and others—well suit Rome. In spite of the arguments for Ephesus, we may take it that there is no necessity to detach chapter sixteen from the *Letter to the Romans*.

But there is a more interesting, and a much more important, problem than that. The early manuscripts show some very curious things with regard to chapters 14, 15 and 16. The only natural place for a doxology to come is at *the very end*. *Romans* 16: 25-27 is a doxology, and in most good manuscripts it comes at the end. But in a number of manuscripts it comes at the end of chapter 14; two good manuscripts have it in *both places*; one ancient manuscript has it at the end of chapter 15; two manuscripts have it in *neither place*, but leave an empty space for it. There is one ancient Latin manuscript which has a series of section summaries. In these summaries the last two are as follows:

> 50: On the peril of him who grieves his brother by meat.

That is obviously *Romans* 14: 15-23.

> 51: On the mystery of the Lord, kept secret before His passion, but after His passion revealed.

That is equally clearly *Romans* 16: 25-27, the doxology. Clearly, these summaries were made from a manuscript which did not contain chapters fifteen and sixteen. Now there is one thing which sheds a flood of light on this. In one manuscript the mention of Rome in *Romans* 1: 7 and 1: 15 is *entirely omitted*. There is no mention of any destination. All this goes to show that *Romans* circulated in two forms—one form as we have it with sixteen chapters, and one with fourteen chapters, and perhaps also one with fifteen chapters. The explanation must be this. As Paul wrote it *to Rome* it had sixteen chapters; but chapters 15 and 16 have reference only to things that were happening in Rome. They are private and personal to Rome. Now there is no letter which gives such a compendium of Paul's doctrine and which so gives the distilled essence of his gospel. What must have happened was that *Romans* began to circulate among all the Churches, *with the last two local chapters omitted*, except for the doxology, It must have been felt that *Romans* was too fundamental to stop at Rome and to stay there, and so the purely local references must have been removed and it must have been sent out to the Church at large. When we probe into this fascinating problem we find that, from very early times, the Church felt that *Romans* was so great an expression of the mind of Paul that it must become, not the possession of a congregation, but of the whole Church. We must remember as we study it that men have always looked on *Romans* as the quintessence of the mind and heart of Paul.

ROMANS

A CALL, A GOSPEL AND A TASK

Romans I: I-7

> This is a letter from Paul, a slave of Jesus Christ, called to be an apostle, set apart to serve the good news of God. This good news God promised long ago, through His prophets, in the sacred writings. It is good news about His Son, who in His manhood was born of David's lineage, who, as a result of His Resurrection from the dead, has been proved by the Holy Spirit to be the mighty Son of God. It is of Jesus Christ, our Lord, of whom I am speaking, through whom we have received grace, and an apostleship to awaken a faithful obedience for His sake amongst all the Gentiles. You are included amongst these Gentiles, you who have been called to belong to Jesus Christ. This is a letter to all the beloved in Rome who belong to God, those who have been called to be dedicated to Him. Grace be to you and peace from God our Father, and from the Lord Jesus Christ.

WHEN Paul wrote his letter to the Romans he was writing to a Church which he did not know personally and in which he had never been. He was writing to a Church which was situated in the greatest city in the greatest empire in the world. Because of that Paul chose his words and thoughts with the greatest care.

Paul begins by giving his own credentials.

(i) He calls himself the slave (*doulos*) of Jesus Christ. In this word slave there are two backgrounds of thought. (*a*) Paul's favourite title for Jesus is LORD (*kurios*). In Greek the word *kurios* describes someone who has undisputed possession of a person or a thing. It means *master* or *owner*, in the most definite and absolute sense. The opposite of the word LORD (*kurios*) is *slave* (*doulos*). Paul thought of himself as the slave of Jesus Christ, his Master and his Lord. Jesus had loved him and given Himself for him, and therefore Paul was sure that he no longer belonged to himself, but entirely to Jesus. On the

H—2   I

one side this word *slave* describes the utter obligation of love. (*b*) But this word slave (*doulos*) has another side to it. In the Old Testament it is the regular word which describes the great men of God. Moses was the servant, the slave, the *doulos* of the Lord (Joshua 1: 2). Joshua himself was the *doulos* of God (Joshua 24: 9). The proudest title of the prophets, the title which distinguishes them from other men, is that they are the servants and the slaves of God (Amos 3: 7; Jeremiah 7: 25). When Paul calls himself the slave of Jesus Christ he is doing nothing less than setting himself in the succession of the prophets. Their greatness and their glory lay in the fact that they were slaves of God, and so did Paul's. So, then, this phrase, *the slave of Jesus Christ*, describes at one and the same time the obligation of a great love and the honour of a great office.

(ii) Paul describes himself as *called to be an apostle*. In the Old Testament the great men were men who heard and answered the call of God. Abraham heard the call of God (Genesis 12: 1-3). Moses answered God's call (Exodus 3: 10). Jeremiah and Isaiah were prophets because, almost against their will, they were compelled to listen to and to answer the call of God (Jeremiah 1: 4, 5; Isaiah 6: 8, 9). Paul never thought of himself as a man who had aspired to an honour; he thought of himself as a man who had been given a task. Jesus said to His men, " Ye have not chosen me, but I have chosen you " (John 15: 16). Paul did not think of life in terms of what he wanted to do, but in terms of what God meant him to do.

(iii) Paul describes himself as *set apart to serve the good news of God*. Paul was conscious of a double setting apart in his life. Twice in Paul's life this very same word (*aphorozein*) is used of him. (*a*) He was set apart *by God*. He thought of God as separating him for the task he was to do even before he was born (Galatians 1: 15). For every man God has a plan. Every man is an expression of the thought of God. No man's life is purposeless. God sent him into the

2

world to do some definite thing. (b) He was set apart
by men. It is this very same word that is used in Acts 13: 2
when the Holy Spirit told the leaders of the Church at
Antioch to separate Paul and Barnabas for the special
mission to the Gentiles. Paul was conscious of having
a task to do for God and for the Church of God.

(iv) In this setting apart Paul was aware of having
received two things. In verse 5 he tells us what these two
things were. (a) He had received *grace*. *Grace* always
describes some gift which is absolutely free and absolutely
unearned. In his pre-Christian days Paul
had sought to earn glory in the eyes of men, and merit
in the sight of God, by meticulous observance of the
works of the law, and he had found no peace that way.
Now he knew that what mattered was not what he could
do, but what God had done. It has been put this way,
" The law lays down what a man must do; the gospel
lays down what God has done." Paul now saw that
salvation depends not on what man's effort can do, but
on what God's love has done. All was of grace, free and
undeserved. (b) He had received *a task*. He was set apart
to be the apostle to the Gentiles. Paul knew himself to
be chosen, not for special honour, but for special responsibility. He knew that God had set him apart, not for
glory, but for toil. It may well be that there is a play on
words here. Once Paul had been a Pharisee (Philippians
3: 5). Now the very name *Pharisee* may very well mean
The Separated One. It may be that the Pharisees were so
called because they had deliberately separated themselves
from all ordinary people, because they would not even
let the skirt of their robe brush against an ordinary man.
The Pharisees would have shuddered at the very thought
of the offer of God being made to the Gentiles. To them
the Gentiles were "fuel for the fires of hell." Once Paul
had been like that. He had felt himself *separated* in such
a way as to have nothing but contempt for all ordinary
men. Now he knew himself to be *separated* in such a

3

way that all his life he must spend, and be spent, to bring the news of good love to every man of every race. Christianity always separates us, but it separates us not for privilege, and self-glory, and pride, but for service, and humility, and love for all men.

Besides giving his own credentials Paul, in this passage, sets out in its most essential outline the gospel which he preached. It was a gospel which centred in Jesus Christ (verses 3 and 4). In particular it was a gospel of two things. (*a*) It was a gospel of the *Incarnation*. He told of a Jesus who was really and truly a man. One of the great early thinkers of the Church summed it up when he said of Jesus, " He became what we are, to make us what He is." Paul preached of someone who was not a legendary figure in an imaginary story, who was not a demi-god, half god and half man. He preached of one who was really and truly one with the men He came to save. (*b*) It was a gospel of *the Resurrection*. If Jesus had lived a lovely life and died an heroic death, and if that had been the end of Him, He might have been numbered with the great and the heroic figures, but He would simply have been one among many heroic ones. The fact that He was unique is guaranteed forever by the fact of the Resurrection. The others are dead and gone, and have left a memory. Jesus lives on and gives us a presence, still mighty with power.

THE COURTESY OF GREATNESS

Romans 1: 8-15

> To begin with, I thank my God for you all through Jesus Christ. I thank Him that the story of your faith is told throughout the whole world. God, whom I serve in my spirit in the work of spreading the good news of His Son, is my witness that I continually talk to Him about you. In my prayers I am always asking that somehow, soon, at last, I may by God's will succeed in finding a way to come to you. For I yearn to see you, that I may give you a share of some gift

which the Spirit gives, so that you may be firmly
founded in the faith—what I mean is, that you and I
may find encouragement together, I through your
faith and you through mine. I want you to know,
brothers, that I have often planned to come to you—
and up until now I have been prevented from doing
so—that I might have some fruit among you too,
as I have amongst the rest of the Gentiles. I am under
a duty to Greeks and to barbarians, to wise and to
foolish. So, then, it is my eager wish to preach the
good news to you too in Rome.

AFTER almost nineteen hundred years the warm affection
of this passage still breathes through it, and we can feel
Paul's great heart throbbing with love for the Church
which he had never seen. Here was Paul's problem in
writing this letter. He had never been in Rome. He had
had no share in founding the Roman Church. He had to
disarm their suspicions. He had to make them feel that
he was not a trespasser on their preserves, and that he
was not interfering where he had no right to intervene.
Before he could do anything else he had to get alongside
them that the barriers of strangeness and suspicion should
be broken down.

(i) Paul, in wisdom and love combined, began with a
compliment. He told them that he thanked God for that
Christian faith of theirs which all the world knew. There
are some people whose tongues are tuned to praise, and
others whose tongues are tuned to criticize. There are some
people whose eyes are focussed to find faults, and others
whose eyes are focussed to discover virtues. It was said
of Thomas Hardy that, if he went into a country field,
he would always see, not the wild flowers, but the dung-heap
in the corner of it. But the fact remains that we will
always get far more out of people by praising them than
by criticizing them. The men who get the best out of
others are the men who insist on seeing others at their best.
There never was, and never has been, anything quite so
beautiful as the civilization of the Greeks at its highest

5

and its best, and T. R. Glover once said that Greek civilization was founded on " a blind faith in the average man." One of the great figures of the 1914-18 war was Donald Hankey, who wrote *The Student in Arms*. He saw men at their best and at their worst. He once wrote home, " If I survive this war I want to write a book called ' The Living Goodness,' analysing all the goodness and nobility inherent in plain people, and trying to show how it ought to find fulfilment and expression in the Church." Donald Hankey himself wrote that great essay entitled *The Beloved Captain*. He describes how the beloved captain picked out the awkward ones and taught them himself. " He looked at them and they looked at him, and the men pulled themselves together and determined to do their best." No one can ever even begin to save men unless he first believes in men. A man is a hell-deserving sinner, but he has also a sleeping hero in his soul, and often a word of praise will awaken that sleeping heroism when criticism and condemnation will only drive to resentment and to despair. Aidan was the apostle to the Saxons. Away back in A.D. 630 the Saxon king had sent to Iona a request that a missionary should be sent to his kingdom to preach the gospel. A missionary was sent. He came back talking of the " stubborn and barbarous disposition of the English." " The English have no manners," he said, " they behave like savages." He reported that the task was hopeless, and then Aidan spoke. " I think, brother," he said, " that you may have been too severe for such ignorant hearers, and that you should have led them on gently, giving them first the milk of religion before the meat." So Aidan was sent to Northumbria, and the gentleness of Aidan won for Christ that very people whom the critical severity of his brother monk had repelled.

(ii) Although Paul did not know the people at Rome personally he nevertheless constantly prayed to God for them. It is ever a Christian privilege and duty to bear our loved ones and all our fellow-Christians to the throne of grace. In one of his sermons on the Lord's Prayer, Gregory of Nyssa has a lyrical passage on prayer:

> "The effect of prayer is union with God, and, if someone is with God, he is separated from the enemy. Through prayer we guard our chastity, control our temper and rid ourselves of vanity. It makes us forget injuries, overcomes envy, defeats injustice and makes amends for sin. Through prayer we obtain physical well-being, a happy home, and a strong, well-ordered society. . . . Prayer is the seal of virginity and a pledge of faithfulness in marriage. It shields the wayfarer, protects the sleeper, and gives courage to those who keep vigil. . . . It will refresh you when you are weary and comfort you when you are sorrowful. Prayer is the delight of the joyful as well as the solace of the afflicted. . . . Prayer is intimacy with God and contemplation of the invisible. . . . Prayer is the enjoyment of things present and the substance of the things to come."

Even if we are separated from people, and even if there is no other gift which we can give to them, we can surround them with the strength and the defence of our prayers.

(iii) Paul, in his humility, was always ready to receive as well as to give. He began by saying that he wished to come to Rome that he might impart to the Roman Church some gift which would confirm them in the faith. And then he changed it. He wished to come to Rome that he and the Roman Church might comfort and strengthen each other, and that each might find precious things in the faith of the other. There are two kinds of teachers. There are the teachers whose attitude is that they are standing above their scholars and they are telling them what they should and must accept. And there are the teachers who, in effect, say, "Come now, let's learn about this together." Paul was the greatest thinker the Early Church ever produced, and yet, when he thought of the people to whom he longed to preach, he thought of himself not only as giving to them but receiving from them. It takes humility to teach as it takes humility to learn.

7

(iv) Verse 14 has in Greek a double meaning that is almost untranslatable. The Authorised Version has it, " I am debtor both to the Greeks and to the Barbarians." Paul was thinking of two things when he wrote that. He was debtor because of all the kindness that he had received, and he was a debtor because of his obligation to preach to them. This highly compressed sentence means, " Because of all that I have received from them, and because of all it is my duty to give to them, I am under an obligation to all sorts of men." It may seem strange that Paul speaks of *Greeks* when he is writing to *Romans*. At this time the word Greek had lost its racial sense altogether. It did not mean a native of the country of Greece. The conquests of Alexander the Great had taken the Greek language and Greek thought all over the world. And a Greek was not a man who was a Greek by race and birth. He was a man who knew the culture and the mind of Greece. A barbarian is literally a man who says *bar-bar*, that is to say, a man who speaks an ugly and an unharmonious tongue in contrast with the man who speaks the beautiful, flexible language of Greek. To be a Greek was to be a man of a certain mind and spirit and culture. One of the Greeks said of his own people, " The barbarians may stumble on the truth, but it takes a Greek to understand." What Paul meant was that his message, his friendship, his debt, his obligation was to wise and simple, cultured and uncultured, lettered and unlettered. He had a message for the world, and it was his ambition some day to deliver that message in Rome too.

GOOD NEWS OF WHICH TO BE PROUD

Romans I: 16-17

> I am proud of the good news, for it is the power of God which produces salvation for every one way believes, to the Jew first and to the Greek. The who to a right relationship with God is revealed in it

when man's faith responds to God's fidelity, just as it stands written, "It is the man who is in a right relationship with God as a result of his faith who will live."

WHEN we come to these two verses the preliminaries are over and the trumpet call of Paul's gospel sounds out. Many of the great classical musical concertos begin with a crashing chord, and then state the theme which they are going to elaborate and develop. The reason for that was that they were often first performed at private gatherings in great houses. When the pianist first seated himself at the piano there was still a buzz and hum of conversation. He played the crashing chord to attract the attention of the company, and then, when that attention was obtained, the theme was stated. Up to these two verses Paul has been making contact with the people to whom he was writing. He has been attracting their attention. And now the introduction is over, and the theme is stated.

There are only two verses here, but they have so much of the quintessence of Paul's gospel in them that we must spend some considerable time on them.

Paul began by saying that he was proud of the gospel which it was his privilege to preach. It is an amazing thing to think of the background of that statement. Paul had been imprisoned in Philippi, chased out of Thessalonica, smuggled out of Beroea, laughed at in Athens. He had preached in Corinth where his message was foolishness to the Greeks and a stumbling-block to the Jews, and out of that background Paul declared that he was proud of the gospel. There was something in the gospel which made Paul triumphantly victorious over all that men could do to him.

In this passage we meet three great Pauline watchwords. They are indeed the three great foundation pillars of his thought and belief.

(i) There is the conception of *salvation* (*sōtēria*). At this time in history salvation was the one thing for which men were searching. There had been a time when Greek philosophy had been speculative. Four and five hundred years before this men had spent their time discussing the problem —what is the one basic element of which the world is composed? Philosophy had been speculative philosophy and it had been natural philosophy. But, bit by bit, as the centuries passed, life fell in. The old landmarks were destroyed. Tyrants and conquerors and perils surrounded men. Degeneracy and weakness haunted them, and philosophy changed its emphasis. It became, not speculative, but practical. It ceased to be *natural* philosophy, and became *moral* philosophy. Its one aim was to build " a ring-wall of defence against the advancing chaos of the world." Epictetus called his lecture room " the hospital for the sick soul." Epicurus called his teaching " the medicine of salvation." Seneca, whose life coincided with the life of Paul, said that all men were looking, *ad salutem*, towards salvation. What we need, he said, is " a hand let down to lift us up." Men, he said, are overwhelmingly conscious of " their weakness and their inefficiency in necessary things." He himself, he said, was *homo non tolerabilis*, a man not to be tolerated. Men love their vices, he said with a sort of despair, and hate them at the same time. In that desperate world, Epictetus said, men were seeking a peace " not of Caesar's proclamation, but of God's." There can seldom have been a time in history when men were more universally seeking for salvation. It was precisely that salvation, that power, that escape, that Christianity came to offer men.

Let us see just what this Christian *sōtēria*, this Christian salvation is.

(*a*) It was *salvation from physical illness*. (Matthew 9: 21; Luke 8: 36). It was not a completely other-worldly thing. It aimed at rescuing a man in body and in soul.

(*b*) It was *salvation from danger*. (Matthew 8: 25; 14: 30). It was not that this salvation gave a man a life which was free from perils and dangers, but it gave him something which gave him a security of soul no matter what was happening. As Rupert Brooke wrote in the days of the First World War in his poem *Safety*:

> " Safe shall be my going,
> Secretly armed against all death's endeavour;
> Safe though all safety's lost; safe where men fall;
> And if these poor limbs die, safest of all."

And as Browning had it in *Paracelsus*:

> " If I stoop,
> Into a dark tremendous sea of cloud,
> It is but for a time; I press God's lamp
> Close to my breast; its splendour, soon or late,
> Will pierce the gloom: I shall emerge one day."

The Christian salvation makes a man safe in a way that is independent of any outward circumstance.

(c) It was *salvation from life's infection*. It is from a crooked and perverse generation that a man is saved (Acts 2: 40). The man who has this Christian civilization has a kind of divine antiseptic which keeps him from infection by the evil of the world.

(d) It was *salvation from lostness* (Matthew 18: 11; Luke 19: 10). It was to seek and to save the lost that Jesus came. The unsaved man is the man who is out on the wrong road, a road that leads to death. The saved man is the man who has been put on the right way.

(e) It was *salvation from sin* (Matthew 1: 21). A man is like a slave to a master from whom he cannot escape. He is like a patient who can diagnose the disease, who knows what is wrong, but who can find no remedy. The Christian salvation liberates him from the tyranny of sin.

(f) It was salvation from *the wrath of God* (Romans 5: 9). We shall have occasion in the next passage to discuss the meaning of this phrase. It is sufficient to note at the moment that there is in this world an inexorable moral law, that there is in the Christian faith an inevitable element of judgment. Without the salvation which Jesus Christ brings a man could only stand condemned.

(g) It was *a salvation which is eschatological*. That is to say it is a salvation which finds its full consummation beyond time. It will find its full meaning and blessedness in the final triumph of Jesus Christ (Romans 13: 11; 1 Corinthians 5: 5; 2 Timothy 4: 18; 1 Peter 1: 5).

The Christian faith came to a desperate world offering a salvation, a *sōtēria*, a safety which would keep a man safe in time and in eternity.

(ii) There is the conception of *faith*. Now *faith* in the thought of Paul is a rich word.

(a) At its simplest it means *loyalty, fidelity*. When Paul wrote to the Thessalonians, he wished to know about their *faith*. That is, he wished to know how their loyalty was standing the test. In 2 Thessalonians 1: 4 *faith* and *patience* are combined. Faith is the enduring loyalty and fidelity which mark the real soldier of Jesus Christ.

(b) *Faith* means *belief*. It means the conviction that something is true. In 1 Corinthians 15: 17 Paul tells the Corinthians that if Jesus did not rise from the dead, then their faith is vain. All that they have believed is wrecked. Faith is the assent that the Christian message is true.

(c) *Faith* sometimes means *the Christian Religion*, as we speak of *The Faith*. In 2 Corinthians 13: 5 Paul tells his opponents to examine themselves to see if they are *in the faith*, that is, to see if they are still within the Christian Religion.

(d) *Faith* is sometimes practically equivalent to *indestructible hope*. " We walk," writes Paul, " by *faith* and not by sight " (2 Corinthians 5: 7).

(e) But in its most characteristic Pauline use *faith* means *total acceptance* and *absolute trust*. It means " betting your life that there is a God." It means being absolutely sure that what Jesus said is true, and staking all time and eternity on that assurance. " I believe in God," said Stevenson, " and if I woke up in hell I would still believe in Him."

Faith begins with *receptivity*. It begins when a man is

at least willing to listen to the message of the truth. It goes on to *mental assent*. A man first hears and then agrees that this is true. But mental assent need not issue in action. Many a man knows very well that something is true, but does not change his actions to meet that knowledge. The final stage is when this mental assent becomes *total surrender*. In full-fledged faith, a man hears the Christian message, agrees that it is true, and then casts himself upon it in a life of total yieldedness to that message.

(iii) There is the conception of *justification*. Now there are no more difficult words to understand than justification, justify, justice and just, in all the New Testament. We shall have much occasion in this epistle to meet them. At this point we can only lay down the broad lines on which all Paul's thought proceeds.

The Greek verb that Paul uses for *to justify* is *dikaioun*, of which the first person singular of the present indication— *I justify*—is *dikaioō*. We have to be quite clear that the word *justify*, used in this sense, has a quite different meaning from its ordinary English meaning. If we justify ourselves we produce reasons to prove that we were right. If someone justifies us he produces reasons to prove that we did act in the right way. But all verbs in Greek which end in *oō* do not mean to *prove* a person or thing to be something, or to *make* a person or thing to be something; they always mean to *treat, or account or reckon* a person to be something. Now if God justifies the sinner, it does not mean that He finds reasons to prove that the sinner was right—far from it. It does not mean that, at this point, He even makes the sinner a good man. What it does mean is that *God treats the sinner as if he had not been a sinner at all.* Instead of treating the sinner as a criminal to be obliterated God treats him as a child to be loved. That is what *justification* means. It means that God reckons us not as His enemies but as His friends, that God treats us not as bad men deserve, but as good men deserve. It means He looks on us not as law-breakers to be punished, but as men and women only to be loved. That is the very essence of the gospel.

That means that *to be justified* is to enter into a new relationship with God, a relationship of love and confidence and friendship, instead of a relationship of distance and enmity and fear. We no longer go to a God radiating terrible but just punishment. We go to a God radiating forgiving and redeeming love. Justification (*dikaiosunē*) is the right relationship between God and man. The man who is just (*dikaios*) is the man who is in this right relationship, and—here is the supreme point—he is not in this right relationship because of anything that he has done, but because of what God has done. He is not in this right relationship because he has meticulously performed the works of the law. He is in it because in utter faith he has cast himself on this amazing mercy and love of God.

In the Authorised Version we read the highly compressed phrase, *The just shall live by faith*, but now we can see that this phrase in Paul's mind meant this—It is the man who is in a right relationship with God, not because of the works of his hands, but because of his utter faith in what the love of God has done, who really knows what life is like in time and in eternity. And to Paul the whole work of Jesus was that Jesus had enabled men to enter into this new and precious relationship with God. Fear was gone, and love had come. The God whom men had thought an enemy had become a friend.

THE WRATH OF GOD

Romans I: 18-23

For the wrath of God is being revealed from Heaven, directed against all impiousness and wickedness of men, who, in their wickedness, wilfully suppress the truth that is struggling in their hearts, for, that which can be known about God is clear within them, for God has made it clear to them, because, from the creation of the world, it has always been possible to understand the invisible things by the created things—I mean His invisible power and divinity—and things have been so ordered in order to leave them without defence, because, although they knew God, they did not glorify God and they did not give Him thanks, but they have involved themselves in futile speculations and their senseless mind was darkened. They alleged themselves to be wise, but they have become fools, and they have exchanged the glory of the immortal God for the image of the likeness of mortal man, and of winged creatures, and of four-footed animals, and of creeping reptiles.

IN the previous passage Paul was thinking about the relationship with God into which a man can enter through the faith which is utter yieldedness and trust. In contrast with that he sets the wrath of God which a man must incur, if he is deliberately blind to God, and if he worships his own thoughts and his own idols instead of worshipping God.

Here we come upon something which is difficult and which must give us seriously to think, for here we meet the conception of *the wrath of God*. Surely this is an alarming and a terrifying phrase. What is the meaning of it? What was in Paul's mind when he used it?

In the Old Testament we meet the wrath of God. In the early parts of the Old Testament the wrath of God is specially connected with the idea of the covenant people. The people of Israel were in a special relationship with God. God had chosen them, and had offered them a special relationship to Himself, a relationship which would obtain so long as they kept the law of God, which was the condition of that relationship (Exodus 24: 3-8). Now that meant two things. (a) It meant that within the nation any breach of the law provoked the wrath of God. A breach of the law broke the relationship, the covenant between God and Israel. Numbers 16 tells of the rebelliousness of Korah, Dathan and Abiram, and at the end of it Moses bade Aaron to make special atonement for the sin of the

people " because there is wrath gone out from the Lord "
(Numbers 16: 43). When the Israelites were led away
into Baal worship, " The anger of the Lord was kindled
against Israel " (Numbers 25: 3). Because Israel was
in such a special relationship to God, any breach of God's
law provoked the wrath of God. (*b*) But, further, because
Israel stood in so special and unique a relationship to
God, any other nation which oppressed Israel and treated
her with cruelty and injustice incurred the wrath of God.
The Babylonians had ill-treated Israel, and " because
of the wrath of the Lord it shall not be inhabited " (Jeremiah 50: 13). Because Israel had this special relationship
with God, her own sin and the sins of others against her
incurred the wrath of God.

In the prophets the idea of the wrath of God occurs,
but the emphasis has changed. Jewish religious thought
from the prophets onwards was dominated by the idea
of the two ages. There was this age which was altogether
bad, and there was the golden age which was altogether
good. There was this present age and the age to come.
These two ages were separated by the Day of the Lord.
That was to be a day of terrible retribution and judgment,
when the world would be shattered, the sinner destroyed,
the universe remade before God's Kingdom came. It
was then that *the wrath of the Lord* would go into terrible
action. " Behold the Day of the Lord cometh, cruel,
both with wrath and fierce anger, to lay the land desolate "
(Isaiah 13: 9). " Through the wrath of the Lord of hosts
is the land darkened " (Isaiah 9: 19). Ezekiel (7: 19)
speaks of " the day of the wrath of the Lord." God will
pour out upon the nations " His indignation and His
fierce anger " (Zephaniah 3: 8).

But the prophets did not regard the wrath of God as
being postponed until that terrible day of judgment.
They saw the wrath of God continuously in action. When
Israel strayed away from God, when she was rebellious

and unfaithful, then the wrath of God operated against her and involved her in ruin, disaster, captivity and defeat.

To the prophets the wrath of God was something which was continually operating, and something that would reach its peak of terror and destruction on the coming Day of the Lord.

A modern scholar has put it this way. Because God is God, because God is characteristically holy, God cannot tolerate sin, and *the wrath of God* is God's " annihilating reaction " against sin.

That is hard for us to grasp and to accept. That is in fact the kind of religion that we associate with the Old Testament rather than with the New Testament. Even Luther found this hard. He spoke of God's love as *God's own work*, and he spoke of God's wrath as *God's strange work*. It was for the Christian mind a baffling thing.

Let us try to see how Paul understood this conception. Dr. C. H. Dodd writes very wisely and profoundly on this matter. Paul speaks frequently of this idea of wrath. But the strange thing is that although Paul speaks of the wrath of God, *he never speaks of God being angry*. Paul speaks of God's love, and he speaks of God loving. He speaks of God's grace, and of God graciously giving. He speaks of God's fidelity, and of God being faithful to His people. But, very strangely, although Paul speaks of the wrath of God, he never speaks about God being angry. So then there is something different here. There is some difference in the connection with God of love and wrath. Now, further, Paul only speaks of the wrath *of God* three times. He does so here, and he does so in Ephesians 5: 6 and Colossians 3: 6 where he, in both passages, speaks of the wrath of God coming upon the children of disobedience. But, quite frequently Paul speaks about *the wrath*, without saying it is the wrath *of God*, and he speaks about it in a kind of impersonal way as if it ought to be spelled with capital letters—The Wrath—as if it was a kind of impersonal force at work in the world. In Romans

3: 5 he speaks of, " God who brings on men The Wrath."
In Romans 5: 9 he speaks about being saved from The
Wrath. In Romans 12: 19 he advises men not to take
vengeance but to leave evil-doers to The Wrath. In
Romans 13: 5 he speaks about The Wrath as being a
powerful motive to keep men obedient. In Romans 4: 5
he says that the law produces wrath. And in I Thessalonians I: 10 he says that Jesus delivered us from The
Wrath to come. Now there is something very strange
here. Paul speaks about The Wrath, and yet from that
very wrath Jesus saves men.

Let us go back to the prophets. The prophets spoke
about the wrath of God, and, very often, their message
was that unless men were obedient the wrath of God would
come upon them. How would that wrath be seen and
operate? It would be seen in captivity and defeat, and
national disaster. In other words the prophetic message
was, " If you are not obedient to God the wrath of God
will involve you in ruin and disaster." In point of fact
Ezekiel put this in another vivid way—" The soul that
sinneth it shall die " (Ezekiel 18: 4). Now if we were to
put this into modern language we would use a different
kind of terminology. We would say, " There is a moral
order in this world, and the man who transgresses the
moral law, soon or late, is bound to suffer." That is exactly
what J. A. Froude the great historian said: " One lesson,
and one lesson only, history may be said to repeat with
distinctness, that the world is built somehow on moral
foundations, that, in the long run, it is well with the good,
and, in the long run, it will be ill with the wicked." The
whole message of the Hebrew prophets was that there is a
moral order in this world. The conclusion is clear—that
moral order is the wrath of God at work. God made this
world in such a way that we break His laws at our peril.
Now if we were left solely at the mercy of that inexorable
and implacable moral order, there could be nothing for
us but death and destruction. True, the world is made

in such a way that the soul that sins must die—if the moral order is to act alone. But into this dilemma of man there comes the love of God, and that love of God, by an act of unbelievable free grace, lifts man out of the consequences of sin and saves him from the wrath he should have incurred.

The wrath of God is the inevitable punishment of sin. It is there in the structure of the universe. And it is precisely from the consequences of our rebellion against that moral order that the love of God saves us, because of what Jesus had done for us.

Paul goes on to insist that men cannot plead ignorance of God. They could have seen what God is like from God's world. It is always possible to tell something of a man from his handiwork. And it is possible to tell something about God from the world He made. The Old Testament writers knew that. Job, chapters 38 to 41, is based on that very idea. Paul knew that. It is from the world that he starts when he is speaking to the pagans at Lystra (Acts 14: 17). Tertullian, the great early Christian Father, has much about this conviction that God can be seen in His world. " It was not the pen of Moses that initiated the knowledge of the Creator. . . . The vast majority of mankind, though they had never heard the name of Moses— to say nothing of his book—know the God of Moses none the less." " Nature," he said, " is the teacher; the soul is the pupil." " One flower of the hedgerow by itself, I think—I do not say a flower of the meadows; one shell of any sea you like—I do not say a pearl from the Red Sea; one feather of a moor fowl—to say nothing of a peacock— will they speak to you of a mean Creator?" " If I offer you a rose, you will not scorn its Creator." In the world we can see God. It is Paul's argument—and it is completely valid—that if we look at the world *suffering follows sin.* Break the laws of agriculture—the harvest fails. Break the laws of architecture—your building collapses. Break the laws of health—your body suffers. Paul was saying ' Look at the world! See how it is constructed! From a world like that you know what God is like." The sinner is left without excuse.

But Paul goes on another step. What did the sinner do? *Instead of looking out to God, he looked into himself.* He involved himself in vain speculations and thought he was wise, while all the time he was a fool. Why? He was a fool because he made *his* ideas, *his* opinions, *his* speculations the standard and the law of life, instead of *the will of God.* The sinner's folly consisted in making " man the master of things." He found his standards in his own opinions and not in the laws of God, because he looked into himself and not out to God. He lived in a self-centred instead of a God-centred universe. Instead of walking looking unto God he walked looking unto himself, and, like any man who does not look where he is going, he fell.

What was the result of this? The result of this was *idolatry.* The glory of God was exchanged for images of human and animal forms. What is the root sin of idolatry? The root sin of idolatry is that it is *selfish.* A man makes an idol. He brings it offerings and addresses prayers to it. Why? *So that his own schemes and dreams and aims may be furthered.* His whole worship is for his own sake and not for God's sake.

In this whole passage we are face to face with the fact that the very essence and basis of sin is to put self in the place of God. Sin is when a man worships himself instead of God.

MEN WITH WHOM GOD CAN DO NOTHING

Romans I: 24, 25

So then God abandoned them to uncleanness in their hearts' passionate desires for pleasure, desires which made them dishonour their bodies among themselves, for they are men who have exchanged the truth of God for falsehood, and who worship and serve the

creation more than they do the Creator, who is blessed
for ever. Amen.

THE word which is translated *desires* (*epithumia*) is the
key to this passage. Aristotle defined *epithumia* as *a
reaching out after pleasure*. The Stoics defined it as a reaching
after pleasure *which defies all reason*. Clement of Alexandria
called it an unreasonable aiming at and reaching for that
which will gratify itself. *Epithumia* is the passionate
desire for forbidden pleasure. It is the desire which makes
men do nameless and shameless things. It is a kind of
insanity which makes a man do things that he would
never have done if this desire had not taken away his
sense of honour and prudence and decency. It is the sign
of a man who has set his heart on the things and the
pleasures which this world can supply and who has completely forgotten the Creator of the world. It is the way
of life of a man who has become so completely immersed
in the world that he has ceased to be aware of God at all.

It is a terrible thing to talk of God *abandoning* anyone.
And yet there are two reasons for that.

(i) God gave man free-will, and God respects that free-
will. In the last analysis not even God can interfere with
that free-will. In Ephesians 4: 19 Paul speaks of men who
have abandoned themselves to lasciviousness. They have
surrendered their whole will to it. Hosea (4: 17) has the
terrible sentence: " Ephraim is joined to idols; let him
alone." Before man there stands an open choice. It has
to be so. Without choice there can be no goodness, and
without choice there can be no love. A coerced goodness
is not real goodness; and a coerced love is not love at all.
If men deliberately choose to turn their backs on God,
then, after God has sent His Son Jesus Christ into the
world, not even He can do anything about it. When
Paul speaks of God *abandoning* men to uncleanness, that
word *abandon* has no angry irritation in it. Indeed, its
main note is not even condemnation and judgment. Its
main note is a wistful, sorrowful regret, as of a lover who

has done all that he can do and can do no more. It describes exactly the feeling of the father when he saw his son turn his back on his home and go out to the far country. There is far more of sorrow than of anger in a man's heart when he sees a thing like that.

(ii) And yet in this word *abandon* there is more than that—there is judgment. It is one of the grim facts of life that sin begets sin. The more a man sins the easier it is to sin. He may begin by sinning with a kind of shuddering awareness of what he is doing, and end by sinning without a second thought. It is not that God is punishing the man. It is that he is bringing punishment upon himself. He is steadily making himself such that he is the slave of sin. The Jews knew this, and they had certain great sayings upon this idea. " Every fulfilment of duty is rewarded by another; and every transgression is punished by another." " Whosoever strives to keep himself pure receives the power to do so; and whosoever is impure, to him is the door of vice thrown open." " He who erects a fence around himself is fenced, and he who gives himself over is given over." The most terrible thing about sin is just this power to beget sin. It is the awful responsibility of free-will that it can be used in such a way that in the end it is obliterated and a man becomes the slave of sin, self-abandoned to the wrong way. And sin is always a lie, because the sinner thinks that his sin will make him happy, whereas in the end it ruins life, both for himself and for others, in this world and in the world to come.

AN AGE OF SHAME

Romans I: 26, 27

> Because of this God abandoned them to dishonourable passions, for their women exchanged the natural relationship, for the relationship which is against nature; and so did the men, for they gave up the natural relationship with women, and were inflamed

with their desire for each other, and men were guilty
of shameful conduct with men. So within themselves
they received their due and necessary reward for
their error.

WHEN we read Romans 1: 26-32 it might seem that this
passage is the work of some almost hysterical moralist
who was exaggerating the contemporary situation and
painting it in colours of rhetorical hyperbole. It describes
a situation of a degeneracy of morals almost without
parallel in human history. But there is nothing that Paul
said that the Greek and Roman writers of the age did
not themselves say.

(i) It was an age when things seemed, as it were, out
of control. Virgil wrote: " Right and wrong are confounded;
so many wars the world over, so many forms of wrong; no
worthy honour is left to the plough; the husbandmen
are marched away and the fields grow dirty; the hook has
its curve straightened into the sword-blade. In the East,
Euphrates is stirring up the war, in the West, Germany;
nay, close-neighbouring cities break their mutual league
and draw the sword, and the war god's unnatural fury
rages over the whole world; even as when in the circus
the chariots burst from their floodgates, they dash into
the course, and, pulling desperately at the reins, the driver
lets the horses drive him, and the car is deaf to the curb."
It was a world where violence had run amok. When
Tacitus came to write the history of this period, he wrote:
" I am entering upon the history of a period, rich in
disasters, gloomy with wars, rent with seditions, savage
in its very hours of peace. . . . All was one delirium of
hate and terror; slaves were bribed to betray their masters,
feedmen their patrons. He who had no foe was destroyed
by his friend." Suetonius, writing of the reign of Tiberius,
said: " No day passed but someone was executed."
It was an age of sheer, utter terror. " Rome," said Livy,
the historian, " could neither bear its ills nor the remedies
that might have cured them." Propertius, the poet,

wrote: " I see Rome, proud Rome, perishing, the victim of her own prosperity." It was an age of moral suicide. Juvenal, the satirist, wrote: " The earth no longer brings forth any but bad men and cowards. Hence God, whoever He is, looks down, laughs at them and hates them." To the thinking man it was an age when things seemed out of control, and when, in the background, a man could hear the mocking laughter of the gods. As Seneca said, it was an age " stricken with the agitation of a soul no longer master of itself."

(ii) It was an age of unparalleled luxury. In the public baths of Rome the hot and cold water ran from silver taps. Caligula had even sprinkled the floor of the circus arena with gold dust instead of sawdust. Juvenal said bitterly: " A luxury more ruthless than war broods over Rome. . . . No guilt or deed of lust is wanting since Roman poverty disappeared." " Money, the nurse of debauchery . . . and enervating riches sapped the sinews of the age with foul luxury." Seneca spoke of " money, the ruin of the true honour of things," and said, " we ask not what a thing truly is but what it costs." It was an age so weary of ordinary things that it was avid for new sensations. Lucretius speaks of, " that bitterness which flows from the very fountain of pleasure." Crime became the only antidote to boredom, until, as Tacitus said, " the greater the infamy, the wilder the delight."

(iii) It was an age of unparalleled immorality. There had not been one single case of divorce in the first 520 years of the history of the Roman republic. The first Roman recorded as having divorced his wife was Spurius Carvilius Ruga in 234 B.C. But now, as Seneca said, " women were married to be divorced and divorced to be married." Roman high-born matrons dated the years by the names of their husbands, and not by the names of the consuls. Juvenal could not believe that it was possible to have the rare good fortune to find a matron with unsullied chastity. Clement of Alexandria speaks

of the typical Roman society lady as " girt like Venus
with a golden girdle of vice." Juvenal writes: " Is one
husband enough for Iberina? Sooner will you prevail
upon her to be content with one eye." He cites the case
of a woman who had eight husbands in five years. He
cites the incredible case of Agrippina, the empress herself,
the wife of Claudius, who at night used to leave the royal
palace and go down to serve in a brothel for the sake of
sheer unsated lust. " They show a dauntless spirit in
those things they basely dare." There is nothing that Paul
said about the heathen world that the heathen moralist
had not themselves already said. And vice did not stop
with the crude and natural vices. Society from top to
bottom was riddled with unnatural vice. Fourteen out
of the first fifteen Roman Emperors were homosexuals.

So far from exaggerating the picture Paul drew it with
restraint—and it was there that Paul was eager to preach
the gospel, and it was there that he was not ashamed
of the gospel of Christ. The world needed the power that
would work salvation, and Paul knew that nowhere else
than in Christ did that power exist.

THE LIFE WHICH HAS LEFT GOD OUT OF THE RECKONING

Romans I: 28-32

> Just as they have given themselves over to a kind of
> knowledge that rejects the idea of God, so God has
> given them over to the kind of mind that all reject.
> The result is that they do things which it is not fitting
> for any man to do. They are replete with all evil,
> villainy, the lust to get, viciousness. They are full
> of envy, murder, strife, deceit, the spirit which puts
> the worst construction on everything. They are
> whisperers, slanderers, haters of God. They are
> insolent men, arrogant, braggarts, inventors of
> evil things, disobedient to their parents, senseless
> breakers of agreements, without natural affections,
> pitiless. They are the kind of men who are well aware

that those who do such things deserve death, and yet they not only do them themselves, but also heartily approve of those who do them.

THERE is hardly any passage which so clearly shows what happens to a man when he leaves God out of the reckoning. It is not so much God who sends a judgment on a man, as a man who brings a judgment on himself when he gives no place to God in his scheme of things. When a man banishes God from his life he becomes a certain kind of man, and here in this passage is one of the most terrible descriptions in literature of the kind of man he becomes. Let us look at the catalogue of dreadful things which enter into the godless life.

Such men do the things which are not fitting for any man to do. The Stoics had a phrase. They talked of *ta kathēkonta,* by which they meant *the things it befits a man to do.* There are certain things which are essentially, naturally, instinctively, inherently part of manhood, and there are certain things which are not. As Shakespeare has it in *Macbeth:*

" I dare do all that may become a man;
Who dares do more is none."

The man who banishes God not only loses godliness; he loses manhood too.

Then there comes the long list of terrible things. Let us take them one by one.

Evil (adikia). Adikia is the precise opposite of *diaiosunē,* which means *justice;* and the Greeks defined *justice* as *giving to God and to men their due.* The *evil* man is the man who robs both man and God of their rights. He has so erected an altar to himself in the centre of things that he worships himself to the exclusion of God and man.

Villainy (ponēria). In Greek this word means more than *badness.* There is a kind of badness which, in the main, hurts only the person concerned. It is not essentially an outgoing badness. When it hurts others, as all badness must, the hurt is not deliberate. It may be thoughtlessly cruel, but it is not callously cruel. But the Greeks defined *ponēria* as *the desire of doing harm*. It is the active, deliberate will to corrupt and to inflict injury. When the Greeks described a woman as *ponēra* they meant that she deliberately seduced the innocent from their innocence. In Greek one of the commonest titles of Satan is *ho ponēros, the evil one,* the one who deliberately assaults, attacks and aims to destroy the innocence and the goodness of men. *Ponēros* describes the man who is not only bad, but who wants to make everyone as bad as himself, the man who wishes to drag others down to his own level. It is destructive badness.

The lust to get (pleonexia). The Greek word is built up of two words which mean *to have more*. The Greeks themselves defined *pleonexia* as *the accursed love of having*. It is an aggressive vice. It has been described as the spirit which will pursue its own interests with complete disregard for the rights of others, and even for the considerations of common humanity. The keynote of it is *rapacity*. Theodoret, the Christian writer, describes it as the spirit that aims at more, the spirit which grasps at things which it has no right to take. It may operate in every sphere of life. If it operates in the material sphere, it means grasping at money and goods, regardless of honour and honesty. If it operates in the ethical sphere, it means the ambition which tramples on others to gain something which is not properly meant for it. If it operates in the moral sphere, it means the unbridled lust which takes its pleasure where it has no right to take. *Pleonexia* is the desire which knows no law.

Viciousness (kakia). *Kakia* is the most general Greek word for badness. It describes the case of a man who is destitute of every quality which would make him good. For instance, a *kakos kritēs* is a judge destitute of the legal knowledge and the moral sense and the uprightness of character which are necessary to make a good judge. It is described by Theodoret as " the *turn* of the soul to the worse." The word he uses for turn is *ropē* which means *the turn of the balance*. A man who is *kakos* is a man the swing of whose life is towards the worse. *Kakia* has been described as the essential viciousness which includes all vice. It has been described as the forerunner of all other sins. It is the degeneracy out of which all sins grow and in which all sins flourish.

Envy (*phthonos*). There is a good and a bad envy. There is the envy which reveals to a man his own weakness and inadequacy, and which makes him eager to copy and to rise to some great example. And there is the envy which is essentially a grudging thing. It looks at a fine person, and is not so much moved to aspire to that fineness, as to resent that the other person is fine. It is the most warped and twisted of human emotions.

Murder (*phonos*). It has always to be remembered that Jesus immeasurably widened the scope of this word. Jesus insisted that not only the deed of violence, but the spirit of anger and hatred must be eliminated. He insisted that it is not enough only to keep life from angry and savage action. The only thing that is enough is when even the desire and the anger are banished from the heart. We may never have struck a man in our lives, but who can say he never wanted to strike anyone? As Aquinas said long ago, " Man regardeth the deed, but God seeth the intention."

Strife (*eris*). The meaning is the *contention* which is born of envy, ambition, the desire for prestige, and place, and office and prominence. It comes from the heart in which there is jealousy. If a man is cleansed of jealousy he has gone far to being cleansed of all that arouses contention and strife. It is a God-given gift to be able to take as much pleasure in the successes of others as in one's own.

Deceit (*dolos*). We get the meaning of this best from the corresponding verb (*doloun*). *Doloun* has two characteristic usages. It is used of debasing precious metals and of adulterating wines. *Dolos* is *deceit*; it describes the quality of the man who has a tortuous and a twisted mind, the man who cannot act in a straightforward way, the man who stoops to devious and underhand methods to get his own way, the man who never does anything except with some kind of ulterior motive. It describes the crafty cunning of the plotting intriguer who is found in every community and every society.

The spirit which puts the worst construction on everything (*kakoētheia*). *Kakoētheia* means literally *evil-naturedness*. At its widest it means *malignity*. Aristotle defined it in a narrower sense which it has always retained. He said it was " the spirit which always supposes the worst about other people." Pliny called it " malignity of interpretation." Jeremy Taylor said that it is " a baseness of nature by which we take things by the wrong handle, and expound things always in the worst sense." It may well be that this is the commonest of all sins. If there are two possible constructions to be put upon the action of any man, human nature will choose the worse. It is terrifying to think how many reputations have been murdered in gossip over the teacups, when people maliciously put a wrong interpretation upon a completely innocent action. When we are tempted so to do we ought to be remembering that God hears and remembers every word we speak.

Whisperers and slanderers (*Psithuristēs* and *katalalos*). These two words describe people with slanderous tongues. But there is a difference between them. *Katalalos*, slanderer, describes the man who trumpets his slanders abroad. He quite openly makes his accusations and tells his tales; but *psithuristēs* describes the man who whispers his malicious stories in the listener's ear, who will take a man apart into a corner and whisper a character-destroying story. Both are bad, but the whisperer is the worse. A man can at least defend himself against an open slander, but he is helpless against the secret whisperer who delights in destroying reputations.

Haters of God (*theostugeis*). This describes the man who hates God because he knows that he is defying God. If

29

there is a God, he knows that it is so much the worse for
him. God is to him the barrier between him and his pleasures.
God is the chain which keeps him from doing exactly
as he likes. He would gladly eliminate God if he could,
for to him a godless world would be a world where he
would have, not liberty, but license.

Insolent men (hubristēs). *Hubris* was to the Greek the
one vice which supremely courted destruction at the hand
of the gods. It has two main lines of thought in it. (i) It
describes the spirit of the man who is so proud that he
defies God. It is the insolent pride that goes before a fall.
It is the forgetting that man is a creature. It is the spirit
of the man who defies fate and fortune. It is the spirit
of the man who is so confident in his wealth, his power,
his own strength that he thinks that he can live life alone.
(ii) It describes the man who is wantonly and sadistically
cruel and insulting. Aristotle describes it as the spirit
which hurts, and harms and grieves someone else, not
for the sake of revenge, and not for any profit or advantage
that may be gained from it, but simply for the sheer pleasure
of hurting. There are people who get pleasure from seeing
someone wince at some cruel saying. There are people
who take a devilish delight in inflicting mental and physical
pain on others. That is *hubris*. It is the sadism which
finds delight in hurting others simply for the sake of hurting
them.

Arrogant men (huperēphanos). This is the word which
is three times used in scripture when it is said that God
resists the *proud*. (James 4: 6; I Peter 5: 5; Proverbs
3: 24). Theophylact called it " the summit of all sins."
Theophrastus was a Greek writer who wrote a series of
famous character sketches, and he defined *huperēphania*
as " a certain contempt for everyone except oneself."
Theophrastus picks out the things in everyday life which
are a sign of this arrogance. The arrogant man, when he
is asked to accept some office, refuses on the ground that
he has not time to spare from his own business. He never

30

looks at people on the street unless it pleases him to do so.
He invites a man to a meal and then does not appear
himself, but sends his servant to attend to his guest.
His whole life is surrounded with an atmosphere of contempt
and he delights to make others feel small.

Braggarts (alazōn). *Alazōn* in Greek is a word with an
interesting history. It literally means *one who wanders
about*. It then became the stock word for wandering
quacks who boast of cures that they have worked, and
for cheapjacks who boast that their wares have an excellence
which they are far from possessing. The Greeks defined
alazoneia as the spirit which pretends to have what it
has not. Xenophon said that the name belongs to those who
pretend to be richer and braver than they are, and who
promise to do what they are really unable to do, and they
do these things in order to make some profit or gain.
Again, Theophrastus has a character study of such a man—
the pretentious man, the snob. He is the kind of man who
boasts of trade deals which exist only in his imagination,
of connections with influential people which do not exist
at all, of gifts to charities and public services which he
never gave or rendered. He says about the house he
lives in it is really too small for him, and that he must
buy a bigger one. The braggart is out to impress others—
and the world is still full of such people.

Inventors of evil (epheuretēs kakōn). The phrase describes
the man who, so to speak, is not content with the usual,
ordinary ways of sinning, but who seeks out new and
recondite vices because he has grown tired and blasé,
and seeks some new thrill in some new sin.

Disobedient to their parents. Both Jews and Romans
set obedience to parents very high in the scale of virtues.
It was one of the Ten Commandments that parents should
be honoured. In the early days of the Roman Republic
the *patria potestas*, the father's power was so absolute that
he had the power of life and death over his family. The
real reason for including this sin in this passage is that once

the bonds of the family are loosened wholesale degeneracy must necessarily follow.

Senseless (*asunetos*). The word describes the man who is a fool, the man who cannot learn the lesson of experience, the man who is guilty of incredible folly, the man who will not use the mind and brain that God has given to him.

Breakers of agreements (*asunthetos*). This word would come with particular force to a Roman audience. In the great days of Rome Roman honesty was a wonderful thing. A man's word was as good as his bond. That was in fact one of the great differences between the Roman and the Greek. The Greek was a born pilferer. The Greeks used to say that if a governor or official was entrusted with one talent— £240—even if there were ten clerks and accountants to check up on him, he was certain to succeed in embezzling some of it; while the Roman, whether as a magistrate in office or a general on a campaign, could deal with thousands of talents on his bare word alone, and never a farthing went astray. By using this word, Paul was recalling the Romans not only to the Christian ethic, but to their own standards of honour in their greatest days.

Without natural affections (*astorgos*). *Storgē* was the special Greek word for family love. It was quite true that this was an age in which family love was dying. Never was the life of the child so precarious as at this time. Children were considered a misfortune. When a child was born, the child was taken and laid at the father's feet. If the father lifted up the child that meant that he ackn ledged it. If he turned away and left it the child literally thrown out. There was never a night when were not thirty or forty abandoned children left i Roman forum. Every night in life children were lite thrown away. Even Seneca, great soul as he was, cou write: " We kill a mad dog; we slaughter a fierce ox; we plunge the knife into sickly cattle lest they taint the

herd; *children who are born weakly and deformed we drown.*"
The natural bonds of human affection had been destroyed.

Pitiless (*aneleēmōn*). There never was a time when
human life was so cheap. The slave could be killed or
tortured by his master, for the slave was only a thing,
and the law gave the master unlimited power over him.
It is told that in a wealthy household a slave was bringing
in a tray of glasses of crystal. He stumbled and a glass
fell and broke. There and then his master had him flung
alive into the fish pond in the middle of the courtyard
where the savage lampreys tore him limb from limb and
devoured his living flesh. It was an age pitiless in its very
pleasures, for it was the great age of the gladiatorial games
where people found their delight in seeing men kill each
other. It was an age when the quality of mercy was gone.

Finally, Paul says one last thing about these people
who have banished God from life. It usually happens that,
even if a man is a sinner, he knows it, and, even if he allows
something in himself, he knows that it is to be condemned
in others. But in those days men had reached such a level
that they sinned themselves and approved of others who
did so and encouraged them to do so. George Bernard
Shaw once said, "No nation has ever survived the loss
of its gods," and here Paul has given us a terrible picture of
what happens when men have deliberately banished God
from the reckoning, and, in due time, Rome too perished.
Disaster and degeneracy went hand in hand and ended in
obliteration.

THE RESPONSIBILITY OF PRIVILEGE

2: 1-11

..., then, O man, everyone of you who judges others,
you yourself have no defence. While you judge others,
you condemn yourself, for you who set yourself up
as a judge do exactly the same things. We know
that God's judgment is directed against all who do

such things, and that it is based on reality. Are you counting on this, O man, you who set yourself up as a judge upon people who do such things and who do them yourself—that you will escape the condemnation of God? Or, are you treating with contempt the wealth of His kindness and forbearance and patience, not realising that God's kindness is meant to lead you to repentance? In your obtuseness, and in your impenitent heart, you are storing up for yourself wrath in the day of wrath, the day when there will be revealed the righteous judgment of God, who will settle accounts with each man according to his deeds. To those who sought glory and honour and immortality in steadfast good work, He will assign eternal life. To those who were dominated by ambition, who were disobedient to truth and obedient to evil, there will be wrath and anger, tribulation and affliction. These things will come upon every soul of man who does the bad thing, upon the soul of the Jew first and then of the Greek. But glory and honour and peace will come to everyone who does the good thing, to the Jew first and then to the Greek, for there is no favouritism with God.

In this passage Paul is directly addressing the Jews. The connection of thought is this. In the foregoing passage Paul had painted a grim and terrible picture of the heathen world, a world which was under the condemnation of God. With every word of that condemnation the Jew thoroughly agreed. The Jew, too, believed that God would blast the heathen out of existence for their sins. But the Jew never for a moment dreamed that he was under a like condemnation. He thought that he occupied a privileged position in the sight of God. God might be the judge of the heathen, but He was the special protector of the Jews. Here Paul is pointing out forcibly to the Jew that the Jew is just as much a sinner as the Gentile is, that when the Jew is condemning the Gentile he is condemning himself, that the fact that he is racially a Jew will certainly not save him from judgment, that he will be judged, not on his racial heritage, but by the kind of life that he himself lived.

34

The Jews always considered themselves in a specially privileged position with God. " God," they said, " loves Israel alone of all the nations of the earth." " God will judge the Gentiles with one measure and the Jews with another." " All Israelites will have part in the world to come." " Abraham sits beside the gates of hell and does not permit any wicked Israelite to go through." When Justin Martyr was arguing with the Jew about the position of the Jews in the *Dialogue with Trypho,* the Jew said, " They who are the seed of Abraham according to the flesh shall in any case, even if they be sinners and unbelieving and disobedient towards God, share in the eternal Kingdom." The writer of the *Book of Wisdom* comparing God's attitude to Jews and Gentiles said: " These as a father, admonishing them, Thou didst prove; but those as a stern king, condemning them, Thou didst search out " (Wisdom 11: 9). " While therefore Thou dost chasten us, Thou scourgest our enemies a thousand times more " (Wisdom 12: 22). The Jew believed that everyone was destined for judgment except himself. It would not be any special goodness which kept him immune from the wrath of God, but simply the fact that he was a Jew.

To meet this situation Paul reminded the Jews of four things.

(i) He told them bluntly that they were trading on the mercy of God. In verse 4 he uses three great words. He asks them: " Are you treating with contempt the wealth of His *kindness,* and *forbearance* and *patience?* " Let us look at these three great words. (*a*) *Kindness* (*chrēstotēs*). Of this word Trench says: " It is a beautiful word, as it is the expression of a beautiful idea." There are two words for *good* in Greek; there is *agathos* and there is *chrēstos.* The difference between them is this. The goodness of a man who is *agathos* may well issue in rebuke and discipline and punishment; but the goodness of a man who is *chrēstos* is always essentially kind. Jesus was *agathos* when He cleansed the Temple and drove the money-changers and the sellers of doves from it in the white heat of His anger. Jesus was *chrēstos* when He treated with loving gentleness the sinning woman who anointed His feet, or the woman taken in adultery. So Paul says, in effect, " You Jews are simply trying to take advantage of the great kindness of God." (b) *Forbearance* (*anochē*). Now *anochē* in Greek is the word for a *truce*. True, it means a cessation of enmity and hostility, but a cessation that has a limit. It is indeed something that gives a chance, but that chance has to be grasped in a given time or it is past. So Paul, in effect, is saying to the Jews, " You think that you are safe because God's judgment has not yet descended upon you. But what God is giving you is not *carte blanche* to sin; He is giving you the opportunity to repent and to amend your ways." A man cannot sin forever with impunity. (c) *Patience* (*makrothumia*). *Makrothumia* in Greek is characteristically a word which expresses *patience with people*. Chrysostom defined it as the characteristic of the man who has it in his power to avenge himself, and who deliberately does not use it. It is the spirit of the man who could wipe out the man who hurts and insults him, but who in patient mercy stays his hand. So, then, Paul is, in effect, saying to the Jews: " Do not think that the fact that God does not punish you is a sign that God cannot punish you. The fact that God's punishment does not immediately follow sin is not a proof of the powerlessness of God; it is a proof of the patience of God. You owe your lives to the patience of God."

One great commentator has said that almost everyone has, what he calls, " a vague and undefined hope of impunity," a kind of feeling that " this cannot happen to me." The Jews went further than that; " they openly claimed exemption from the judgment of God." The Jews traded on the mercy of God, and there are many who to this day seek to do the same.

(ii) The Jew regarded the mercy of God as an invitation to sin rather than as an incentive to repentance. It was Heine who made the famous, cynical statement. He was obviously not worrying about the world to come. He was asked why he was so confident, and his answer was, " God will forgive." He was asked why he was so sure of that, and his reply was, " *C'est son métier* " " It is His trade." Let us think of it in human terms. There are two attitudes to human forgiveness. Suppose a young person does something which is a shame, a sorrow and a heart-break to his parents, and suppose that in love he is freely forgiven, and the thing is never held against him, he can do one of two things. He can either go and do the same thing all over again, trading on the fact that he will be forgiven all over again; or he can be so moved to wondering gratitude by the free forgiveness that he has received that he spends his whole life in trying to be worthy of it. It is one of the most shameful things in the world to use mercy and love's forgiveness as an excuse to go on sinning. That is what the Jews were doing. That is what so many people still do. The mercy of God, the love of God, is not meant to make us feel that we can sin and get away with it; it is meant so to break our hearts in love that we will seek never to sin again.

(iii) Paul insists that there is no favouritism with God. He insists that in God's economy there is no most favoured nation clause. There may be nations which are picked out for a special task and for a special responsibility, but there are no nations which are picked out for special privilege and special consideration. It may be true, as Milton said, that " When God has some great work He gives it to His Englishmen," but it is a great *work* that is in question, not a great *privilege*. The whole of Jewish religion was based on the conviction that the Jews held a special position of privilege and favour in the eyes of God. We may feel that that is a position which nowadays we are far past. But is it? Is there no such thing nowadays as a colour bar? Is there no such thing as a conscious feeling of superiority to what Kipling called " lesser breeds without the law "? This is not to say that all nations are the same in talent, in genius, in ability. But it is to say that those nations who have advanced further than others are forbidden to look with contempt on the others, and are under the responsibility to help the others up to their own standards.

(iv) Of all passages of Paul this passage deserves most carefully to be studied in order to arrive at a correct idea of Paulinism. It is often argued that Paul's position was that all that matters is faith. A religion which stresses the importance of works is often contemptuously waved aside as being quite out of touch with the New Testament. Nothing could be further from the truth. " God," said Paul, " will settle with each man according to his deeds." To Paul a faith which did not issue in deeds would be a travesty and a parody of faith. In fact it would not be a faith at all. Paul would have said that the only way in which you can see a man's faith at all is by his deeds. One of the most dangerous of all religious tendencies is to talk as if faith and works were entirely different and separate things. There can be no such thing as a faith which does not issue in works, and there can be no such thing as works which are not the product of faith. Works and faith are inextricably bound up together. How, in the last analysis, can God judge a man any other way than by his deeds? We cannot comfortably say, " I have faith," and leave it at that. That faith of ours must issue in deeds, for it is by our deeds we are accepted or condemned.

THE UNWRITTEN LAW

Romans 2: 12-16

> As many as sinned without the law shall also perish without the law; and as many as sinned in the law shall be judged by the law; for it is not the hearers

of the law who are righteous in the sight of God, but it is the doers of the law who will be accounted righteous, in that day when God judges the hidden things of men according to my gospel through Jesus Christ. For whenever the Gentiles, who do not possess the law, do by nature the deeds of the law, they, although they do not possess the law, are a law to themselves. They show the work of the law written on their hearts, while their consciences bear them witness, and while their thoughts within accuse or excuse them.

IT is to be noted that in the translation we have slightly changed the order of the verses. In the sense of the passage verse 16 ought to come after verse 13, and verses 14 and 15 are a long parenthesis. It is to be remembered that Paul was not writing this letter sitting at a desk and thinking out every word and every construction. We are to think of him striding up and down the room dictating it to his secretary, Tertius (Romans 16: 22), who struggled to get it down. That explains the long parenthesis, but it is easier to get the correct meaning in English if we take out the parenthesis, and if we go straight from verse 13 to verse 16, and add verses 14 and 15 afterwards, as an explanation.

In this passage Paul turns to the Gentiles. He has dealt with the Jews and with their claims to special privilege and special favour. But one advantage the Jew did have, and that was the Law. It might well be that a Gentile might retaliate by saying, " It is only right that God should condemn the Jews who had the Law and who ought to have known better; but we, the Gentiles, will surely escape judgment altogether because we had no opportunity to know the Law and did not know any better." In answer to that claim Paul lays down two great principles.

(i) A man will be judged by what he had the opportunity to know. If he knew the Law, he will be judged as one who knew the Law. If he did not know the Law, he will be judged as one who did not know the Law. God is fair.

And here is the answer to those who ask what is to happen to the people who lived in the world before Jesus came into the world and who had no opportunity to hear the Christian message. The Christian answer is that a man will be judged by his fidelity to the highest that it was possible for him to know. If he has been true to the highest that he knew, God cannot and will not ask any more.

(ii) But Paul goes on to say that even those who did not know the written Law had an unwritten law within their hearts. We would call it the instinctive knowledge of right and wrong. The Stoics said that in the universe there were certain laws operative which a man broke at his peril—the laws of health, the moral law, the laws which govern life and living. The Stoics called these laws *phusis*, which means *Nature*, and the Stoics urged men to live *kata phusin*, according to nature. It is Paul's argument that in the very nature of man there is implanted an innate, inherent and instinctive knowledge of what he ought to do. The Greeks would have agreed with that. Aristotle said: " The cultivated and free-minded man will so behave as being *a law to himself*." Plutarch asks: " Who shall govern the governor? " And he answers: " Law, the king of all mortals and immortals, as Pinder calls it, which is not written on papyrus rolls or wooden tablets, but is his own reason within the soul, which perpetually dwells with him and guards him and never leaves his soul bereft of leadership."

Paul saw the world divided into two classes of people. He saw the Jews with their Law given to them direct from God and written down so that all could read it. He saw the other nations, without this written law, but nonetheless with a God-implanted, instinctive knowledge of right and wrong within their hearts. Neither could claim exemption from the judgment of God. The Jew could not claim exemption because he had a special place in God's plan. The Gentile could not claim exemption because he had never received the written Law. The Jew would be judged as one who had known the Law; the Gentile would be judged as one who, though he had no written law, nevertheless had a God-given conscience. God will judge a man according to what he knows and has the chance to know.

THE REAL JEW

Romans 2: 17-29

If you are called by the name of Jew, if you take your rest in the Law, if you boast in God and know His will, if you give your approval to the excellent things, if you are instructed in the Law, if you believe yourself to be a leader of the blind, a light in darkness, and educator of the foolish, a teacher of the simple, if you believe yourself to have the very shape of knowledge and of truth in the Law—do you, then, who instruct another, not instruct yourself? Do you, who proclaim to others that stealing is forbidden, steal yourself? Do you, who forbid others to commit adultery, commit adultery yourself? Do you, who shudder at idols, rob temples? Do you, who boast in the Law, dishonour others by transgressing the Law? As it stand written, " Because of your conduct, God's name is ill-spoken of among the Gentiles." Circumcision is indeed an advantage if you do the Law. But if you are a transgressor of the Law your circumcision has become the equivalent of uncircumcision. For if uncircumcision observes the moral requirements of the Law, shall not uncircumcision be reckoned as the equivalent of circumcision, and will natural uncircumcision which keeps the Law, not become the judge of you who are a transgressor of the Law, although you have the letter and the circumcision? For he is not a real Jew who is externally a Jew; nor is the real circumcision the external circumcision in the flesh; but he is a real Jew who is a Jew in inward things; and real circumcision is the circumcision of the heart, in spirit, and not in letter. The praise of such a man comes not from men but from God.

To a Jew a passage like this must have come as a shattering experience. The Jew was certain that he stood in a special relationship to God, and that God regarded him with special favour, simply and solely because of his national descent from Abraham, and because he bore the badge of circumcision in his flesh. But here Paul introduces an idea to which he will return again and again. Jewishness, he insists, is not a matter of race at all; Jewishness has nothing to do with circumcision. Jewishness is a matter of conduct. If that is so, there is many a so-called Jew who is a pure descendant of Abraham, and who bears the mark of circumcision in his body, who is no Jew at all; and equally there is many a Gentile who never heard of Abraham, and who would never dream of being circumcised, who is a Jew in the real sense of the term. To a Jew this would have sounded the wildest heresy. With one stroke Paul was abolishing the very basis of Jewish thought. He was shutting out from real Jewishness many and many a Jew, and he was introducing a new conception which made Jewishness a thing available to every nation, a thing as wide as the earth itself. A statement like that would leave a Jew angry and aghast.

The very last verse of this passage contains a pun which is completely untranslatable. " The praise of such a man comes not from men but from God." The Greek word for praise is *epainos*. Now when we turn back to the Old Testament (Genesis 29: 35; 49: 8), we find that the original and traditional meaning of the word *Judah* is *praise* (*epainos*). So that this phrase means two things. (*a*) It means the *praise* of such a man comes not from men but from God. (*b*) It means the Jewishness of such a man comes not from men but from God. The whole sense of the passage is that God's promises are not to people of a certain race and to people who bear a certain mark on their bodies. God's promises are to people who live a certain kind of life irrespective of what race they may belong to. To be a real Jew is not a matter of pedigree;

it is a matter of character; and it can often happen that the man who is not racially a Jew at all is a better Jew than the man who is.

In this passage Paul says that there are Jews whose conduct makes the name of God to be ill-spoken of among the Gentiles. It is a simple fact of history that the Jews were, and often still are, the best hated and the most unpopular people in the world. Let us see just how the Gentiles did regard the Jews in New Testament times.

The Gentiles regarded Judaism as a " barbarous superstition." They regarded the Jews as " the most disgusting of races," and as " a most contemptible company of slaves." The origins of Jewish religion were twisted with a malicious ignorance. It was said that the Jews had originally been a company of lepers who had been sent by the king of Egypt to work in the sand quarries; that Moses had rallied this band of leprous slaves and led them through the desert to Palestine. It was said that they worshipped an ass's head, because in the wilderness a herd of wild ass's had led them to water when they were perishing with thirst. It was said that they abstained from swine's flesh because the pig is specially liable to a skin disease called the itch, and it was that skin disease that the Jews had suffered from in Egypt.

Certain of the Jewish customs were mocked at by the Gentiles. Their abstinence from swine's flesh provided the Gentiles with many a jest. Plutarch thought that the reason for that abstinence might well be that the Jews worshipped the pig as a god. Juvenal declares that Jewish clemency has accorded to the pig the privilege of living to a good old age, and that swine's flesh is more valuable to them than the flesh of a man. The custom of observing the Sabbath was regarded as pure laziness and indolence.

Certain things which the Jews enjoyed infuriated the Gentiles. It was the odd fact that, unpopular as they were, the Jews had nonetheless received extraordinary privileges from the Roman government. (a) They were allowed to transmit the temple tax every year to Jerusalem. This remitting of the temple tax to Jerusalem became so serious in Asia about the year 60 B.C. that the export of currency was forbidden and, according to the historians, no less than twenty tons of contraband gold was seized which the Jews had been about to despatch to Jerusalem. (b) They were allowed, at least to some extent, to have their own courts, and live according to their own laws. There is a decree issued by a governor called Lucius Antonius in Asia about the year 50 B.C. in which the governor wrote: " Our Jewish citizens came to me and informed me that they had their own private gathering, carried out according to their ancestral laws, and their own private place, where they settle their own affairs and deal with cases between each other. When they asked that this custom should be continued, I gave judgment that they should be allowed to retain this privilege." The Gentiles detested the spectacle of a race of people living as a kind of separate and specially privileged nation. (c) The Roman government respected the Jewish observance of the Sabbath. It was laid down that the Jew could not be called to give evidence in a law court on the Sabbath. It was laid down that if special doles and favours were being distributed to the populace, and the distribution fell on the Sabbath, the Jews could claim their share on the following day. And—what was a specially sore point with the Gentiles—the Jews enjoyed *astrateia*, that is exemption from conscription to serve in the Roman army. This exemption was directly due to the fact that the Jewish strict observance of the Sabbath obviously made it impossible for him to carry out military duties on the Sabbath. The result was that he was exempted altogether, and it can easily be imagined with what resentment the rest of the world would look on this special exemption from what to others was a burdensome duty.

But there were two special things of which the Jews were accused. (a) They were accused of *atheism* (*atheotēs*). It was the odd fact that the ancient world had great difficulty in conceiving of the possibility of any religion without any visible images of worship. Pliny called them, " a race distinguished by their contempt for all deities." Tacitus said, " The Jews conceive of their deity as one, by the mind alone. . . . Hence no images are erected in their cities or even in their temples. This reverence is not paid to kings, nor this honour to the Caesars." Juvenal said, " They venerate nothing but the clouds and the deity of the sky." But the truth is that what really moved the Gentile to such dislike, was not so much the imageless worship of the Jews, as the cold contempt in which the Jews held all other religions. No man whose main attitude to his fellow men is contempt can ever be a missionary. This contempt for others was one of the things which Paul was thinking of when he said that the Jews brought the name of God into disrepute.

(*b*) They were accused of *hatred of their fellow-men* (*misanthrōpia*) and *complete unsociability* (*amixia*). Tacitus said of them: " Among themselves their honesty is inflexible, their compassion quick to move, but to all other persons they show the hatred of antagonism." In Alexandria the story was that the Jews had taken an oath never to show kindness to a Gentile, and that they even offered a Greek in sacrifice to their God every year. Tacitus said that the first thing that Gentiles who had been converted to Judaism were taught to do was " to despise the gods, to repudiate their nationality, and to disparage parents, children and brothers." Juvenal declared that if a Jew was asked the way to any place he refused to give any information except to another Jew, and that if anyone was looking for a well from which to drink, they would not lead him to it unless he was circumcised. Here we have the same thing again. The basic Jewish attitude to other men was contempt, and contempt must ever invite hatred in answer.

It was all too true that the Jews did bring the name of God into disrepute because they shut themselves into a rigid little community from which all others were shut out, and because they showed to the heathen an attitude of contempt for their worship, and complete lack of charity for their needs. Real religion is a thing of the open heart and the open door; Judaism was a religion of the shut heart and the shut door.

GOD'S FIDELITY AND MAN'S INFIDELITY

Romans 3: 1-8

What, then, is the something plus which belongs to a Jew? Or what special advantage belongs to those who have been circumcised? Much in every way. In the first place, there is this advantage—that the Jews have been entrusted with the oracles of God. Yes, you say, but what if some of them were unfaithful to them? Surely you are not going to argue that their infidelity invalidates the fidelity of God? God forbid! Let God be shown to be true, though every man be shown to be a liar, as it stands written: " In order that you may be seen to be in the right in your arguments, and that you may win your case when you enter into judgment." But, you say, if our unrighteousness merely provides proof of God's righteousness, what are we to say? Surely you are not going to try to argue that God is unrighteous to unleash the Wrath upon you? (I am using human arguments). God forbid! For, if that were so, how shall God judge the world? But, you say, if the fact that I am false merely provides a further opportunity to demonstrate the fact that God is true, to His greater glory, why should I still be condemned as a sinner? Are you going to argue—just as some slanderously allege that we suggest—that we should do evil that good may come of it? Anyone can see that statements like that merit nothing but condemnation.

HERE is one of these passages where Paul is arguing in the closest and the most difficult way. It will make it easier to understand if we remember that Paul is carrying on an argument with an imaginary objector. The argument stated in full, would run something like this.

The objector: The result of all that you have been saying is that there is no difference between Gentile and Jew, that they are in exactly the same position. Do you really mean that?

Paul: By no means.

The objector: What, then, is the difference?

Paul: For one thing, the Jew possesses what the Gentile never so directly possessed—the Commandments of God.

The objector: Granted! But what if some of the Jews disobeyed these commandments and were unfaithful to God, and came under the condemnation of God? You have just said that God gave the Jews a special position and a special promise. Now you go on to say that at least some of the Jews are under the condemnation of God. Does that mean that God has broken His promise, and has therefore shown Himself to be unjust and unreliable?

Paul: Far from it! What it does show is that there is no favouritism with God, that God punishes sin wherever He sees it. The very fact that God condemns the unfaithful Jews is the best possible proof of the absolute justice of God. He might have been expected to overlook the sins of this special people of His but He did not. Nothing could so demonstrate His impartial justice, and His right to be the Judge of all the earth.

The objector: Very well then! All you have done is to succeed in showing that my disobedience has given God an opportunity to demonstrate His righteousness. You are saying that my infidelity has given God a marvellous opportunity to demonstrate His fidelity. Why call me a sinner for that? My sin is an excellent thing! It has given God a chance to show how good He is! I may have done evil, but nothing but good has come of it! You can't surely condemn a man for giving God a chance to show His justice!

Paul: An argument like that is beneath contempt! You have only to state it to see how intolerable it is!

When we disentangle this passage in this way, we see that there are in it certain basic thoughts of Paul in regard to the Jews.

(i) To the end of the day Paul believed the Jews to be in a special position in regard to God. That, in fact, is what the Jews believed themselves. But the difference was that Paul believed that that special position was a position of special *responsibility*; the Jew believed it to be a position of special *privilege*. What did Paul say that the Jew had specially been entrusted with? *The oracles of God*. What does he mean by that? The word he uses is *logia*, which is the regular word in the Greek Old Testament for a special statement or pronouncement of God. Here it means *The Ten Commandments*. What God entrusted the Jews with was *commandments*, not privileges. He said to them, " You are a special people; therefore you must live a special life." He did *not* say, " You are a special people; therefore you can do what you like." He did say, " You are a special people; *therefore you must do what I like.*" This special choice of God brought special duty, not special exemption from duty. When Lord Dunsany was brought in safety through the 1914-18 war he tells us that he said to himself, " In some strange way I am still alive. I wonder what God means me to do with a life so specially spared? " It was just that thought that never struck the Jews. They never could grasp the fact that God's special choice was for special duty.

(ii) All through his writings there are three basic facts in Paul's mind about the Jews. They occur in embryo here; and they are in fact the three thoughts that it takes this whole letter to work out. We must note that Paul did not place all the Jews under the one condemnation. He puts it in this way: "What if *some of them* were unfaithful? " (*a*) Paul was quite sure that God was justified in condemning the Jews. They had their special place; they had their special promises; and the very fact that they had proved unfaithful to God made their condemnation all the greater. Responsibility is always the obverse of privilege. The more chances a man has to do right, the greater his condemnation if he does wrong. (b) *But not* all of them were unfaithful. Paul never forgot the faithful remnant; and he was quite sure that that faithful remnant —however small it was in numbers—was the true Jewish race. The others had lost their privileges and were under condemnation. They were no longer Jews at all. The remnant was the real nation. (c) Paul was always sure that this rejection by God of Israel *was not final*. Because of this rejection, a door was opened to the Gentiles; and, *in the end*, some day the Gentiles would actually bring the Jews back within the fold, and Gentile and Jew would be one in Christ. The tragedy of the Jew was that the great task of world evangelisation that he might have had, and was designed to have, was refused by him. It was therefore given to the Gentiles, and, in the end, God's plan was, as it were, reversed, and it was not, as it should have been, the Jew who evangelised the Gentile, but the Gentile who evangelised the Jew—a process which is still going on.

But, further, this passage has in it two great universal human truths.

(i) The root of all sin is disobedience. The root of the sin of the Jew was disobedience to the known law of God. As Milton wrote, it was " man's first disobedience " which was responsible for paradise lost. When pride sets up the will of man against the will of God there is sin. If there were no disobedience there would be no sin.

(ii) Once a man has sinned, he displays an amazing ingenuity in justifying his own sin. Here we come across an argument that reappears again and again in religious thought. The argument was that sin gives God a chance to show at once His justice and His mercy; therefore sin is a good thing, because it has good results. It is a twisted argument. One might as well argue—it would, in fact, be the same argument—that it is a good thing to break a person's heart, because it gives that person a chance to show how much he or she loves you. It is the argument that only a man blindly, and callously insensitive, would ever use. When a man does sin, the need is not for ingenuity to justify the sin, but for humility to confess it in penitence and in shame.

THE CHRISTLESS WORLD

Romans 3: 9-18

> What then? Are we Jews out ahead? By no means. For we have already charged all Jews and Greeks with being under the power of sin, as it stands written: " There is none righteous, no not one. There is no man of understanding. There is none who seeks the Lord. All have swerved out of the way, and all together have gone bad. There is none whose acts are good, not one single one. Their throat is an open tomb. They practise fraud with their tongues. The poison of asps is under their lips. Their mouths are laden with curses and bitterness. Their feet are swift to shed blood. Destruction and wretchedness are in their ways, and they have not known the way of peace. There is no fear of God before their eyes."

IN the last passage Paul had insisted that, in spite of everything, the Jew had a special position in the economy of God. Not unnaturally the Jewish objector then asks f that means that the Jews are out ahead of other peoples. Paul's answer was that Jew and Gentile alike, so long as they are without Christ, are under the dominion of sin. The phrase that Paul uses for under sin is very suggestive. In the Greek it is *hupo hamartian*. In this sense *hupo* means definitely *in the power of, under the authority of*. In Matthew 8: 9 the centurion says: " I have soldiers *upo emauton, under me.*" That is, I have soldiers *under my command*. A schoolboy is *upo paidagōgon, under the direction* of the slave who is in control of him. A slave is *hupo zugon, under the yoke*, in the power of his master.

In the Christless state a man is under the command, under the authority, under the control of sin, and helpless to escape from it.

There is one other interesting word in this passage. It is the word in verse 11 which we have translated, " They have gone bad." The word is *achreioō*, which literally means *to render useless*. One of its uses is that it is used of milk that has gone sour, that has turned bad. Human nature without Christ is a soured and useless thing.

We see Paul doing here what Jewish Rabbis customarily did. In verses 10-18 he has strung together a collection of Old Testament texts. He is not quoting accurately because he is quoting from memory, but he includes quotations from Psalm 14: 1-3; Psalm 5: 9; Psalm 140: 3; Psalm 10: 7; Isaiah 59: 7, 8; Psalm 36: 1. It was a very common method of Rabbinic preaching to string texts together like this. It was called *charaz*, which literally means *stringing pearls*.

It is indeed a terrible description of human nature in its Christless state. Vaughan has pointed out that, when we examine these Old Testament quotations, they describe three things. (i) A *character* whose characteristics are ignorance, indifference, crookedness and unprofitableness. (ii) A *tongue* whose notes are destructive, deceitful, malignant. (iii) A *conduct* whose marks are oppression, injuriousness, implacability. These things are the result of disregard of God.

There is no one who saw so clearly the evil of human nature as Paul did; but it must always be noted that the evil of human nature was to Paul, not a call to hopelessness, but a challenge to hope. When we say that Paul believed in original sin, when we say that he believed in the depravity of human nature, we must never take that to mean that Paul despaired of human nature, or that he looked on it with cynical contempt. Once when William Jay, of Bath, was an old man, he said: " My memory is failing, but there are two things that I never forget—that I am a great sinner, and that Jesus Christ is a great Saviour." Paul never under-rated the sin of man, and he never under-rated the redeeming power of Jesus Christ. Once, when he was a young man, William Roby, the great Lancashire Independent, was preaching at Malvern. His lack of success drove him to despair, and he wished to leave the work. Then came a seasonable reproof from a certain Mr. Moody, who asked him, " Are they, then, too bad to be saved? " The challenge of that sent William Roby back to his work. Paul believed men without Christ to be bad, but he never believed men too bad to be saved. He was confident that what Christ had done for him He could do for any man.

THE ONLY WAY TO BE RIGHT WITH GOD

Romans 3: 19-26

We know that whatever the law says, it says to those who are within the law, and the function of the law is that every mouth should be silenced and that the whole world should be shown to be liable to the judgment of God, because no one will ever get into a right relationship with God by doing the works which the law lays down. What does come through the law is a full awareness of sin. But now a way to a right relationship to God lies open before us quite apart from the law, and it is a way attested by the law and the prophets. For a right relationship to God comes through faith in Jesus Christ to all who believe. For there is no distinction, for all have sinned and all fall short of the glory of God, but they are put into a right relationship with God, freely, by His grace, through the deliverance which is wrought by Jesus Christ. God put Him forward as one who can win for us forgiveness of our sins through faith in His blood. He did so in order to demonstrate His righteousness because, in the forbearance of God, there had been a passing over of the sins which happened in previous times; and He did so to demonstrate His righteousness in this present age, so that He Himself should be just and that He should accept as just the man who believes in Jesus.

HERE again is a passage which is not easy to understand, but which is full of riches when its true meaning is grasped. Let us see if we can penetrate to the basic truth behind it.

The supreme problem of life is, How can a man get into a right relationship with God? How can a man feel at peace, at ease, at home with God? How can a man escape the feeling of estrangement and fear in the presence of God? The older religion, the religion of Judaism, answered: "A man can attain to a right relationship with God by keeping meticulously all that the law lays down. If he fulfils all the works of the law, he will be right with God." But to say that is simply to say that there is no possibility of any man ever attaining to that right relationship with God. No man ever can keep or ever will keep every commandment of the law. Simply because man is an imperfect creature he can never render a perfect obedience. No man can ever render a perfect service to the infinite perfection of God.

> " Not the labours of my hands
>   Can fulfil Thy law's demands."

What then is the use of the law? The use of the law is that it makes a man aware of sin. It is only when a man knows what he ought to do that he can realize that he is not doing it. It is only when a man knows the law and tries to satisfy it that he realizes he can never satisfy it. The law is designed to show a man his own weakness and his own sinfulness. Is a man then shut out from God? Far from it, because the way to God is not the way of law, but the way of grace. It is not the way of works, it is the way of faith.

To show what he means Paul uses three metaphors.

(i) He uses the metaphor from the *law courts*, that is the metaphor which we call *justification*. Let us remind ourselves again, the whole problem is, How can a man enter into a right relationship with God? This metaphor thinks of man on trial before God. Now the Greek word which is translated *to justify* is *diakioun*. All Greek verbs which end in *-oun* mean, not to *make* someone something, but to *treat*, to *reckon*, to *account* someone as something. If a man appears before a judge and that man *is* innocent, then to treat him as innocent is to *acquit* him. But the whole point about God and man is this—that when man appears before God he is anything but innocent; he is utterly guilty; and yet God, in His amazing mercy, treats him, reckons him, accounts him as if he were an innocent man. That is what justification means. When Paul says that "God justifies the ungodly," he means that God, in His incredible mercy, treats the ungodly as if he had been a good man. That is what shocked the Jews to the core of their being. To them to treat the bad man as if he was a good man was the sign of a wicked judge. " He that justifieth the wicked is an abomination to the Lord " (Proverbs 17: 15). " I will not justify the wicked " (Exodus 23: 7). But Paul says that that is precisely what God does. But how can I know that God is like that? I know that God is like that *because Jesus said so.* Jesus came to tell us that God loves us, bad as we are. He came to tell us that we may be sinners—we are sinners—but we are still dear to God. Now, note, when we discover that, and believe that, *it changes our whole relationship to God.* We are conscious of our sin, but we are no longer in terror; we are no longer estranged; penitent and broken-hearted we come to God, like a sorry child coming to his mother, and we know that the God we come to is love. That is what *justification by faith in Jesus Christ* means. It means that we are in a right relationship with God, because we believe with all our hearts that what Jesus told us about God is true. We are no longer terrorized strangers from an angry God. We are children, erring children, trusting in their Father's love for forgiveness. *And we could never have known that if Jesus had not come to live and to die to tell us so.* And we only know it when we trust absolutely that what Jesus said about God is true.

54

(ii) Paul uses the metaphor from *sacrifice*. He says of Jesus that God put Him forward as one who can win forgiveness for our sins. The word that Paul uses to describe Jesus is the Greek word *hilastērion*. This word comes from a Greek verb which means *to propitiate*. It is a verb which has to do with sacrifice. Under the old system, when a man broke the law, he brought to God a sacrifice. His aim was that that sacrifice should make God gracious to him, that the sacrifice should avert the wrath of God, that the sacrifice should turn aside the punishment that should fall upon him. To put it in another way—a man sinned; that sin put him at once in a wrong relationship with God; to get back into the right relationship he offered his sacrifice. *But* it was the whole of human experience that an animal sacrifice failed entirely to do that. " Thou desirest not sacrifice, else would I give it; thou delightest not in burnt-offering " (Psalm 51: 16). " Wherewith shall I come before the Lord, and bow myself before the high God? Shall I come before him with burnt-offerings, with calves of a year old? Will the Lord be pleased with thousands of rams, or with ten thousands of rivers of oil? Shall I give my first-born for my transgression, the fruit of my body for the sin of my soul? " (Micah 6: 6, 7). Instinctively men felt that once they had sinned the paraphernalia of earthly sacrifice could not put matters right. So Paul says, " Jesus Christ, by His life of obedience and His death of love, made the one sacrifice to God which really and truly atones for sin." Paul insists that that which happened on the Cross opens the door back to the right relationship with God, a door which every other sacrifice is powerless to open.

(iii) Paul uses the metaphor from *slavery*. He speaks of the *deliverance* wrought through Jesus Christ. The word is *apolutrōsis*. It means a ransoming, a redeeming, a liberating. It means that man was in the power, the grip, the dominion of sin, and that Jesus Christ alone can free him from it.

Finally, Paul says of God that God did all this because He is, and accepts as just, all who believe in Jesus. Paul never in his life said a more startling thing than this. Bengel called it " the supreme paradox of the gospel." Think what it means. It means that God is just and accepts the sinner as a just man. The natural thing to say, the inevitable thing to say, would be, " God is just, and, therefore, condemns the sinner as a criminal." But here we have the great and precious paradox—God is just, and somehow, in that incredible and miraculous grace that Jesus came to bring to me, He accepts the sinner, not as a criminal, but as a son whom He still loves.

Now what is the essence of all this? Where is the difference between all this and the old way of the law? The basic difference is this—the way of obedience to the law is concerned with what a man can do for himself; the way of grace is concerned with what God can do, and has done, for a man. Paul is insisting that nothing that we can ever do can win for us the forgiveness of God; only what God has done for us can win that; therefore the way to a right relationship with God lies, not in a frenzied, desperate, doomed attempt to win acquittal by our performance; it lies in the humble, penitent acceptance of the love and the grace which God offers us in Jesus Christ.

THE END OF THE WAY OF HUMAN ACHIEVEMENT

Romans 3: 27-31

Where, then, is there any ground for boasting? It is completely shut out. Through what kind of law? Through the law of works? No, but through the law of faith. So, then, we reckon that a man enters into a right relationship with God by faith quite apart from works of the law. Or, is God the God of the Jews only? Is He not the God of the Gentiles? Yes, He is the God of the Gentiles too. If, indeed, God is one, He is the God who will bring those who are of the circumcision into a right relationship with Himself

56

by faith, and those who never knew the circumcision through faith. Do we then through faith completely cancel out all law? God forbid! Rather, we confirm the law.

PAUL deals with three points here.

(i) If the way to God is the way of faith and of acceptance, then all boasting in human achievement is gone. There was a certain kind of Judaism which kept a kind of profit and loss account with God. There was a certain kind of Jew who strictly kept every detail of the ceremonial law, and for every time he carried out one of the law's little regulations he made an entry on the credit side. In the end he came to a frame of mind in which he rather held that God was in his debt. Paul's whole position was that every man is a sinner, that no man could ever have put himself back into a right relationship with God through his own efforts, that every man is God's debtor, and that all grounds for self-satisfaction and boasting in one's own achievement are forever gone.

(ii) But, a Jew might answer, that way might be well enough for a Gentile who never knew the law, but what about Jews who do know the law? Paul's answer was to turn them to the sentence which is the basis of the Jewish creed, the sentence with which every Synagogue service always began and still begins. " Hear, O Israel, the Lord thy God is one God " (Deuteronomy 6: 4). There is not one kind of God for the Gentiles and another for the Jews. God is *one*. The way to Him is the same for Gentile and Jew. It is not the way of human achievement; it is the way of trusting and accepting faith.

(iii) But, says the Jew, does this mean an end of all law? We might have expected Paul to say, " Yes." In point of fact he says, " No." He says that, in fact, it strengthens the law. What does he mean by this? He means this. Up to this time the Jew had tried to be a good man, he had tried to keep the commandments, he had tried to serve God, because he was afraid of God, and was terrified of the punishment that breaches of the law would bring. True, that day has for ever gone. But what has taken its place? The thing that has taken its place is *the love of God.* Now a man must try to be good, must try to keep God's law, not because he fears God's punishment, but because he feels that somehow, with his last drop of energy, he must strive to deserve that amazing love. He strives for goodness, not because he is afraid of God, but because he loves God. He knows now that sin is not so much breaking God's law as it is breaking God's heart, and, therefore, sin is doubly terrible. Take a human analogy. Many a man is tempted to do a wrong thing, and does not do it. Why does he not do it? It is not so much that he fears the law. He would not greatly care if he were fined, or even imprisoned. What keeps him right is the simple fact that he could not meet the sorrow in the eyes of the one who loves him if he shipwrecked life. It is not the law of fear but the law of love which keeps him right. It must be that way with us and God. We are rid forever of the terror of God, but that is no reason for doing as we like. We can never again do as we like for we are now for ever sentenced to goodness by the law of love. And the law of love is a far stronger law than ever the law of fear can be.

THE FAITH WHICH TAKES GOD AT HIS WORD

Romans 4: 1-8

> What, then, shall we say that Abraham, our forefather from whom we take our human descent, found? If Abraham entered into a right relationship with God by means of work, he has some ground for boasting—but not in regard to God. For what does scripture say? " Abraham trusted in God and it was accounted to him for righteousness." The man who works does not receive his pay as a favour; he receives it as a debt due to him. But, as for the man who does not depend on work, but who trusts in the God who

treats the ungodly as He would treat a good man, his faith is accounted as righteousness. Just so, David speaks of the counting happy of the man to whom God accounts righteousness apart from works—" Happy they whose transgressions are forgiven and whose sins are covered! Happy the man to whom God does not account sin!"

PAUL moves on to speak of Abraham for three reasons.

(i) The Jew regarded Abraham as the great founder of the race, and the pattern of all that a man should be. Very naturally the Jew must ask, " If all that you say is true, what was the special thing that was given to Abraham when God picked him out to be the ancestor of His special people? Wherein lies the special position of Abraham? What makes him different from other people?" That is the question which Paul is going to go on to answer.

(ii) Paul has just been seeking to prove that what makes a man right with God is not the performance of the works that the law lays down, but the simple trust of complete yieldedness which takes God at His word, and which believes that God still loves us when we have done nothing to deserve that love. The immediate reaction of the Jew was, " This is something entirely new. This is a contradiction of all that we have been taught to believe. This is doctrine which is completely incredible and unheard of." Paul's answer is, " So far from being new, this doctrine is as old as the Jewish faith. So far from being an heretical novelty, this teaching is the very basis of Jewish religion." That is what Paul is going on to prove.

(iii) Paul begins to speak about Abraham because Paul was a wise teacher who knew the human mind and the way in which it works. He has been talking about *faith*. Now faith is an abstract noun and an abstract idea. The ordinary human mind finds abstract ideas very hard to grasp and to understand. The wise teacher knows that every word must become flesh, every idea must become a person, that the only way in which an ordinary person can grasp an abstract idea is to see that idea in action, and to see it embodied in a person. So Paul, in effect, says, " I have been talking about faith. If you want to see what faith is, look at Abraham." Paul moves on to Abraham in order to make his readers see the abstract idea of faith in concrete action, so that they will really grasp what he means by faith.

When Paul began to speak about Abraham he was on ground that every Jew knew and understood. In the thoughts of the Jews Abraham held a unique position. He was the founder of the nation. He was the man to whom God had first spoken. He was the man who had in a unique way been chosen by God and who had heard and obeyed God. The Rabbis had their own discussions about Abraham. To Paul the essence of Abraham's greatness was this. God had come to Abraham, and God had bidden Abraham leave home and friends and kindred and livelihood, and had said to him, " If you make this great venture of faith, you will become the father of a great nation and a great people." Thereupon Abraham had taken God at His word. He had not argued; he had not hesitated; he went out not knowing whither he went (Hebrews II: 8); he completely and unquestioningly trusted God and took God at His word. It was not the fact that Abraham had meticulously performed the demands of the law that put him into this special relationship with God; it was his complete trust in God, his complete acceptance in God, his complete willingness to abandon his life to God. That for Paul was faith, and it was that faith of Abraham which made God regard Abraham as a good man.

Now some few, some very few, of the more advanced Rabbis believed that. There was a rabbinic commentary which said, " Abraham, our father, inherited this world and the world to come solely by the merit of faith whereby he believed in the Lord; for it is said, ' And he believed in the Lord, and He accounted it to him for righteousness.' "

But the great majority of the Rabbis turned the Abraham story to suit their own beliefs. They held that because Abraham was the only righteous man of his generation, *therefore* he was chosen to be the ancestor of God's special people. The immediate answer is, " But how could Abraham keep the law when he lived hundreds of years before the law was given? " The Rabbis advanced the odd theory that he kept it by *intuition* or *anticipation*. " At that time," says the Apocalypse of Baruch (57: 2), " the unwritten law was named among them, and the works of the commandment were then fulfilled." "He kept the law of the Most High," says Ecclesiasticus (44: 20, 21), " and was taken into covenant with God. . . . Therefore God assured him by an oath that the nations should be blessed in his seed." The Rabbis were so in love with their theory of works that they insisted that it was because of his works that Abraham was chosen, even if it meant that they had to argue that he knew the law by anticipation, although the law had not yet come.

Here, again, we have the root cleavage between Jewish legalism and Christian faith. The basic thought of the Jews was that a man must *earn* God's favour. The basic thought of Christianity is that a man can never earn God's favour, that all that he can do is to take God at His word and stake everything on the faith that God's promises are true. Paul's argument was—and, of course, Paul was unanswerably right—that Abraham entered into a right relationship with God, not because he did all kinds of legal works, but because he cast himself, just as he was, on the promise of God.

> " If our love were but more simple,
>   We should take Him at His word;
> And our lives would be all sunshine,
>   In the sweetness of our Lord."

It is the supreme discovery of the Christian life that we do not need to torture ourselves with a losing battle to earn God's love, that what we need to do is to accept in perfect trust the love which God offers to us. True, after that any man of honour is under the life-long obligation to see to be worthy of that love. But he is no longer a criminal seeking to obey an impossible law; he is a lover offering his all to one who loved him when he never deserved it.

Sir James Barrie once told a story about Robert Louis Stevenson. " When Stevenson went to Samoa he built a small hut, and afterwards went into a large house. The first night he went into the large house he was feeling very tired and sorrowful that he had not had the forethought to ask his servant to bring him coffee and cigarettes. Just as he was thinking that, the door opened, and the native boy came in with a tray carrying cigarettes and coffee. And Mr. Stevenson said to him, in the native language, ' Great is your forethought '; and the boy corrected him, and said, ' Great is the love.' " The service was rendered, not because of the coercion of servitude, but because of the compulsion of love. That also is the motive of Christian goodness.

THE FATHER OF THE FAITHFUL

Romans 4: 9-12

Did, then, this pronouncing of blessedness come to Abraham when he was circumcised? Or when he was uncircumcised? We are just saying, " His faith was accounted to Abraham for righteousness." Under what circumstances was it then accounted? Was it while he was circumcised? Or was it while he was uncircumcised? It was not while he was circumcised, but while he was uncircumcised. And he received the sign of circumcision as a seal of that relationship to God whose source was faith while he was still uncircumcised. This happened that he might be the father of all who believe while they are uncircumcised, so that the accounting of righteousness may come to them too; and that he might also be the father

of those who are circumcised, and by that I mean,
not those who are circumcised only, but who walk
in the steps of that faith which our father Abraham
showed when he was still uncircumcised.

To understand this passage we must understand the
importance that the Jew attached to circumcision. To
the Jew, a man who was not circumcised was quite literally
not a Jew, no matter what his parentage was. The Jewish
circumcision prayer runs: " Blessed is He who sanctified
His beloved from the womb, and put His ordinance upon
His flesh, and sealed His offspring with the sign of the holy
covenant." The rabbinic ordinance lays it down: " Ye
shall not eat of the Passover unless the seal of Abraham
be in your flesh." If a Gentile accepted the Jewish faith,
he could not enter fully into it without three things—
baptism, sacrifice and circumcision. To the Jew no uncircumcised man was a Jew.

So the Jewish objector, whom Paul is answering all
the time, is still fighting a rear-guard action. " Suppose
I admit," he says, " all that you say about Abraham and
about the fact that it was his complete trust that gained
him an entry into a right relationship with God, you will
still have to agree that Abraham was circumcised." Paul
has an unanswerable argument. The story of Abraham's
call, and of God's blessing on Abraham, is in Genesis 15: 6;
the story of Abraham's circumcision is in Genesis 17: 10ff.
Abraham was not, in fact, circumcised until fourteen
years after he had answered God's call, and had entered
into the unique relationship with God. Circumcision was
not the gateway to the right relationship with God; it was
only the sign and the seal that a man had already entered
into that relationship. It was while he was still uncircumcised that Abraham was accounted righteous. His
being accounted righteous had nothing to do with circumcision and everything to do with his act of faith. From
this unanswerable historic fact Paul makes two great
deductions.

(i) Abraham is not the father of those who have been circumcised; he is the father of those who make the same act of faith in God as he made. He is the father of every man who in every age takes God at His word as he did. This means that the real Jew is not the man who is racially a Jew and who is physically circumcised. The real Jew is the man who trusts God as Abraham did, no matter what his race is. And all the great promises of God are made not to the Jewish nation, but to the man who is Abraham's descendant because he trusts God as Abraham did. The word Jew has ceased to be a word which describes a nationality and has come to describe a way of life and a reaction to God. The descendants of Abraham are not the members of any particular nation, but those who in every nation belong to the family of God.

(ii) The converse of this is also true. A man may be a Jew of pure lineage. He may be circumcised; and yet in the real sense he may be no descendant of Abraham. He has no right to call Abraham his father, he has no right to claim the promises of God, because he did not make that venture of trust and faith that Abraham made.

In one short paragraph Paul has shattered all Jewish thought. The Jew always believed that just because he was a Jew he automatically enjoyed the privilege of God's blessings and immunity from God's punishment. The proof that he was a Jew was circumcision. So literally did some of the Rabbis take this that they actually said that, if a Jew was so bad that he had to be condemned by God, there was an angel whose task it was to obliterate his circumcision, and to make him uncircumcised again, before he entered into punishment.

Paul has laid down the great principle that the way to God is not through membership of any nation, not through any ordinance which makes a mark upon a man's body; the only way to God is by the faith which takes God at His word, which makes everything dependent, not on man's achievement or record, but solely upon God's grace.

64

ALL IS OF GRACE

Romans 4: 13-17

It was not through law that there came to Abraham
or to his seed the promise that he would inherit the
earth, but it came through that right relationship
with God which has its origin in faith. If they who
are vassals of the law are heirs, then faith is drained
of its meaning, and the promise is rendered inoperative;
for the law produces wrath, but where law does not
exist, neither can transgression exist. So, then, the
whole process depends on faith, in order that it may
be a matter of grace, so that the promise should be
guaranteed to all Abraham's descendants, not only
to those who belong to the tradition of the law, but
also to those who are of Abraham's family in virtue
of faith, Abraham who is the father of us all — as
it stands written, " I have appointed you a father
of many nations "—in the sight of that God in whom
he believed, that God who calls the dead into life,
and who calls into being even things which do not exist.

To Abraham God made a very great and wonderful promise.
He promised that Abraham would become a great nation,
and that in him all families of the earth would be blessed
(Genesis 12: 2, 3). In truth, the earth would be given to him
as his inheritance. Now that promise came to Abraham
because of the faith, and the trust, and the confidence
and the yieldedness that Abraham showed towards God.
It did not come because he piled up merit by doing works
of the law. It did not come from anything that Abraham
had done. It was the outgoing of God's generous grace
in answer to Abraham's absolute faith. The promise, as
Paul saw it, was dependent on two things and two things
only—the free grace of God and the perfect faith of
Abraham. The Jews were still asking, " How can a man
enter into the right relationship with God so that he too
may inherit this great promise? " Their answer was,
" He must do so by winning, earning, acquiring merit
in the sight of God by doing works which the law prescribes."
That is to say, he must do it by his own efforts. Now

Paul saw with absolute clearness just what that Jewish attitude had done—*it had completely destroyed the promise.* It had done so for this reason—no man can fully keep the law; no man ever lived such a perfect life that he never transgressed the law; no man, in his imperfection, can ever satisfy the perfection which is God; therefore, if the promise depends on keeping the law, the promise can never be fulfilled.

Paul saw things in terms of black and white. He saw two mutually exclusive ways of trying to get into a right relationship with God. On the one hand there was dependence on human effort; on the other, dependence on divine grace. On the one hand there was the constant losing battle to obey an impossible law; on the other, there was the faith which simply takes God at His word.

On each side there were three things.

(i) On the one side there was God's *promise.* There are two words which mean *promise* in Greek. There is *huposchesis*, which means a promise which is entered into upon conditions. " I promise to do this if you promise to do that." There is *epaggelia,* which means a promise made out of the goodness of someone's heart and made quite unconditionally. It is *epaggelia* that Paul uses of the promise of God. It is as if he was saying, " God is like a human father; God promises to love His children no matter what they do." True, He will love some of them with a love that makes Him glad, and He will love some of them with a love that makes Him sad, but in either case it is a love which will never let us go. It is not dependent on our merit, but only on God's own generous heart.

(ii) There is *faith.* Faith is the certainty that God is indeed like that. It is staking everything on the love of God. It is resting back in this love from which fear is banished for ever.

(iii) There is *grace.* A gift of grace is always something which is unearned and undeserved. The truth is that man

66

can never earn the love of God. Man must always find his glory, not in what he can do for God, but in what God has done for him.

(i) On the other side there is *law*. Now the trouble about law has always been that it can diagnose the trouble but cannot effect a cure. Law shows a man where he goes wrong, but does not help him to avoid going wrong. There is in fact, as Paul will later stress, a kind of terrible paradox in law. It is human nature that when a thing is forbidden it has a tendency to become desirable. " Stolen fruits are sweetest." And, therefore, law can actually have the effect of moving a man to desire the very thing which it forbids. The essential complement of law is judgment, and so long as a man lives in a religion whose dominant thought is law he cannot see himself as anything other than a condemned criminal at the bar of the justice of God.

(ii) There is *transgression*. Whenever law is introduced transgression follows. No one can break a law which does not exist; and no one can be condemned for breaking a law of the existence of which he was ignorant. If we introduce law and stop there, if we make religion solely a thing of obeying law, then life consists of one long series of transgressions waiting to be punished.

(iii) There is *wrath*. Think of *law*, think of *transgression*, and inevitably the next thought is *wrath*. Think of God in terms of law and you cannot do other than think of God in terms of outraged justice. Think of man in terms of law and you cannot do other than think of man as destined for the condemnation of God.

So Paul sets before the Romans the two ways. The one is a way in which a man seeks a right relationship with God through his own efforts. It is a way which is doomed to failure. The other is the way in which a man, in trusting faith, enters into a relationship with God, which by the grace of God already exists, and into which he has only to come in trust.

BELIEVING IN THE GOD WHO MAKES THE IMPOSSIBLE POSSIBLE

Romans 4: 18-25

In hope Abraham believed beyond hope that he would become the father of many nations, as the saying had it, " So will be your seed." He did not weaken in his faith, although he was well aware that by this time his body had lost its vitality (for he was a hundred years old), and that the womb of Sarah was without life. He did not in unfaith waver at the promise of God, but he was revitalized by his faith, and he gave glory to God, and he was firmly convinced that He who had made the promise was also able to perform it. So this faith was accounted to him as righteousness. It was not only for his sake this " it was accounted to him for righteousness " was written. It was written also for our sakes; for it will be so reckoned to us who believe in Him who raised Jesus, our Lord, from the dead, who was delivered up for our sin and raised to bring us into a right relationship with God.

THE last passage ended by saying that Abraham believed in the God who calls the dead into life, and who brings into being even things which have no existence at all. This saying turns Paul's thoughts to another outstanding example of Abraham's willingness to believe God, to trust God, and to take God at His word. The promise that all families of the earth would be blessed in his descendants was given to Abraham when he was an old man. His wife, Sarah, had always been childless; and now, when Abraham was one hundred years old, and when Sarah was ninety years old (Genesis 17: 17), there came the promise that a son would be born to them. It seemed a promise, which, on the face of it, was beyond all belief and beyond all hope of fulfilment, for Abraham was long past the age of begetting, and Sarah long past the age of bearing a son. And yet, once again, Abraham took God at His word; he believed that God's promises were true; he believed that what God said God would do. Once again, it was this faith that was accounted to Abraham for righteousness. It was this willingness to take God at His word which put Abraham into the right relationship with God. Now the Jewish Rabbis had a saying to which Paul here refers. They said, " What is written of Abraham is written also of his children." They meant that any promise that God made to Abraham extends to his children also. Therefore if Abraham's willingness to take God at His word brought him into a right relationship with God, so it will be with us. It is not works of the law, it is this trusting faith which establishes the relationship between God and a man which ought to exist.

The essence of Abraham's faith in this case was that he believed that God could make the impossible possible. So long as we believe that everything depends on our efforts we are bound to be pessimists, for experience has taught the grim lesson that our own efforts can achieve very little. When we realize that it is not our effort but God's grace and power which matter, then we become optimists, because we are bound to believe that with God nothing is impossible.

It is told that once Saint Theresa set out to build a convent with a sum the equivalent of half a crown as her complete resources. Someone said to her, " Not even Saint Theresa can accomplish much with half a crown." " True," she answered, " but Saint Theresa and half a crown *and God* can do anything." A man may well hesitate to attempt a great task by himself; there is nothing which he need hesitate to attempt with God. Ann Hunter Small, the great missionary teacher, tells how her father, himself a missionary, used to say: " Oh! the wickedness as well as the stupidity of the croakers! " And she herself had a favourite saying: " A Church which is alive dares to do anything." That daring only becomes possible to a man and to a Church who take God at His word.

AT HOME WITH GOD

Romans 5: 1-5

> Since, then, we have been put into a right relationship
> with God in consequence of faith, let us enjoy peace
> with Him through our Lord Jesus Christ. Through
> Him, by faith, we are in possession of an introduction
> to this grace in which we stand; and let us glory in
> the hope of the glory of God. Not only that, but let
> us find a cause of glorying in our troubles; for we
> know that trouble produces fortitude; and fortitude
> produces character; and character produces hope;
> and hope does not prove an illusion, because the love
> of God has been poured out into our hearts through
> the Holy Spirit who has been given unto us.

HERE is one of Paul's great lyrical passages in which he
almost sings the intimate joy of his confidence in God.
Trusting faith, the accepting of God at His word has done
what the labour to produce the works of the law could
never do; it has given a man peace with God. Before
Jesus came, and until a man accepts as true that which
Jesus says about God, no man could ever be intimate with
God. There are some who have seen God, not as the
supreme good, but as the supreme evil. Swinburne wrote:

> " His hidden face and iron feet,
> Hath not man known and felt them in their way
> Threaten and trample all things every day?
> Hath He not sent us hunger? Who hath cursed
> Spirit and flesh with longing? Filled with thirst
> Their lips that cried to Him? "

There are some who have seen God as the complete stranger,
the utterly untouchable. In one of H. G. Wells' books
there is the story of a man of affairs whose mind was so
tensed and strained that he was in serious danger of a complete nervous and mental breakdown. His doctor told him
that the only thing that could save him was to find the
peace that fellowship with God can give. " What! " he
said, " to think of that, up there, having fellowship with
me! I would as soon think of cooling my throat with the

milky way or shaking hands with the stars!" God, to him, was the completely unfindable. Rosita Forbes, the traveller, tells of finding shelter one night in a Chinese village temple because there was nowhere else to sleep. In the night she woke and the moonlight was slanting in through the window on to the faces of the images of the gods, and on every face there was a snarl and a sneer, as of those who hated men. It is only when we realize that God is the God who is the God and Father of our Lord Jesus Christ that there comes into life that intimacy with God, that new relationship which Paul calls justification.

Through Jesus, says Paul, we have an introduction to this grace in which we stand. The word Paul uses for introduction is *prosagōgē*. It is a word with two great pictures in it. (i) It is the regular word for introducing or ushering someone into the presence of royalty; and it is the regular word for the approach of the worshipper to God. It is as if Paul was saying, "Jesus ushers us into the very presence of God. Jesus opens the door for us to the presence of the King of Kings; and when that door is opened what we find is grace; not condemnation, not judgment, not vengeance, but the sheer, undeserved, unearned, unmerited, incredible kindness of God." (ii) But this word *prosagōgē* has another picture in it. In late Greek it is the word for the place where ships come in. It is the word for a *harbour* or a *haven*. If we take it in that meaning, it means that so long as we tried to depend on our own efforts we were tempest-tossed, like mariners striving with a sea which threatened to overwhelm them completely, but now that we have heard the word of Christ, we have reached at last the haven of God's grace, and we know the calm of depending, not on what we can do for ourselves, but on what God has done for us. Because of Jesus we have entry to the presence of the King of Kings; we have entry to the haven of God's grace.

But no sooner has Paul said that than the other side of the matter strikes him. All this is true; all this is glory;

71

but the fact remains that in this life the Christians are up against it. It was hard to be a Christian in Rome. Remembering that, Paul produces a great climax. "Trouble," he said, "produces fortitude." The word he uses for trouble is *thlipsis*, and thlipsis literally means *pressure*. All kinds of things may press in upon the Christian —the pressure of want and need, and straitened circumstances, the pressure of sorrow, the pressure of persecution, the pressure of unpopularity and loneliness. All that pressure, says Paul, produces fortitude. The word he uses for *fortitude* is *hupomonē*. *Hupomonē* means more than endurance; it means the spirit which can overcome the world; it means the spirit which does not passively endure but which actively overcomes and conquers the trials and the tribulations of life. When Beethoven was threatened with deafness, that most terrible of troubles for a musician, he said: " I will take life by the throat." That is *hupomonē*. When Scott was involved in ruin because of the bankruptcy of his publishers, he said: " No man will say ' Poor fellow! ' to me; my own right hand will pay the debt." That is *hupomonē*. Someone once said to a gallant soul who was undergoing a great sorrow: " Sorrow fairly colours life, doesn't it? " Back came the reply: " Yes! And I propose to choose the colour! " That is *hupomonē*. When Henley was lying in Edinburgh Infirmary with one leg amputated, and the prospect that the other must follow, he wrote *Invictus*.

> " Out of the night that covers me,
>   Black as the Pit from pole to pole,
> I thank whatever gods may be
>   For my unconquerable soul."

That is *hupomonē*. *Hupomonē* is not the spirit which lies down and lets the floods go over it; it is the spirit which meets things breastforward and overcomes them. " Fortitude," Paul goes on, " produces character." The word he uses for *character* is *dokimē*. *Dokimē* is used of metal

which has been passed through the fire so that everything
base has been purged out of it. It is used of coinage as
we use the word *sterling*. It describes something out of
which every alloy of baseness has been eliminated. When
affliction is met with fortitude, out of the battle a man
emerges stronger, and purer, and better and nearer God.
" Character," Paul goes on, " produces hope." Two
men can meet the same situation. It can drive one of
them to despair, and it can spur the other to triumphant
action. To the one it can be the end of hope, to the other
it can be a challenge to greatness. " I do not like crises,"
said Lord Reith, " but I do like the opportunities they
provide." Now the difference corresponds to the difference
within the man. If a man has let himself become weak,
and slack and flabby, if he has allowed circumstances to
beat him, if he has allowed himself to whine and grovel
under affliction, he has made himself such that when the
challenge of the crisis comes he cannot do other than
despair. If, on the other hand, a man has insisted on meeting
life with head up, if he has always faced and, by facing,
conquered things, then when the challenge comes he meets
it with eyes aflame with hope. The character which has
endured the test always emerges in hope. And then Paul
makes one last great statement: " The Christian hope
never proves an illusion for it is founded on the love of
God." Omar Khayyam wrote wistfully of human hopes:

> " The Worldly Hope men set their hearts upon
> Turns Ashes—or it prospers; and anon,
>   Like Snow upon the Desert's dusty Face
> Lighting a little Hour or two—is gone."

When a man's hope is in God it cannot turn to dust and
ashes. When a man's hope is in God it cannot be disap-
pointed. When a man's hope is in the love of God it can
never be an illusion, for God is loving us with an everlasting
love, which is backed by an everlasting power.

THE FINAL PROOF OF LOVE

Romans 5: 6-11

> While we were still helpless, in God's good time, Christ died for the ungodly. A man will hardly die for a just man. It may be that a man would even dare to die for the good cause. But God proves His love to us by the fact that while we were still sinners Christ died for us. Since we have been brought into a right relationship with God at the price of His life's blood, much more through Him we shall be saved from the Wrath. For if while we were still at enmity with God, we were reconciled to God through the death of His Son, much more, now that we have been reconciled, we shall go on being saved by His life. Not only that, but we glory in God through our Lord Jesus Christ, through whom we have received this reconciliation.

THE fact that Jesus Christ died for us is the final proof of God's love. It would be difficult enough to get a man to die for a just man. It might be possible for a man to be persuaded to die for some great and good principle. A man might have the greater love that would make him lay down his life for his friend. But the wonder of Jesus Christ is that He died for us when we are sinners, bad men, and in a state of enmity and hostility to God. Love can go no further than that.

Rita Snowden relates an incident from the life of Colonel T. E. Lawrence. In 1915 he was journeying across the desert with some Arabs. Things were desperate. Food was almost done, and water was at its last drop. Their hoods were over their heads to shelter them from the wind which was like a flame, and which was full of the stinging sand of the sandstorm. Suddenly someone said, " Where is Jasmin? " Another said, " Who is Jasmin? " A third answered, " That yellow-faced man from Maan. He killed a Turkish tax-collector and fled to the desert." The first said, " Look, Jasmin's camel has no rider. His rifle is strapped to the saddle, but Jasmin is not there." A second said, " Someone has shot him on the march." A third

74

said, " He is not strong in the head, perhaps he is lost in mirage; he is not strong in the body, perhaps he has fainted and fallen off his camel." Then the first said, " What does it matter? Jasmin was not worth half a crown." And the Arabs hunched themselves up on their camels and rode on. But Lawrence turned and rode back the way he had come. Alone, in the blazing heat, at the risk of his life, he went back. After an hour and a half's ride he saw something against the sand. It was Jasmin, blind and mad with heat and thirst, Jasmin being murdered by the desert. Lawrence lifted him up on his camel, gave him some of the last drops of the precious water, slowly plodded back to his company. When he came up to them the Arabs looked in amazement. " Here is Jasmin," they said, "Jasmin, not worth half a crown, saved at his own risk by Lawrence, our lord." That is a parable. It was not good men Christ died to save; it was sinners. It was not God's friends Christ died to rescue; it was men who were at enmity with God.

And then Paul goes on a step. <u>Through Jesus our *status* with God was changed</u>. Sinners though we were, we were put into a <u>right relationship with God</u>. *But that is not enough*. Not only our *status* must be changed but our *state.* The saved sinner cannot go on being a sinner; he must become a good man. Now Christ's death changed our *status*; and Christ's risen life changes our *state*. He is not dead; He is alive; He is with us always to help us and guide us and direct us, to fill us with His strength to enable us to overcome temptation, to clothe our lives with something of His radiance if we live for ever in His risen presence. He who changed our *status* with God can also change our *state*. He begins by putting sinners into a right relationship with God even when they are still sinners; He goes on, by His grace, to enable these sinners to quit their sin and to become good men. There are technical names for these things. The change of our *status* is *justification*; that is where the whole saving process begins. The change of our *state* is *sanctification*; that is where the saving process goes on, and never ends, until we see Him face to face and are like Him.

There is one thing to note here. It is a thing of quite extraordinary importance. Paul is quite clear that the whole saving process, the coming of Christ, the death of Christ, is the proof of *God's* love. It all happened to show how much *God* loves us. It all happened because *God* loves us. Now, sometimes the thing is stated as if on the one side there was a gentle and loving Christ, and on the other an angry and vengeful God. The thing is sometimes stated as if Christ had done something which changed the attitude of God to men, which changed God from being angry into being gracious. Nothing could be further from the truth. The whole matter springs from the love of God. Jesus did not come to change God's attitude; He came to show what God's attitude to men is and always was. He came to prove unanswerably to men that God is love.

RUIN AND RESCUE

Romans 5: 12-21

> Therefore, just as through one man sin entered into the world, and, through sin, death entered into the world, and so death spread to all men, in that they had sinned; for up to the coming of the law sin was in the world, but sin was not debited against men because the law did not yet exist; but death reigned from the time of Adam to the time of Moses even over those who had not sinned in the way that Adam had, Adam, who was the symbol of the one who was to come. But the gift of free grace was not like the trespass. For if the many died in consequence of the sin of the one, much more the grace of God and His free gift in the grace of the one man Jesus Christ abounded to many. The free gift is not like the effect of the one man who sinned. The sentence which followed the one sin was a sentence of condemnation; but the free gift which followed the many trespasses

was a sentence of acquittal. For if, because of the trespass of one, death reigned because of one, much more they who receive the superabundance of grace and of that free gift which establishes a right relationship between man and God, shall reign in life through the one Jesus Christ. So, then, as by one sin it came to all men to fall under sentence, so by one supreme act of righteousness it came to men to enter into that relationship with God which gives them life. Just as through the disobedience of one man the many were constituted sinners, so, through the obedience of one man, the many were constituted righteous. But the law slipped in that trespass might abound; but where sin abounded grace superabounded, so that just as sin reigned in death, grace might reign by putting men into a right relationship with God that they might enter into eternal life because of what Jesus Christ our Lord has done.

THERE is no passage of the New Testament which has had such an influence on theology as this passage; and there is no passage which is more difficult for a modern mind to understand. It is difficult because Paul expresses himself in a difficult way. We can see, for instance, that the first sentence, having begun, never ends, but breaks off in mid-air, while Paul pursues another idea down a sideline. But, still more, it is difficult, because it is thinking and speaking in terms which were familiar to Jews and perfectly understandable to them, but which are unfamiliar to us.

If we were to put the thought of this passage into one sentence, which, indeed, was the sentence which Paul set out to write at the very beginning, and which got sidetracked, it would be this: " By the sin of Adam all men became sinners and were alienated from God; by the righteousness of Jesus Christ all men become righteous and are restored to a right relationship with God." Paul, in fact, said this very much more clearly in I Corinthians 15: 21: " As by man came death, by man comes also the resurrection of the dead. For as in Adam all die, so in Christ shall all be made alive."

What, then, are the basic Jewish ideas in the light of which this passage must be read? There are two such ideas which are supremely important.

(i) There is the idea of *solidarity*. The Jew never really thought of himself as an individual; he always thought of himself as part of a clan, a family, a nation; and apart from that society he had no real existence. To this day it is said that if an Australian aborgine is asked his name, he does not give his name; he gives the name of his tribe or clan. He does not think of himself as a person, but as a member of a clan. One of the clearest instances of this kind of thing in recognizable action is the blood feud amongst primitive people. Suppose a man from one tribe murders a man from another tribe. It then becomes the duty of the tribe of which the murdered man was a member to take vengeance on the other tribe; the feud becomes, not a quarrel between persons, but a quarrel between tribes. It is the tribe that has been hurt, and the tribe which takes vengeance. In the Old Testament there is one vivid case of this. It is the case of Achan as it is related in Joshua 7. At the siege of Jericho Achan had kept to himself certain spoils in direct defiance of the commandment of God that all spoils should be destroyed. Achan had sinned. The next item in the campaign was the siege of Ai, which should have fallen without trouble. The campaigns against it, however, failed disastrously. Why? Because Achan had sinned, and, since Achan had sinned, the whole nation was branded as a sinner and was being punished by God. Achan's sin was not one man's sin, it was the nation's sin. The nation was not a collection of individuals; it was a solid mass. What the individual did, the nation did. When Achan's sin was admitted and discovered it was not Achan alone who was executed. Achan's whole family was wiped out. Again, Achan was not a solitary, self-responsible individual; he was one of a solid mass of people from whom he could not be separated. Now that is how Paul sees Adam. Adam was not an

individual. Adam was one of mankind, and because Adam
was one of mankind, all mankind sinned in him. His sin
was the sin of all men.

Paul says that all men sinned in Adam. If we are ever
to understand Paul's thought here we must be quite sure
of what Paul means, and we must be quite sure that Paul
meant what he said. All through the history of Christian
thinking there have been efforts to interpret this conception
of the connection between Adam's sin and mankind in
different ways. (i) The passage has been taken to mean
that " each man is his own Adam." This really means
that, just as Adam sinned, all men have sinned, but that
there is no real connection between the sin of Adam and
the sin of mankind, other than that it could be said that
Adam's sin is typical of the sin of all mankind. (ii) There
has been what has been called the legal interpretation.
This interpretation would hold that Adam was *the representative* of mankind, and the human race shares in the
deed of its representative. But a representative must be
chosen by the people he represents ; and in no sense can
we say that of Adam. (iii) There is the interpretation
that what we inherit from Adam is *the tendency* to sin.
That is true enough, but that is not what Paul meant.
It would not, in fact, suit his argument at all. (iv) The
only possible interpretation of the passage is what is
called the realistic interpretation, that, because of the
solidarity of the human race, all mankind literally and
actually sinned in Adam. This was not an idea that was
strange to a Jew. It was the actual belief of the Jewish
thinkers. The writer of 2 Esdras is quite clear about it.
" A grain of evil was sown in the heart of Adam from the
beginning and how much wickedness has it brought forth
unto this time; and how much shall it yet bring forth
till the time of the threshing come " (4: 30). " For the
first Adam, bearing a wicked heart, transgressed and was
overcome; and not only he but all they also who are born
of him " (3: 21).

(ii) The second basic idea is intimately connected with this in Paul's argument. *Death is the direct consequence of sin.* It was the Jewish belief that if Adam had not sinned man would have been immortal. Death came into this world as a consequence of sin. Sirach (2: 23) writes, " A woman was the beginning of sin and through her all die." The Book of Wisdom has it, " God created man for immortality and made him the image of his own proper nature; but by the envy of the devil death entered into the world." In Jewish thought sin and death are integrally connected. This is what Paul is getting at in the involved and difficult line of thought in verses 12-14. We may trace his thought in these verses in a series of ideas.

(i) Adam sinned because he broke a direct commandment of God—the commandment not to eat of the fruit of the forbidden tree—and because Adam sinned, Adam, who was meant to be immortal, died.

(ii) The law did not come until the time of Moses; now, if there is no law there can be no breach of the law; that is to say, if there is no law, and no commandment, there can be no sin. Therefore, the men who lived between Adam and Moses did in fact sin, but it was not reckoned against them because there was as yet no law, and they could not be condemned for breaking a law which did not exist.

(iii) But, in spite of the fact that sin could not be reckoned to them, they still died. Death reigned over them although they could not be accused of breaking a non-existent law.

(iv) Why, then, did they die? They died because they had sinned in Adam. It was their involvement in the sin of Adam that caused their deaths, although there was no law for them to break. That, in fact, is Paul's proof that all men did sin in Adam.

So, then, we have extracted the essence of one side of Paul's thought. Because of this idea of the complete solidarity of mankind, all men literally sinned in Adam; and because death is the consequence of sin death reigned over all men.

But this very same conception, which can be used to produce so desperate a view of the human situation, can be used in reverse to fill the whole situation with a blaze of glory. Into this situation there comes Jesus. To God Jesus offered perfect obedience, perfect righteousness, perfect goodness. And, just as all men were involved in Adam's sin, all men are involved in Jesus Christ's perfect goodness; and just as Adam's sin was the cause of death, so Jesus' perfect goodness conquers death and gives men life eternal. Paul's triumphant argument is that as mankind was solid with Adam, and was therefore condemned to death, so mankind is solid with Christ and is therefore acquitted to life. Even when the law came and made sin much more terrible, this grace of Christ overcomes the condemnation which the law must bring.

That is Paul's argument, and on Jewish grounds it is unassailable. But it has one great flaw as it has one great shining truth.

(i) The flaw is this. Suppose we assume the literal truth of the Adam story, *our connection with Adam is a physical connection*. We have nothing to do with it; we have no choice whatever in the matter, any more than a child chooses his father. We are connected with Adam simply by physical descent which we can neither choose nor reject. It is a connection which is simply there independent of anything we can do. On the other hand *our connection with Christ is voluntary*. Union with Christ is something a man can accept or reject. He can unite himself with Christ, or he can refuse to do so. The connection is in reality quite different. That is a serious flaw in the argument of Paul.

(ii) The great virtue is this. Paul does conserve the great truth that mankind was involved in a situation from which there was no escape. Sin had man in its power. There was no hope. Into this situation there came Jesus Christ, and He brought with Him something that broke through the old situation. By what He did, by what He is,

81

by what He gives, He enabled man to escape from a situation in which man was hopelessly dominated by sin. Whatever else we may say about Paul's argument this we can say— it is completely true that man was ruined by sin and rescued by Christ.

DYING TO LIVE

Romans 6: 1-11

> What, then, shall we infer? Are we to persist in sin that grace may abound? God forbid! How shall we who have died to sin still live in it? Can you be unaware that all who have been baptized into Jesus Christ have been baptized into His death? We have therefore been buried with Him through baptism until we died, in order that, just as Christ was raised from the dead through the glory of the Father, so we, too, may live in newness of life. For, if we have become united to Him in the likeness of His death, so also shall we be united to Him in the likeness of His resurrection. For this we know, that our old self has been crucified with Him, that our sinful body might be rendered inoperative, in order that we should no longer be slaves to sin. For a man who has died stands acquitted from sin. But, if we have died with Christ, we believe that we shall also live with Him, for we know that, after Christ was raised from the dead, He dies no more. Death has no more lordship over Him. He who died, died once and for all to sin; and He who lives, lives to God. So you, too, must reckon yourselves to be dead to sin, but alive to God in Christ Jesus.

As he has so often done in this letter, in this passage Paul is once again carrying on an argument against a kind of imaginary opponent. The argument springs from the great saying at the end of the last chapter: " Where sin abounded, grace superabounded." The argument would run something like this.

The Objector: You have just said that God's grace is great enough to find forgiveness for every sin.

Paul: That is so.

The Objector: You are, in fact, saying that God's grace is the greatest and the most wonderful thing in all this world.

Paul: That is so.

The Objector: Well, if that is so, let us go on sinning. The more we sin the more grace will abound. Sin does not matter, for God will forgive anyway. In fact we can go further than that and say that sin is an excellent thing, because sin gives the grace of God a chance to operate. The conclusion of your argument is that sin produces grace; therefore sin is bound to be a good thing if it produces the greatest thing in the world.

Paul's first reaction is to recoil from that argument in sheer horror. " Do you suggest," he demands, " that we should go on sinning in order to give grace more chance to operate? " " God forbid," he answers, " that we should pursue so incredible a course as that."

But then, having recoiled like that, he goes on to something else. " Have you never thought," he demands, " what happened to you when you were baptized? " Now, when we try to understand what Paul is going to go on to say, we must remember that baptism in the time of Paul was different from what baptism commonly is to-day. (*a*) It was adult baptism. That is not to say that the New Testament is in any sense opposed to infant baptism, but infant baptism is the result of the Christian family, and the Christian family could hardly be said to have come into being as early as the time of Paul. A man came to Christ as an individual, often leaving his family behind, in the Early Church. (*b*) Baptism in the Early Church was intimately connected with confession of faith. A man was baptized when he entered the Church. And he was entering the Church direct from paganism. Baptism marked a dividing line in his life. In baptism a man came to a decision which cut his life in two, a decision which often meant that he had to tear himself up by the roots, a decision which was so definite that for him it often meant nothing less than beginning life all over again. (c) Commonly, baptism was by total immersion, and that practice lent itself to a symbolism which sprinkling does not so readily lend itself to. When a man descended into the water, and the water closed over his head, it was like being buried in a grave. When he emerged from the water, it was like rising from the grave. Baptism was symbolically like dying and rising again. The man died to one kind of life and rose to another kind of life. He died to the old life of sin and rose to the new life of grace. He went down into the water a man of the world and rose a man in Christ.

Now, again, if we are fully to understand this, we must remember that Paul was using language and pictures that almost anyone of his day and generation would understand. It may seem strange to us, but it was not at all strange to Paul's contemporaries. The very language he was using was the very language they used.

The Jews would understand it. When a man entered the Jewish religion from heathenism it involved three things—sacrifice, circumcision and baptism. The Gentile entered the Jewish faith by baptism. The ritual was as follows. The person to be baptized cut his nails and hair; he undressed completely; the baptismal bath must contain at least forty *seahs*, that is two hogsheads, of water. Every part of his body must be touched by the water. As he was in the water he made confession of his faith before three fathers of baptism, and certain exhortations and benedictions were addressed to him. Now the effect of this baptism was held to be complete regeneration; the man was a new man; he was born anew. He was called a little child just born, the child of one day. All his sins were remitted because God cannot punish sins committed before he was born. The completeness of the change is seen in the fact that certain Rabbis held that a man's child born after baptism was his first-born, even if he had had children before baptism. Theoretically it was held—although the belief was never put into practice—

that a man was so much a completely new man that he might marry his own sister or his own mother. He was not only a changed man, he was a new man, a different man. Any Jew would fully understand Paul's words about the necessity of a baptized man being a completely new man.

The Greek would understand. At this time the only real Greek religion was found in the mystery religions. These mystery religions were wonderful things. They offered men release from the cares and sorrows and fears of this earth; and the release was by union with some god. All the mysteries were passion plays. They were based on the story of some god who suffered and died and rose again. The story of the god was played out as a drama. Before a man could see the drama he had to be initiated. He had to undergo a long course of instruction on the inner meaning of the drama. He had to undergo a course of ascetic discipline. He was carefully wrought up and prepared. The drama was played out with all the resources of music and lighting, and incense and mystery. As the drama was played out the man felt himself one with the god; he underwent an emotional experience of identification with the god. Before he entered on this he was initiated. Now initiation was always regarded as a death followed by a new birth, by which the man was *renatus in aeternum*, reborn for eternity. One who went through the initiation tells us that he underwent " a voluntary death." We know that in one of the mysteries the man to be initiated was called *moriturus*, the one who is to die, and that he was buried up to the head in a trench. When he had been initiated he was addressed as a little child and fed with milk, as one newly born. In another of the mysteries the person to be initiated prayed: " Enter thou into my spirit, my thought, my whole life; for thou art I and I am thou." Any Greek who had been through this would have no difficulty in understanding what Paul meant by dying and rising again in baptism, and, in so doing, becoming one with Christ. We are not for one moment saying that Paul borrowed either his ideas or his words from such Jewish or pagan practices; what we do say is that he was using words and pictures that both Jew and Gentile would understand and recognize.

In this passage there lie three great permanent truths.

(i) It is a terrible thing to seek to trade on the mercy of God. It is a terrible thing to make the mercy of God an excuse for sinning. Think of it in human terms. How despicable it would be for a son or a daughter to consider himself or herself free to sin, because he or she knew that a father or a mother would forgive. That would be taking advantage of love to break love's heart.

(ii) The man who enters upon the Christian way is committed to a different kind of life. He has died to one kind of life and has been born to another. He is essentially a different man. In modern times we have tended to stress the fact that acceptance of the Christian way need not make so very much difference in a man's life. Paul would have said that it ought to make all the difference in the world.

(iii) But there is more than a mere ethical change in a man's life when he accepts Christ. There is a real union with a real identification with Christ. It is in fact the simple truth that the ethical change is not possible without the union with Christ. A man is *in Christ*. A great scholar has suggested this analogy for that phrase. We cannot live our physical life unless we are in the air, and the air is in us. It is so with Christ. Unless we are in Christ, and Christ is in us, we cannot live the life of God. To limit Christianity to an ethical demand, and to leave out this essential union with Christ, is to leave Christianity less than half-way.

THE PRACTICE OF THE FAITH

Romans 6: 12-14

> Let not sin reign in your mortal body to make you
> obey the body's desires. Do not go on yielding your
> members to sin as weapons of evil; but yield yourselves
> once and for all to God, as those who were dead and
> are now alive, and yield your members to God as
> weapons of righteousness. For sin will not lord it
> over you. You are not under law but under grace.

THERE is no more typical transition in Paul than the
transition between this passage and the passage which
went before it. The passage which went before it was the
writing of a mystic. It spoke of the mystical union between
the Christian and Christ which came in baptism. It spoke
of the way in which a Christian should live so close to
Christ that all his life can be said to be lived in Christ.
And now, after the mystical experience, there comes the
practical demand. Christianity is not an emotional experience; it is a way of life. The Christian is not meant to
luxuriate in an experience however wonderful; he is
meant to go out and to live a certain kind of life in the
teeth of the world's attacks and problems. It is the commonest thing in the world of religious life to sit in church
and to feel a wave of feeling sweep over us. It is a not
uncommon experience when we sit alone to feel Christ
very near to us. But the Christianity which has stopped
there has stopped half-way. That emotion must be translated into action. Religious feeling can never be a substitute
for religious doing. Christianity can never be only an
experience of the secret place; it must be a life in the
market place.

When a man goes out into the world he is confronted
with an awesome situation. As Paul thinks of it, both
God and sin are looking for weapons to use. God cannot
work without men. If God wants a word spoken, He has
to get a man to speak it. If God wants a deed done, He
has to get a man to do it. If God wants a person cheered,

encouraged, strengthened, helped, He has to get a man
to do the lifting up. God, as it has been said, is everywhere
looking for hands to use. And it is the same with sin.
Every man has to be given the push into sin. The invitation
to sin has to be offered to every man. Sin is looking for
men who will by their words, or example, seduce and invite
others into sinning. It is as if Paul was saying: " In this
world there is an eternal battle between sin and God;
choose your side." We are faced with the tremendous
alternative of making ourselves the weapons in the hand
of God, or the weapons in the hand of sin.

A man may well answer: " Such a choice is too much
for me. I am bound to fail." Paul's answer is: " Don't
be discouraged and don't be despairing; sin will not lord
it over you." Why? The answer is that we are no longer
under law but under grace. Why should that make all
the difference? It makes the difference because we are no
longer trying to satisfy the demands of law; we are trying
to be worthy of the gifts of love. We are no longer regarding
God as the stern judge; we are regarding Him as the lover
of the souls of men. There is no inspiration in all the world
like love. Who ever went out from the presence of his
loved one without the burning desire to be a better person?
The Christian life is no longer an intolerable burden to be
borne; it is a privilege to be lived up to. As Denney put
it: " It is not restraint but inspiration which liberates
from sin; not Mount Sinai but Mount Calvary which
makes saints." There is many a man who has been saved
from sin, not because of the regulations and commands
of the law, but because he could not dare to hurt and grieve
and disappoint someone whom he loved and someone
whom, he knew, loved him. At best, the law restrains a
man through fear; but love redeems a man by inspiring
him to be better than his own best. The inspiration of the
Christian comes, not from the fear of what God will do
to him, but from the inspiration of what God has done
for him.

THE EXCLUSIVE POSSESSION

Romans 6: 15-23

> What then? Are we to go on sinning because we are
> not under the law but under grace? God forbid!
> Are you not aware that if you yield yourselves to
> anyone as slaves, in order to obey them, you are the
> slaves of the person whom you have chosen to obey—
> in this case, either of sin, which leads to death, or of
> obedience, which leads to righteousness. But, thank
> God, you, who used to be slaves of sin, have come to a
> spontaneous decision to obey the pattern of teaching
> to which you were committed, and, since you have
> been liberated from sin, you have become the slaves
> of righteousness. I speak in human terms, because
> unaided human nature cannot understand any others.
> Just as you yielded your members as slaves to unclean-
> ness and lawlessness which issues in still more law-
> lessness, so now you have yielded your members
> as slaves to righteousness and have started on the
> road that leads to holiness. When you were slaves
> of sin, you were free as regards righteousness; but
> then what fruit did you have? All you had was things
> of which you are now heartily ashamed, for the end
> of these things is death. But now, since you have
> been liberated from sin, and since you have become
> the slaves of God, the fruit you enjoy is designed to
> lead you on the road to holiness and its end is eternal
> life. For sin's pay is death, but God's free gift is
> eternal life in Christ Jesus our Lord.

To a certain type of mind the doctrine of free grace is
always a temptation. There is always a temptation to say,
" If forgiveness is as easy and as inevitable as all that, if
God's one desire is to forgive men, and if God's grace is
wide enough to cover every spot and stain, why worry
about sin? Why not do as we like? It will be all the same
in the end." No sooner had Paul said that the Christian
is no longer under law but under grace than that was
precisely what was said.

Paul counters this argument by using a vivid picture.
He says: " Once you gave yourselves to sin as the slave
of sin; when you did that, righteousness had no claim

over you. But now you have given yourselves to God as the slave of righteousness; when you did that sin has no claim over you." To understand this we must understand the status of the slave. When we think of a servant, in our sense of the word, we think of a man who gives a certain agreed part of his time to his master, and who receives a certain agreed wage for doing so. Within that agreed time he is at the disposal and in the command of his master. But, when that time ends, he is free to do exactly as he likes. As we see it, during his working hours a servant belongs entirely to his master, but in his free time he belongs to himself. Thus, for instance, a man may be a clerk in an office during the day, but might well play the violin in an orchestra at night. But, in Paul's time, the status of the slave was quite different. Quite literally he had no time which belonged to himself. He had no moment when he was free. Every single moment of his time belonged to his master. He was the absolutely exclusive possession of his master, and there was not one single moment of his life when he could do as he liked. In Paul's time a slave could never do what he liked; it was impossible for him to serve two masters, because he was the exclusive possession of one master. That is the picture that is in Paul's mind. He says: " At one time you were the slave of sin. Sin had exclusive possession of you. At that time you could not talk of anything else but sinning. But now you have taken God as your master. God has exclusive possession of you. And now you cannot even talk about sinning; you must talk about nothing but holiness."

Paul actually apologizes for using this picture. He says: " I am only using a human analogy so that your human minds can understand it." He apologized because he did not like to compare the Christian life to any kind of slavery. But the one thing that this picture does show is the fact that the Christian can have no master but God. He cannot give a part of his life, a part of his time to God, and another part to the world. With God it is all—or nothing. So long as a man keeps some corner of his life without God, so long as a man wants to keep some part of his life without God, he is not really a Christian. A Christian is a man who has given complete control of his life to Christ and who has held nothing back. And no man who has done that can ever think of using grace as an excuse for sin.

But Paul has something more to say. He says, " You took a spontaneous decision to obey the pattern of the teaching to which you were committed." In other words, Paul is saying, " You knew what you were doing, and you did it of your own free will." This is interesting. Remember that this passage has arisen from a discussion of baptism at the beginning of the chapter. This therefore means that baptism was instructed baptism. Now we have already seen that baptism in the Early Church was in the nature of things, adult baptism, and it was confession of faith. It is, then, quite clear that no man was ever allowed into the Christian Church on a moment of emotion. He was instructed. He had to know what he was doing. The case was deliberately put to him. He was shown what Christ offered and what Christ demanded. Then, and then only, could he take the decision to come in. It is said that when a man wishes to become a member of the great Benedictine order of monks he is accepted for a year on probation. During all that time his clothes, which he wore in the world, hang in his cell. At any time he can put off his monk's habit, put on his worldly clothes, and walk out, and no one will think any the worse of him. Only at the end of the year are his clothes finally taken away. He must know what he is doing; it is with open eyes and a full appreciation of what he is doing that he must enter the order. It is so with Christianity. Jesus does not want followers who have not stopped to count the cost. He does not want a man to express an impermanent loyalty on the crest of a wave of emotion. The Church has a duty to present the faith in all the riches of its offer and the heights of its demands to those who wish to become members of the Church.

Paul draws a distinction between the old life and the new life. The old life was characterized by *uncleanness* and *lawlessness*. The pagan world was an unclean world. The pagan world did not know the meaning of chastity. Justin Martyr has a terrible jibe. He is talking about the exposure of infants. In Rome unwanted children, especially girls, were literally thrown away. Every night numbers of them were left lying in the forum. They were collected by dreadful characters, who ran brothels, and nurtured up to be prostitutes with whom the brothels were stocked. So Justin turns on his heathen opponents and tells them that, in their immorality, they had every chance of going into a city brothel, and, all unknown to them, having intercourse with their own child. That is what pagan life was like. The pagan world was lawless. It was lawless in the sense that men's lusts were their only laws. And that lawlessness begot more lawlessness. That, indeed is the law of sin. Sin begets sin. The first time we do a wrong thing we may do it with a hesitation, and a tremor and a shudder. The second time we do it, it is easier; and if we go on doing it, it becomes effortless; sin loses its terror. The first time we allow ourselves some indulgence we may be satisfied with very little of it; but the time comes when we need more and more of it to produce the same thrill. Sin leads on to sin. Lawlessness produces lawlessness. To start on the path of sin is to go on to more and more. But the new life is different. It is a life which is righteous. Now the Greeks defined righteousness as *giving to man and to God their due*. The Christian life is a life which gives God His proper place, and which respects the rights of human personality. The Christian will never disobey God, nor will he ever use a human being in any way to gratify his desire for pleasure or for lust. That life leads to what the Authorised Version calls *sanctification*. The word in Greek is *hagiasmos*. All Greek nouns which end in

-asmos describe, not a completed state, but a *process.*
Sanctification is not a completed state; it is the road to
holiness. When a man gives his life to Christ, he does not
stop there and then become a perfect man; the struggle
is by no means over. But Christianity has always regarded
the direction in which a man is facing as more important
than the particular stage to which he has achieved. Once
he is Christ's he has started on the process of sanctification,
on the road to holiness.

> " Leaving every day behind
>   Something which might hinder;
>   Running swifter every day;
>   Growing purer, kinder."

Robert Louis Stevenson said: " To travel hopefully is
better than to arrive." What is true is that it is a great
thing to set out to a great goal, even if we never get the
whole way to it.

Paul finishes this section with a great saying with a
double metaphor in it. " Sin's pay is death," he says,
" but God's free gift is eternal life." Here Paul uses two
military words. For *pay* he uses the word *opsōnia*. *Opsōnia*
was the soldier's pay, something that he earned with the
risk of his body and the sweat of his brow, something that
was due to him and could not be taken from him. For
gift he uses the word *charisma*. The *charisma* or, in Latin,
the *donativum*, was a totally free and unearned gift which
the army sometimes received. On special occasions, for
instance on his birthday, or on his accession to the throne,
or the anniversary of it, an emperor handed out a free
gift of money to the army. It had not been earned; it
was a present; a gift of the emperor's kindness and grace.
So Paul says: " Sin has earned death. If we got the pay
we had earned it would be death. It is death that is due
to us as a right." And then he goes on: " But what we
have received is a free gift; we did not earn it; we did
not deserve it; we have earned death; but out of His
grace God has given us life."

THE NEW ALLEGIANCE

Romans 7: 1-6

> You are bound to know, brothers—for I speak to men who know what law means—that the law has authority over a man only for the duration of his life. Thus, a married woman remains bound by law to her husband as long as he is alive; but, if her husband dies, she is completely discharged from the law concerning her husband. Accordingly, she will be called an adulteress if she marries another man while her husband is still alive; but, if her husband dies, she is free from the law, and she is no longer an adulteress if she marries another man. Just so, my brothers, you have died to the law, through the body of Jesus Christ (for you shared in His death by baptism) in order that you should enter into union with another, I mean, with Him who has been raised from the dead, in order that we may bear fruit to God. In the days of our unaided human nature, the passions of our sins, which were set in motion by the law, worked in our members to bear fruit for death. But now we are completely discharged from the law, because we have died to that by which we were held captive, so that we serve, not under the old written law, but in the new life of the spirit.

SELDOM did Paul write so difficult and so complicated a passage as this. C. H. Dodd has said of this passage that when we are studying it we should try to forget what Paul says and to find out what he means. The basic thought of the passage is founded on the legal maxim that death cancels all contracts. Paul begins with the illustration of this truth, and he wishes to use this picture as a symbol of what happens to the Christian. So long as a woman's husband is alive, she cannot marry another. If she does, she is an adulteress. But if her husband dies, the contract is, so to speak, cancelled, and she is free to marry anyone she likes. Now, in view of that, Paul could have said that we were married to sin; that sin was slain by Christ; and that, therefore, now we are free to be married to God. That is undoubtedly what Paul set out to say. But into this picture there came the Law. Paul could still have put the thing quite simply. He could have said that we were married to the law; that the law was killed by the work of Christ; and that now we are free to be married to God. But, quite suddenly, he puts it the other way, and, in his suddenly changed picture, it is *we* who die to the law. How can that be? By baptism we share in the death of Christ. That means, that having died, we are discharged from all obligations and duties to the law, and become free to marry again. This time we marry, not the law, but Christ. When that happens Christian obedience becomes based, not on an externally imposed obedience to some written code of laws, but on an inner allegiance of our spirit to Jesus Christ.

Paul is drawing a contrast between the two states of man—the state without Christ and the state with Christ. Before we knew Christ we tried to rule life by obedience to the written code of the law. That was when we were *in the flesh*. Now, by *the flesh*, Paul does not simply mean the body, because a man retains a physical body to the end of the day. In man there is something which answers to the seduction of sin; if there was nothing in man for sin to appeal to, the attack of sin would be harmless; but there is something in man which provides a bridgehead for sin. It is that part of man which provides a bridgehead for sin that Paul calls *the flesh*. The flesh is human nature, apart from and unaided by God. Paul says that, when our human nature was unaided by God, the law actually moved our passions to sin. What does he mean by that? More than once Paul has the thought that the law actually produces sin, because the very fact that a thing is forbidden by the law lends it a certain attraction. Forbidden fruit has a fascination all its own; and, therefore, the very prohibitions of the law awakened the desire to sin. When we had nothing but the law we were at the mercy of sin. Then Paul turns to the state of a man with Christ. When a man rules life by union with Christ he rules his life not by obedience to a written code of law which may actually awaken the desire to sin; he rules it by an allegiance to Jesus Christ within his spirit and his heart. Not law, but love, is the motive of his life; and the inspiration of love can make him able to do what the restraint of law was powerless to help him to do.

THE EXCEEDING SINFULNESS OF SIN

Romans 7: 7-13

> What then are we to infer? That the law is sin? God forbid! So far from that, I would never have known what sin meant except through the law. I would never have known desire if the law had said, " You must not covet." For, when sin had, through the commandment, obtained a foothold, it produced every kind of desire in me; for, without law, sin is lifeless. Once I lived without the law; but, when the commandment came, sin sprang to life, and in that moment I knew that I had incurred the penalty of death. The commandment that was meant for life—I discovered that that very commandment was in me for death. For, when sin obtained a foothold through the commandment, it seduced me, and, through it, killed me. So the law is holy, and the commandment is holy, just and good. Did then that which was good become death to me? God forbid! But the reason was that sin might be revealed as sin by producing death in me, through the very thing which was in itself good, so that, through the commandment, sin might become surpassingly sinful.

WITH this passage there begins one of the greatest of all passages in the New Testament, and one of the most moving passages; because here Paul is giving us his own spiritual autobiography and laying bare his very heart and soul.

Here Paul deals with the torturing paradox of the law. In itself the law is a fine and a splendid thing. It is *holy*. That is to say it is the very voice of God. The root meaning of the word *holy* (*hagios*) is *different*. It describes something which comes from a sphere other than this world, something which belongs to a realm of life and being far beyond human life. The law is divine and has in it the very voice of God. It is *just*. We have seen that the root Greek idea of justice is that justice consists in giving to man, and to God, their rights and their due. Therefore the law is that which settles all relationships, human and divine. If a man perfectly kept the law he would be in a perfect relationship both with his God and with his fellow men. The law is _good._ That is to say, the law is designed for nothing other than our highest welfare and our highest good. It is meant to make a man a good man. All that is true. And yet the fact remains that this same law is the very thing through which sin gains an entry and a bridgehead into a man. How does that happen? There are two ways in which the law may be said to be, in one sense, the source and the origin of sin. (i) *The law defines sin*. Sin without the law, as Paul said, is lifeless; it has no existence. Until a thing is defined as sin by the law, a man cannot know that it is sin. We can take a kind of remote analogy in the rules of any game. Let us take tennis. A man might not know the rules, and he might, when he was playing, allow the ball to bounce more than once before he returned it over the net. So long as there were no rules he could not be accused of any fault. But then the rules are made, and it is laid down that the ball must be struck over the net after only one bounce, and that to allow it to bounce twice becomes a fault. The rules define what a fault is, and that which was allowable before the rules were made, becomes a fault after the rules are made. So the law defines sin. Again, we may take a better analogy. That which is pardonable in a child, or in an uncivilized man from a savage country, is not allowable in a mature person from a civilized land. The mature, civilized person is aware of laws of conduct which the child and the savage do not know; therefore, what is pardonable in them is fault in him. The law creates sin in the sense that it defines sin.

It may for long enough be legal to drive a motor car in either direction along a street; then that street is declared a one-way street; after that law is made a new breach of the law is actually created—the fault of driving in a forbidden direction. The new regulation actually created a new fault. The law, by making men aware of what sin is, creates sin. (ii) But there is a much more serious sense in which the law produces sin. One of the strange, odd facts of life is the fascination of the forbidden thing. In point of fact, the Jewish rabbis and thinkers saw that human tendency at work in the Garden of Eden. Adam at first lived in innocence; a commandment was given to him not to touch the forbidden tree, and that commandment was meant for nothing but his good; it was a safeguard. But the serpent came and subtly turned that very prohibition into a temptation. The fact that the tree was forbidden actually made it desirable; so Adam was seduced into sin by the forbidden fruit; and death was the result. Philo allegorised the whole story. The *serpent* is pleasure; *Eve* stands for the *senses*; pleasure, as it always does, wanted the forbidden thing; it attacked through the senses; *Adam* is the *reason*; and, through the attack of the forbidden thing on the senses, reason was led astray, and death came. In Augustine's *Confessions* there is a famous passage in which Augustine tells of the fascination of the forbidden thing.

" There was a pear tree near our vineyard, laden with fruit. One stormy night we rascally youths set out to rob it and carry our spoils away. We took off a huge load of pears—not to feast upon ourselves, but to throw them to the pigs, though we ate just enough to have the pleasure of forbidden fruit. They were nice pears, but it was not the pears that my wretched soul coveted, for I had plenty better at home. I picked them simply in order to become a thief. The only feast I got was a feast of iniquity, and that I enjoyed to the full. What was it that I loved in that theft? Was it the pleasure of acting against the law, in order that I, a prisoner under

> rules, might have a maimed counterfeit of freedom by
> doing what was forbidden, with a dim similitude of
> impotence?. . . . The desire to steal was awakened
> simply by the prohibition of stealing."

Set a thing in the category of forbidden things, put a
place out of bounds, and immediately that place, and that
thing, become fascinating. In that sense the law produces sin.

Paul has one revealing word which he uses of sin. "Sin,"
he says, " *seduced* me." There is always deception in sin.
Vaughan says that sin's deception and delusion works in
three directions. (i) We are deluded regarding the *satis-
faction* to be found in sin. No man ever took a forbidden
thing without thinking that it would make him happy,
and no man ever found that it did. (ii) We are deluded
regarding the *excuse* that can be made for it. Every man
thinks that he can put up a defence for doing the wrong
thing; but no man's defence ever sounded anything else
but futile when it was made in the presence of God. (iii) We
are deluded regarding the *probability of escaping the consequences of it.* No man sins without the hope, and even the
certainty, that he can, as we say, get away with it. But it is
true that, soon or late, our sin will find us out.

Is, then, the law a bad thing because it actually produces
sin? Paul is certain that there is wisdom in the whole
sequence. (i) First he is convinced that, whatever be the
consequence of the law, sin had to be demonstrated as
sin. Whatever the consequence, sin has to be defined.
(ii) The whole process shows the terrible nature of sin,
because sin took a thing—the law—which was holy, and
just and good, and twisted it into something which served
the ends of evil. The awfulness of sin is shown by the fact
that it could take a fine, and splendid and lovely thing,
and make it a weapon of evil. That is what sin does.
Sin can take the loveliness of love and turn it into lust.
Sin can take the honourable desire for independence and
turn it into the lust for money and for power. Sin can take
the beauty of friendship and use it as a seduction to the

wrong things. That is what Carlyle called " the infinite damnability of sin." The very fact that sin took the law and made the law a bridgehead to sin shows the supreme sinfulness of sin. The whole terrible process is not accidental; it is all designed to show us how awful a thing sin is, because sin can take the loveliest things, and defile them with a polluting touch.

THE HUMAN SITUATION

Romans 7: 14-25

> We are aware that the law is spiritual; but I am a creature of flesh and blood under the power of sin. I cannot understand what I do. What I want to do, that I do not do; but what I hate, that I do. If what I do not want to do I in point of fact do, then I acquiesce in the law, and I agree that it is fair. As it is, it is no longer I who do it, but the sin which resides in me—I mean in my human nature. To will the fair thing is within my range, but not to do it. For I do not do the good that I want to do; but the evil that I do not want to do, that is the very thing I do. And if I do that very thing that I do not want to do, it is no longer I who do it, but the sin which resides in me. My experience of the law, then, is that I wish to do the fine thing and that the evil thing is the only thing that is within my ability. As far as my inner self is concerned, I fully agree with the law of God; but I see another law in my members, continually carrying on a campaign against the law of my mind, and making me a captive by the law of sin which is in my members. O wretched man that I am! Who will deliver me from this fatal body? God will! Thanks be to Him through Jesus Christ our Lord. Therefore with my mind I serve the law of God, but with my human nature the law of sin.

IN this passage Paul is baring his very soul; and he is telling us of an experience which is of the very essence of the human situation. He knew what was right; he wanted to do what was right; and yet, somehow, he could never do it. He knew what was wrong; the last thing that he wanted to do was to do it; and yet, somehow, he did it.

allusion-I know good but education!

He felt himself to be a split personality. It was as if two men were inside the one skin. He felt himself pulled in two directions. He knew himself to be a walking civil war. He was haunted by this feeling of frustration, this ability to see what was good, and this inability to do it; this ability to recognize what was wrong, and this inability to refrain from doing it.

Paul's contemporaries well knew this feeling, as, indeed, we know it ourselves. Seneca talked of " our helplessness in necessary things." He talked about how men hate their sins and love them at the same time. Ovid, the Roman poet, had penned the famous tag: " I see the better things, and I approve them, but I follow the worse."

No one knew this problem better than the Jews. The Jews had solved it by saying that in every man there were two natures, two tendencies, two impulses. They called them the *Yetser hatob* and the *Yetser hara*. It was the Jewish conviction that God had made men like that, that all men had a good impulse and an evil impulse inside them. There were Rabbis who believed that that evil impulse was in the very embryo in the womb, that it was there before a man was born at all. It was " a malevolent second personality." It was " man's implacable enemy." It was there waiting, if need be for a life-time, for a chance to ruin man in the end. But the Jew was equally clear, in theory, that no man need ever succumb to that evil impulse. To the Jew it was all a matter of choice. Ben Sirach wrote:

" God Himself created man from the beginning.
And He left him in the hand of his own counsel.
If thou so desirest thou shalt keep the commandments,
And to perform faithfulness is of thine own good pleasure.
He hath set fire and water before thee,
Stretch forth thy hand unto whichever thou wilt.
Before man is life and death,
And whichever he liketh shall be given unto him. . . .
He hath commanded no man to do wickedly,
Neither have He given any man licence to sin."
    (15: 11-20).

There were certain things which would keep a man from falling to the evil impulse. There was *the law*. They thought of God as saying:

> " I created for you the evil impulse; I created for you the law as an antiseptic."
> " If you occupy yourself with the law you will not fall into the power of the evil impulse."

There was *the will and the mind*.

> " When God created man, He implanted in him his affections and his dispositions; and then, over all, He enthroned the sacred, ruling mind."

When the evil impulse attacked, the Jew held that wisdom and reason can defeat it; to be occupied with the study of the word of the Lord is safety ; the law is a prophylactic; at such a time the good impulse can be called up in defence.

Now, Paul knew all that; and no doubt that was all theoretically true; no doubt it *ought* to be true; and equally, no doubt, it is not true. There remains in man this battle. There are things in man's human nature—that is what Paul means by *this fatal* body—which answer to the seduction and the temptation of sin. It is part of the human situation that we know the right and yet do the wrong, that we are never as good as we know we ought to be. It is part of the human situation that at one and the same time we are haunted by goodness and haunted by sin.

From one point of view this passage might be called a demonstration of inadequacies.

(i) It demonstrates *the inadequacy of human knowledge*. If to know the right thing was to do the right thing, then life would be easy. But knowledge by itself does not make a man a good man. It is the same in every walk of life. We may know exactly how golf should be played—but that is very far from being able to play it. We may know how poetry ought to be written—but that is very far from being able to write it. We may know how we

ought to behave in any given situation—but that is very
far from being able so to behave. That is the difference
between religion and morality. Morality is knowledge of
what to do; religion is knowledge of Jesus Christ. Morality
is knowledge of a code; religion is knowledge of a person;
and it is only when we know Christ that we are able to do
what we know we ought to do.

(ii) It demonstrates the inadequacy of *human resolution*.
To resolve to do a thing is very far from doing it. There
is in human nature an essential weakness of the will.
The will comes up against the facts, the problems, the
difficulties, the opposition—and the will fails. Once Peter
took a great resolution. " Though I should die with Thee,"
he said, " yet will I not deny Thee " (Matthew 26: 35).
The human will unstrengthened by Christ is bound to
crack.

(iii) It demonstrates *the limitations of diagnosis*. Paul
knew quite clearly what was wrong; but he was quite
unable to put it right. He was like a doctor who could
accurately diagnose a disease but who was quite powerless
to prescribe a cure. Jesus is the one person who not only
knows what is wrong, but who can also put the wrong to
rights. It is not criticism He offers but help.

THE LIBERATION OF OUR HUMAN NATURE

Romans 8: 1-4

> There is, therefore, now no condemnation against
> those who are in Christ Jesus. For the law which
> comes from the Spirit and leads to life has in Christ
> Jesus set me free from the law which begets sin and
> leads to death. As for the impotency of the law, that
> weakness of the law which resulted from the effects
> of our sinful human nature—God sent His own Son
> as a sin offering with that very same human nature
> which in us had sinned; and thereby, while He existed
> in the same human nature as we have, He condemned
> sin, so that as a result the righteous demand of the
> law might be fulfilled in us, who live our lives not

after the principle of sinful human nature, but after the principle of the Spirit.

THIS is a very difficult passage because it is so highly compressed, and because, all through it, Paul is making allusions to things which he has already said.

All through this chapter two words keep repeating themselves and occurring again and again. These two words are *flesh* (*sarx*) and *spirit* (*pneuma*). We will not understand the passage at all unless we understand the way in which Paul is using these words.

(i) First of all, let us take the word *sarx*. Literally it means flesh, and the most cursory reading of Paul's letters will show how often he uses the word, and how he uses it in a sense that is all his own. Broadly speaking, he uses it in three different ways. (*a*) He uses it quite literally. He speaks of circumcision in the flesh (Romans 2: 28). That simply means bodily circumcision. (*b*) Over and over again he uses the phrase *kata sarka*, which literally means *according to the flesh*. Most often that phrase means *looking at things from the human point of view*. For instance, Paul says that Abraham is our forefather *kata sarka, according to flesh*, that is, *from the human point of view*. He says that Jesus is the son of David *kata sarka, according to the flesh* (Romans 1: 3). That is to say, on the human side of His descent Jesus is the Son of David. He speaks of the Jews being his kinsmen *kata sarka* (Romans 9: 3). That is to say, speaking of human relationships and human terms, the Jews are Paul's kinsmen. When Paul uses the phrase *kata sarka* it always implies that he is looking at things from the human point of view. (*c*) But Paul has a use of this word *sarx* which is all his own. When he is talking of the Christians, he talks of the days when we were *in the flesh* (*en sarki*) (Romans 7: 5). He speaks of those *who walk according to the flesh* in contradistinction to those who live the Christian life (Romans 8: 4, 5). He says that those who are *in the flesh* cannot please God (Romans 8: 8). He says that *the mind of the flesh* is death,

and that it is hostile to God (Romans 8: 6, 8). He talks
about *living according to the flesh* (Romans 8: 12). He
says to his Christian friends, " You are not *in the flesh* "
(Romans 8: 9). Now it is quite clear, especially from the
last instance, that Paul is not using the term flesh simply
in the sense of the body, as we say *flesh and blood.* How,
then, is he using it? When Paul uses the word *flesh* in
this way he really means human nature in all its weakness,
its impotence and its helplessness. He means human
nature in its vulnerability to sin and to temptation. He
means that part of man which gives sin its chance and its
bridgehead. He means sinful human nature, apart from
Christ and apart from God. He means everything that
attaches a man to the world instead of to God. *To live
according to the flesh* is to live a worldly life, to live life
dominated by the dictates and desires of sinful human
nature instead of a life dominated by the dictates and the
love of God. The flesh is the lower side of man's nature.
It is to be carefully noted that when Paul thinks of the
kind of life that a man dominated by the *flesh, the sarx,*
lives he is *not* by any means thinking exclusively of sexual
and bodily sins. He is not thinking altogether of what we
call fleshly sins. When he gives a list of the works of the
flesh in Galatians 5: 19-21 he includes the bodily and the
sexual sins; but he also includes idolatry, hatred, wrath,
strife, heresies, envy, murder. The flesh to Paul was not a
physical thing; it was a spiritual thing. The flesh was
human nature in all its sin and weakness, and impotence and
frustration; the flesh is all that man is without God and
without Christ.

(ii) There is the word *Spirit*. In this single chapter the
word *Spirit* occurs no fewer than twenty times. Now, the
word *Spirit* has a very definite Old Testament background.
In Hebrew the word is *ruach,* and it has two basic thoughts.
(*a*) *Ruach* is not only the word for *Spirit*; it is also the
word for *wind*. It has always the idea of power about it,
power as of a mighty rushing wind. (*b*) *Ruach*, in the Old

Testament, always has the idea of something that is more than human, something that is not of man and not within the power of man. *Spirit*, to Paul, represented a power which was divine.

So Paul says in this passage that there was a time when the Christian, before he was a Christian, was at the mercy of his own sinful human nature. In that state the law simply became something that moved him to sin, and in that state he went from bad to worse, a defeated and frustrated man. But, when he became a Christian, into his life there came the surging power of the Spirit of God, and, because in his life there was now a power that was not his power, he entered into victorious living instead of defeated existence.

In the second part of the passage Paul speaks of the effect of the work of Jesus on us. It is a very complicated and a very difficult passage, but what Paul is getting at is this. Let us remember that he began all this by saying that all men sinned in Adam. We saw how the Jewish conception of solidarity made it possible for Paul to argue that, quite literally, all men sinned in Adam and all men were involved in that sin and in its consequence—death. But there is another side to this picture. Into this world came Jesus. He came as a man; He came with a completely and truly human nature. As He lived as a man He was sinless; He defeated sin; He condemned sin; in Him sin was vanquished and conquered; and He brought to God a life of perfect obedience, of perfect fulfilment of the law of God. Now, because Jesus was fully a man, just as we were one with Adam, we are now one with Him; and, just as we were involved in Adam's sin, we are now involved in Jesus' perfection. In Him mankind fulfilled God's law just as in Adam mankind broke God's law. In Him mankind brought to God the perfect obedience just as in Adam mankind brought to God the fatal disobedience. Men are saved because they were once involved in Adam's sin but are now involved in Jesus' goodness.

That is Paul's argument, and to him and to those who heard it, it was completely convincing however hard it is for us to grasp it. Because of what Jesus did there opens out to the Christian a life which is no longer dominated by the flesh, by sinful, impotent, human nature, but a life that is dominated by that Spirit of power, that Spirit of God, which fills a man with a power not his own. The penalty of the past is removed, strength for the future is assured.

THE TWO PRINCIPLES OF LIFE

Romans 8: 5-11

> Those who live according to the dictates of sinful human nature are absorbed in worldly human things. Those who live according to the dictates of the Spirit are absorbed in the things of the Spirit. To be absorbed in worldly human things is death; but to be absorbed in the things of the Spirit is life and peace, because absorption in the things which fascinate our sinful human nature is hostility to God, for it does not obey the law of God, nor, indeed, can it do so. Those whose life is a purely worldly thing cannot please God; but you are not dominated by the pursuits which fascinate our sinful human nature; you are dominated by the Spirit, if so it be that the Spirit of God dwells in you. If anyone does not possess the Spirit of Christ he does not belong to Christ. But if Christ is in you, even if because of sin your body is mortal, your Spirit has life through righteousness. If the Spirit of Him who raised Jesus from the dead dwells in you He will make even your mortal bodies alive through His Spirit indwelling in you.

IN this passage Paul is drawing a contrast between two kinds of life.

(i) There is the life which is dominated by sinful human nature; the life whose focus and centre is self; the life that is absorbed in the things that fascinate sinful human nature; the life whose only law is its own desires; the life which takes what it likes where it likes. In different people that life will be differently described. It may be passion-controlled, or lust-controlled, or pride-controlled, or ambition-controlled. Its characteristic is its absorption in the things that human nature without Christ sets its heart upon.

(ii) There is the life that is dominated by the Spirit of God. In the man's heart is the Spirit. As he lives in the air, he lives in Christ, never separated from Him. As he breathes in the air, and the air fills him, so Christ fills him. He has no mind of his own. Christ is his mind. He has no desires of his own; the will of Christ is his only law. He is Spirit-controlled, Christ-controlled, God-focussed.

These two lives are going in diametrically different directions. The life that is dominated by the desires and activities of sinful human nature is on the way to death. In the most literal sense, there is no future in it. That is because it is getting further and further away from God. To allow the things of the world completely to dominate life is self extinction; it is spiritual suicide; it is, again in the most literal sense, soul destroying. By living it a man is making himself totally unfit ever to stand in the presence of God. He is hostile to God; he is resentful of God's law and God's control. God is not his friend but his enemy, and no man ever won the last battle against God.

The Spirit-controlled life, the Christ-centred life, the God-focussed life is on the way to life. Daily it is coming nearer heaven even when it is still on earth. Daily it is becoming more Christlike, more one with Christ. It is a life which is such a steady progress to God that the final transition of death is only a natural and inevitable stage on the way. It is like Enoch who walked with God and God took him. As the child said: " Enoch was a man who went walks with God—and one day he didn't come back."

But no sooner has Paul said this than an inevitable objection strikes him. Someone may say: " You say that the Spirit-controlled man is on the way to life; but in point of fact every man must die. Just what do you mean? " Paul's answer is this. He says that all men die because all men are involved in the human situation. Sin came into this world, and with sin came death. Death is the consequence of sin. Inevitably, therefore, all men die; but the man who is Spirit-controlled, and whose heart is Christ-occupied, dies only to rise again. It is Paul's basic thought that the Christian is indissolubly one with Christ. Now Christ died and rose again; He conquered death; and the man who is one with Christ is one with death's conqueror and shares in that victory. It still remains true that the Spirit-controlled, Christ-possessed man is on the way to life; death is but an inevitable interlude that has to be passed through on the way.

ENTRY INTO THE FAMILY OF GOD

Romans 8: 12-17

> So then, brothers, a duty is laid upon us—and that duty is *not* to our own sinful human nature, to live according to the principles of that same nature; for, if you live according to the principles of sinful human nature, you are on the way to death; but if, by the spirit, you kill the deeds of the body, you will live. For all who are guided by the Spirit of God, these, and only these, are the children of God. For you did not receive a state whose dominating condition is slavery so that you might relapse into fear; but you received a state whose dominating characteristic is adoption, in which we cry, " Abba! Father! " The Spirit itself bears witness with our spirit that we are children of God. If we are children then we are also heirs; and if we are the heirs of God then we are joint-heirs with Christ. If we suffer with Him we shall also be glorified with Him.

IN this passage Paul is introducing us to another of the great metaphors in which he describes the new relationship of the Christian to God. Here Paul speaks of the Christian being adopted into the family of God. It is only when we understand how serious and complicated a step Roman adoption was that we really understand the depth of meaning in this passage. Roman adoption was always rendered more serious and more difficult by the Roman *patria potestas*. The *patria potestas* was the father's power over his family; that power was absolute; it was actually the power of absolute disposal and control, and in the early days it was actually the power of life and death. In regard to his father a Roman son never came of age. No matter how old he was, he was still under the *patria potestas*, in the absolute possession, and under the absolute control, of his father. Obviously this made adoption into another family a very difficult and a very serious step. In adoption a person had to pass from one *patria potestas* to another. He had to pass out of the possession and control of one father into the equally absolute possession and control of another. There were two steps. The first was known as *mancipatio*, and it was carried out by a symbolic sale, in which copper and scales were symbolically used. Three times the symbolism of sale was carried out. Twice the father symbolically sold his son, and twice he bought him back; and the third time he did not buy him back, and thus the *patria potestas* was held to be broken. After the sale there followed a ceremony called *vindicatio*. The adopting father went to the *praetor*, one of the Roman magistrates, and presented a legal case for the transference of the person to be adopted into his *patria potestas*. When all this was completed then the adoption was complete. Clearly this was a serious and an impressive step.

But it is the consequences of adoption which are most significant for the picture that is in Paul's mind. There were four main consequences. (i) The adopted person lost all rights in his old family, and gained all the rights of a fully legitimate son in his new family. In the most literal sense, and in the most binding legal way, he got a new father. (ii) It followed that he became heir to his new father's estate. Even if other sons were afterwards born, who were real blood relations, it did not affect his rights.

He was inalienably co-heir with them. (iii) In law, the
old life of the adopted person was completely wiped out.
For instance, legally all debts were cancelled; they were
wiped out as if they had never been. The adopted person
was regarded as a new person entering into a new life
with which the past had nothing to do. (iv) In the eyes
of the law the adopted person was literally and absolutely
the son of his new father. Roman history provides an _e.g._
outstanding case of how literally and completely this was
held to be true. The Emperor Claudius adopted Nero,
in order that Nero might succeed him on the throne.
They were not in any sense blood relations. Claudius
already had a daughter, Octavia. To cement the alliance
Nero wished to marry Octavia. Now, Nero and Octavia
were in no sense connected; they were in no sense blood
relations; yet, in the eyes of the law, they were brother
and sister; and before they could marry the Roman senate
had to pass special legislation to enable Nero to marry
a girl who was legally his own sister. Nothing shows better
how complete adoption in Rome was.

That is what Paul is thinking of. He uses still another
picture from Roman adoption. He says that God's Spirit
witnesses with our spirit that we really are children of
God. The adoption ceremony was carried out in the presence
of seven witnesses. Now, suppose the adopting father died,
and then suppose that there was some dispute about the
right of the adopted son to inherit, one or more of the
seven original witnesses stepped forward and swore that
the adoption was genuine and true. Thus the right of the
adopted person was guaranteed and he entered into his
inheritance. So, Paul is saying, it is the Holy Spirit Himself
who is the witness to our adoption into the family of God.

We see then that every step of Roman adoption was
meaningful in the mind of Paul when he transferred the
picture to our adoption into the family of God. Once we
were in absolute possession of sin, in absolute control
of our own sinful human nature; but God, in His mercy,

has brought us into absolute possession of Himself. The old life has no more rights over us; God has an absolute right. The past is cancelled; the debts of the past are wiped out; we begin again a new life, a life with God. We become heirs of all the riches of God. If that is so, we become joint-heirs with Jesus Christ, God's own Son. That which Christ inherited, and inherits, we also inherit. If Christ had to suffer we also inherit that suffering, but if Christ was raised to life and glory we also inherit that life and glory.

It was Paul's picture that when a man became a Christian he entered into the very family of God. He did nothing to earn it; he did nothing to deserve it; God, the great Father in His amazing love and mercy, has taken the lost, helpless, poverty-stricken, debt-laden sinner and adopted him into His own family, so that the debts are cancelled and the unearned love and glory inherited.

THE GLORIOUS HOPE

Romans 8: 18-25

For I am convinced that the sufferings of this present age cannot be compared with the glory which is destined to be disclosed to us. The created world awaits with eager expectation the day when those who are the sons of God will be displayed in all their glory. For the created world has been subjected to chaos, not because of its own choice, but through Him who passed the sentence of such subjugation upon it, and yet it still has the hope that the created world also will be liberated from this slavery to decay and will be brought to the freedom of the glory of the children of God; for we know that the whole creation unites together in groans and agonies. Not only does the created world do so, but so do we, even though we have received the first-fruits of the spirit as a foretaste of the coming glory, yes, we too groan within ourselves earnestly awaiting the full realisation of our adoption into the family of God, I mean the redemption of our body. For it is by hope that we

> are saved; but a hope which is already visible is
> not a hope; for who hopes for what he already sees?
> But if we hope for what we do not see, then in patience
> we eagerly wait for it.

PAUL has just been speaking of the glory of adoption
into the family of God; and then, after the thought of
the glory, he comes back to the troubled state of this present
world. Here he draws a great picture. He speaks with a
poet's vision. He sees creation itself, the created world,
all nature waiting for the glory that shall be. At the moment
creation is in bondage to decay.

> " Change and decay in all around I see."

The world is a world where beauty fades and loveliness
decays; the world is a dying world; but the world is waiting
for its liberation from all this and the coming of the state
of freedom and of glory.

Now, when Paul was painting this picture, he was
working with ideas that any Jew would recognize and
understand. He talks of this present age and of the glory
that will be disclosed. Jewish thought divided time into
two sections—there was this present age and the age
which is to come. This present age was wholly bad, subject
to sin, and death and decay. Some day there would come
The Day of the Lord. That would be a day of judgment
and a day when the world would be shaken to its foundations
and shattered; but out of it there would come a new world.
The renovation of the world was one of the great Jewish
thoughts. The Old Testament speaks of it without elabor-
ation and without detail. " Behold I create new heavens
and a new earth " (Isaiah 65: 17). But in the days between
the Testaments, days when the Jews were oppressed, and
enslaved and persecuted, they dreamed their dreams of
that new earth and that renovated world.

> " The vine shall yield its fruit ten thousand fold,
> and on each vine there shall be a thousand branches;
> and each branch shall produce a thousand clusters;

and each cluster produce a thousand grapes; and each grape a cor of wine. And those who have hungered shall rejoice; moreover, also, they shall behold marvels every day. For winds shall go forth from before me to bring every morning the fragrance of aromatic fruits, and at the close of the day clouds distilling the dews of health." (The Apocalypse of Baruch 29: 5).

" And earth, and all the trees, and the innumerable flocks of sheep shall give their true fruit to mankind, of wine and of sweet honey and of white milk and corn, which to men is the most excellent gift of all." (Sibylline Oracles 3: 620-633).

" Earth, the universal mother, shall give to mortals her best fruit in countless store of corn, wine and oil. Yea, from heaven shall come a sweet draught of luscious honey. The trees shall yield their proper fruits, and rich flocks, and kine, and lambs of sheep and kids of goats. He will cause sweet fountains of white milk to burst forth. And the cities shall be full of good things, and the fields rich; neither shall there be any sword throughout the land or battle-din; nor shall the earth be convulsed any more with deep-drawn groans. No war shall be any more, nor shall there by any more drought throughout the land, no famine, or hail to work havoc on the crops." (Sibylline Oracles 3: 744-756).

The dream of the renovated world was dear to the Jews. Paul knew that, and here he, as it were, endows creation with consciousness. He thinks of nature longing for the day when sin's dominion would be broken, when death and decay would be gone, and when God's glory would come. With a touch of imaginative insight, Paul says that the state of nature was even worse than the state of men. Man had sinned deliberately; but it was involuntarily, not of her own choice, that nature was subjected. Unwittingly nature was involved in the consequences of the sin of man. " Cursed be the ground for thy sake," God said to Adam after his sin (Genesis 3: 17). So here, with a poet's eye, Paul sees nature waiting for liberation from the death and decay that man's sin had brought into the world.

If that is true of nature, it is still truer of man. So
Paul goes on to think of human longing. In the experience
of the Holy Spirit men have had a foretaste, a first instal-
ment, of the glory that shall be; now they long with all
their hearts for the full realization of what adoption into
the family of God means. That final adoption will be the
redemption of their bodies. In the state of glory Paul
did not think of man as a disembodied spirit. Man in
this world is a body and a spirit; and in the world of glory
the total man will be saved. Only his body will no longer
be the victim of decay and the instrument of sin; it will
be a spiritual body fit for the life of a spiritual man.

And then there comes a great saying. " We are saved
by hope." The one blazing truth that lit life for Paul
was the tremendous fact that the human situation is not
a hopeless situation. Paul was no pessimist. H. G. Wells
once said: " Man, who began in a cave behind a wind-
break, will end in the diseased soaked ruins of a slum."
Not so Paul. He saw man's sin; he saw the state of the
world and the state of the human situation; but he also
saw God's redeeming power, and the end of it all for Paul
was hope. And because of that, to Paul life was not a
despairing waiting for an inevitable end in a world encom-
passed by sin and death and decay; life was an eager
anticipation of a liberation, a renovation and a re-creation
wrought by the glory and the power of God.

In verse 19 he uses a wonderful word for *eager expectation.*
The word is *apokaradokia*; it describes the attitude of a
man who scans the horizon with head thrust forward
eagerly searching the distance for the first signs of the dawn
break of glory. To Paul life was not a weary, defeated
waiting; life was a throbbing, vivid expectation. The
Christian is involved in the human situation. Within he
must battle with his own evil human nature; without
he must live in a world of death and decay. But, nonetheless,
the Christian does not only live in the world; he also
lives in Christ. He does not only see the world; he looks

beyond the world to God. The Christian does not only see the consequence of man's sin; he sees the power of God's mercy and God's love. And, therefore, the key-note of the Christian life is always hope and never despair. The Christian waits, not for death, but for life.

ALL IS OF GOD

Romans 8: 26-30

> Even so, the Spirit helps us in our weakness; for we do not know what we should pray, if we are to pray as we ought. But the Spirit Himself intercedes for us with groanings which baffle speech to utter; but He who searches the hearts knows the mind of the Spirit, because it is by God's will that He intercedes for those whose lives are consecrated to God. We know that God intermingles all things for good for those who love Him, for those who are called according to His purpose. For those whom He knew long ago He long ago designed to be conformed to the likeness of His Son, that He might be the first born among many brothers. Those whom He long ago designed for this purpose, He also called; and those whom He called He put into a right relationship with Himself; and those whom He put into a right relationship with Himself He also glorified.

THE first two verses of this passage form one of the most important passages on prayer in the whole New Testament. Paul is saying that, because of our weakness, we do not know what to pray for, but the prayers we ought to offer are offered for us by the Holy Spirit of God. C. H. Dodd defines prayer in this way—" Prayer is the Divine in us appealing to the Divine above us." There are two very obvious reasons why we cannot pray as we ought. First, we cannot pray aright because we cannot foresee the future. We cannot see a year or even an hour ahead; and we may well pray to be saved from things which are for our good, and we may well pray for things which would be to our ultimate harm simply because we cannot see ahead and know what is to happen. Second, we cannot pray aright because even in any given situation we do not know what is best for us. We are often in the position of a child who wants something which would be bound only to hurt him; and God is often in the position of a parent who has to refuse his child's requests, or who has to compel the child to do something he does not want to do, because he knows what is to the child's good far better than the child does himself. Even the Greeks knew that. Pythagoras forbade his disciples to pray for themselves, because, he said, they could never in their ignorance know what was expedient for them. Xenophon tells us that Socrates taught his disciples simply to pray for good things, and not to attempt to specify them, but to leave God to decide what the good things were. C. H. Dodd puts it in this way. We cannot know our own real need; we cannot with our finite minds grasp God's plan; in the last analysis all that we can bring to God is an inarticulate sigh which the Spirit will translate to God for us. As Paul saw it, prayer, like everything else, is of God. Paul knew that by no possible human effort can a man justify himself; and he also knew that by no possible effort of the human intelligence can a man know for what to pray. In the last analysis the perfect prayer is simply, " Father, into Thy hands I commend my spirit. Not my will, but Thine be done."

But Paul goes on from there. He says that those who love God, and who are called according to His purpose, know well that God is intermingling all things for good to them. It is the experience of life for the Christian that all things do work together for good. We do not need to be very old to look back on life and see that things that we thought were disasters worked out to our good; things that we thought were disappointments worked out to greater blessings. We can look back, and we can see a guiding and a directing hand in it and through it all.

But we have to note that that experience comes only

to those who love God. The Stoics had a great idea and it may well be that the Stoic idea was actually in Paul's mind when he wrote this passage. One of the great Stoic conceptions was the conception of the *logos* of God. The *logos* was the mind or the reason of God. The Stoic believed that this world was permeated and interpenetrated with that *logos.* It was the *logos* which put order and sense into the world. It was the *logos* which kept the stars in their courses and the planets in their appointed tracks. It was the *logos* which controlled the ordered succession of night and day, and summer and winter and spring and autumn. The *logos* was the reason and the mind of God in the universe, making the universe an order and not a chaos. Now the Stoic went further. The Stoic believed that the *logos* of God not only had an order for the universe, but that it also had an order and a plan and a purpose for the life of every individual man. To put it in another way, the Stoic believed that nothing could happen to a man which did not come from God and which was not part of the plan of God for that man. Epictetus writes: "Have courage to look up to God and to say, ' Deal with me as Thou wilt from now on. I am as one with Thee; I am Thine; I flinch from nothing so long as Thou dost think that it is good. Lead me where Thou wilt; put on me what raiment Thou wilt. Wouldst Thou have me hold office or eschew it, stay or flee, be rich or poor? For this I will defend Thee before men.' " So then the Stoic taught that the duty of every man was *acceptance.* If he accepted the things that God sent him, he knew peace. If he struggled against them, he was uselessly battering his head against the ineluctable purpose of God.

Now Paul has the very same thought. He says that all things work together for good, but only *to them that love God.* If a man loves God and trusts God and accepts God, if a man feels and knows and is convinced that God is the all-wise and all-loving Father, then he can humbly accept all that God sends to him. A man may go to a physician or a surgeon, and the physician or surgeon may prescribe a course of treatment which at the time is unpleasant or even painful; but the man trusts the wisdom of the man of skill and accepts the thing that is laid upon him. It is so with us if we love God. But if a man does not love and trust God, he may well resent what happens to him; he may well fight against the will of God; he may well find that the pains and the sorrows and the trials of life move him to anger and rebellion. It is only to the man who loves and trusts that all things do work together for good, for to him they come from a Father who in perfect wisdom, love and power is working ever for the best.

But Paul goes further; he goes on to speak of the spiritual experience of every Christian. In the Authorised Version's translation there follows a famous passage. " For whom He did foreknow He also did predestinate to be conformed to the image of His Son, that He might be the first-born among many brethren. Moreover, whom He did predestinate, them He also called; and whom He called, them He also justified; and whom He justified, them He also glorfied." This is a passage which has been very seriously mis-used. If we are ever to understand this passage we must grasp the basic fact that Paul never meant it to be the expression of theology or philosophy; he meant it to be the almost lyrical expression of Christian experience. If we take this as philosophy and theology and if we apply the standards of cold logic to it, it must mean that God chose some and did not choose others, that there is a strange and terrible selectiveness in the love of God. But that is not what the passage means. Think of the Christian experience. The more a Christian thinks of his experience the more he becomes convinced that he had nothing to do with it and all is of God. Jesus Christ came into this world; He lived; He went to the Cross; He rose again. We did nothing to bring that about; that is God's work. We heard the story of this wondrous love. We did not *make* the story; we only *received* the story.

Love woke within our hearts; the conviction of sin came; and with it there came the experience of forgiveness and of salvation; we did not achieve that. All is of God. That is what Paul is thinking of here. The Old Testament has an illuminating use of the word *to know*. " I did *know* thee in the wilderness," said God to Hosea about the people Israel (Hosea 13: 5). " You only have I *known* of all the families in the earth," said God to Amos (Amos 3: 2). When the Bible speaks of God *knowing* a man, it means that God has a purpose and a plan and a design and a task for that man. And when we look back upon our Christian experience, all that we can say is, " I did not do this; I could never have done this; God did everything." And we know well that this does not take free-will away. God knew Israel, but the day came when Israel refused the destiny God meant her to have. God's unseen guiding is in our lives, but to the end of the day we can refuse it and take our own way. It is the deep experience of the Christian that all is of God; that he did nothing and that God did everything. That is what Paul means here. He means that from the beginning of time God marked us out for salvation; that in due time His call came to us; but Paul also knew that the pride of the heart of man can wreck the plan of God and the disobedience of the will of man can refuse the call.

THE LOVE FROM WHICH NOTHING CAN SEPARATE US

Romans 8: 31-39

> What then shall we say to these things? If God is for us, who is against us? The very God who did not spare His own Son but who delivered Him up for us all, how shall He not with Him also freely give us all things? Who shall impeach the elect of God? It is God who acquits. Who is He who condemns? It is Jesus Christ who died, nay rather, who was raised from the dead, and who is at the right hand of

God, who also intercedes for us. Who will separate us from the love of Christ? Shall trial, or distress, or persecution, or famine, or nakedness, or peril, or sword? As it stands written, " For Thy sake we are killed all the day long; we are reckoned as sheep for the slaughter." But in all these things we are more than conquerors through Him who loved us. For I am convinced that neither death, nor life, nor angels, nor principalities, nor the present age, nor the age to come, nor powers, nor height, nor depth, nor any other creation will be able to separate us from the love of God which is in Christ Jesus our Lord.

THIS is one of the most lyrical passages that Paul ever wrote. In verse 32 there is a very wonderful allusion and reminiscence which would stand out to any Jew who knew his Old Testament well. Paul says in effect: " God for us did not spare His own Son; surely that is the final guarantee that He loves us enough to supply all our needs." Now the words that Paul uses of God are the very words that God used of Abraham when Abraham proved his utter loyalty to God by being willing to sacrifice his son Isaac at God's command. God said to Abraham: " You did not spare your only son for my sake " (Genesis 22: 16). Paul seems to say: " Think of the greatest human example in the world of a man's loyalty to God; God's loyalty to you is like that." Just as Abraham was so loyal to God that he was prepared to sacrifice his dearest possession for the sake of God, God is so loyal to men that He is prepared to sacrifice His only Son for them. Surely we can trust a loyalty like that for anything.

It is difficult to know just how to take verses 33-35. There are two ways of taking them and both give excellent sense and precious truth.

(i) We can take these verses as two statements, followed by two questions which give the inferences to be made from these statements. (*a*) It is God who acquits men— that is the statement. If that be so who can possibly condemn men? If man is acquitted by God, then he is saved from every other condemnation. (*b*) Our belief is in a Christ who died and rose again and who is alive for evermore—that is the statement. If that be so is there anything in this or any other world that can separate us from our Risen Lord? If we take it that way two great truths are laid down. (*a*) God has acquitted us; therefore no one can condemn us. (*b*) Christ is risen; therefore nothing can ever separate us from Him.

(ii) But there is another way to take it. God has acquitted us. Who then can stand in judgment over us and condemn us? The answer is that the Judge of all men is Jesus Christ. He is the one who has the right to condemn—but so far from condemning, He is at God's right hand interceding for us, and therefore we are safe. It may be that in verse 34 Paul is doing a very wonderful thing. See what he is saying of Jesus. He is saying four things about Jesus. (*a*) He died. (*b*) He rose again. (*c*) He is at the right hand of God. (*d*) He makes intercession for us and pleads for us there. Now the earliest creed of the Church, a creed which is still the essence of all Christian creeds, ran like this: " He was crucified dead and buried; the third day He rose again from the dead; and sitteth at the right hand of God; *from thence He shall come to judge the quick and the dead.*" Now note, three items in Paul's statement and in the early creed are the same. The three are that Jesus died, rose again, and is at the right hand of God. *But the fourth is different.* In the creed the fourth is that Jesus will come *to be the judge of the quick and the dead.* In Paul the fourth is that Jesus is at God's right hand *to intercede for us and to plead our case.* It is as if Paul said: " You think of Jesus as the Judge who is there to condemn; and well He might for well He has won the right; but you are wrong; He is not there to be our prosecuting counsel; He is there to be the advocate to plead our cause; He is not there to state the case against us; He is there to state the case for us; He is not there to be our Judge; He is there to be the friend who pleads our cause."

I think that the second way of taking this is right. With one tremendous leap and adventure of thought Paul has seen Christ, not as the Judge of the creed, but as the lover of the souls of men.

So Paul goes on with a poet's fervour and a lover's rapture to sing of how nothing can separate us from the love of God in our Risen Lord.

(i) No affliction, no hardship, no peril can separate us. (Verse 36). Though the world be falling about our ears, we can still have sweet times with Christ. The disasters of the world do not separate a man from Christ; they bring him closer yet.

(ii) In verses 38 and 39 Paul makes a list of terrible things. Neither *life nor death* can separate us from Christ. In life we live with Christ; in death we die with Him; and because we die with Him, we also rise with Him; and death so far from being a separation is only a step into His nearer presence. Death is not the end; it is only " the gate on the skyline " leading to the presence of Jesus Christ. *The angelic powers* cannot separate us from Him. At this particular time the Jews had a highly developed belief in angels. Everything in the world had its angel. There was an angel of the winds, of the clouds, of the snow and hail and hoarfrost, of the thunder and the lightning, of cold and heat, of the seasons. The Rabbis said that there was nothing in the world, not even a blade of grass, that had not got its angel. These angels were divided into classes and families and ranks. According to the Rabbis there were three ranks of angels. The first rank included thrones, cherubim and seraphim. The second rank included powers, lordships and mights. The third rank included angels and archangels and principalities. More than once Paul speaks of these angels (Ephesians I: 21; 3: 10; 6: 12; Colossians 2: 10, 15; I Corinthians 15: 24). Now the Rabbis—and Paul had once been a Rabbi—believed that these angels were grudgingly hostile to men. They believed that the angels had been angry when God created man. It was as if they did not want to share God with anyone and they had grudged man his creation and his share in God. The Rabbis had a legend that when God appeared on Sinai to give Moses the law He was attended by His hosts of angels, and the angels grudged Israel the law, and assaulted Moses on his way up the mountain and tried to stop him, and would have stopped him had not God intervened. So Paul, thinking in terms of his own day, says, " Not even the grudging, jealous angels can separate us from the love of God, much as they would like to do so." *No age in time* can separate us from Christ. Paul speaks of *things present and things to come.* We know that the Jews divided all time into *this present age* and *the age to come.* Paul is saying: ." In this present world nothing can separate us from God in Christ; the day will come when this world will be shattered and the new age will dawn. It does not matter; even then, when this world has passed and the new world come, the bond is still the same." *No malign influence* will separate us from Christ. Paul speaks about *height and depth.* Now these are astrological terms. The ancient world was haunted by the tyranny of the stars. They believed that a man was born under a certain star and thereby his destiny was settled. There are some who still believe that; but the ancient world was really haunted by this supposed domination of a man's life by the influence of the stars. *Height* (*hupsōma*) was the time when a star was at its zenith, and when its influence was greatest; *depth* (*bathos*) was the time when a star was at its lowest, waiting to rise and to put its influence on some man. Paul says to these haunted men of his age: " The stars cannot hurt you. In their rising and their setting they are powerless to separate you from God's love." *No other world* can separate us from God. The word that Paul uses for *other* (*heteros*) when he speaks of any *other* creation has really the meaning of *different.* So Paul is saying: " Suppose that by some wild flight of imagination there emerged another and a different world, you would still be safe; you would still be enwrapped in the love of God."

Here is a vision to take away all loneliness and all fear. Paul is saying: " You can think of every terrifying thing that this or any other world can produce. Not one of them is able to separate the Christian from the love of God which is in Jesus Christ, who is Lord of every terror and Master of every world." Of what then shall we be afraid?

THE PROBLEM OF THE JEWS

In chapter 9 to 11 Paul tries to deal with one of the most bewildering problems that the Church has to solve—the problem of the Jews. The Jews were God's chosen people; they had had a unique and special place in God's purposes; and yet when God's Son had come into the world they had rejected Him and crucified Him. How is this tragic paradox to be explained? How are we to explain the fact that God's people crucified God's Son? That is the problem with which Paul seeks to deal in these chapters. They are complicated and difficult chapters, and, before we begin to study them in detail, it will be well to set out the ideas with which Paul worked, and the broad lines of the solution which Paul presented.

One thing we must note before we begin to disentangle Paul's thought—the chapters were not written in anger; they were written in heart-break. Paul could never forget that he was a Jew and he would gladly have laid down his own life if, by so doing, he could have brought his brethren to Jesus Christ.

Paul never denies that the Jews were the chosen people. God adopted them as His own people; He gave them the covenants and the service of the Temple, and the law; He gave them the presence of His own glory; He gave them the patriarchs; and, above all, in his human descent, Jesus was a Jew. The special place of the Jews in God's economy of salvation Paul accepts as an axiom and as the starting-point of the whole problem.

The first point which he makes is this—it is true that the Jews as a nation rejected and crucified Jesus, but it is also true, that *not all the Jews rejected Him*; some of them received Him and believed in Him, for all the early followers of Jesus, in the first days, were Jews. Paul then looks back on history, and he insists that racial descent from Abraham does not make a Jew. Over and over again in Jewish history there was in God's ways a process of selection—Paul calls it *election*—whereby some of those who were racial descendants of Abraham were chosen and some rejected. In the case of Abraham, Isaac, the son who was born according to the promise of God, was chosen, but Ishmael, the son who was born of purely natural processes and desires, was not. In the case of Isaac, his son Jacob was chosen, but Esau, who was Jacob's twin, was not. This selection had nothing to do with merit; it was not something which those selected had earned as a right; it was the work entirely of God's electing wisdom and power.

Further, the real nation of Israel, the real chosen people, never lay in the whole nation; it always lay in *the righteous remnant*, the few who were true to God when all others denied Him. It was so in the days of Elijah, when seven thousand remained faithful to God when the rest of the nation had gone after Baal. It was an essential part of the teaching of Isaiah, who said: "Though the number of the children of Israel be as the sand of the sea, *a remnant shall be saved*." (Isaiah 10: 22; Romans 9: 27). So then, Paul's first point is that at no time were the whole people the chosen people. There were always selection, *election* on the part of God.

But, is that fair? Is it fair of God to elect some and to reject others? Is this election just and reasonable, equitable and fair? And, if some men are elected and others are rejected, through no virtue or fault of their own, how can you blame them if they reject Christ, and how can you praise them if they accept Him? It is here that Paul uses an argument at which the mind staggers, and from which we quite properly recoil. Bluntly, Paul's argument is that God can do what He likes and that man has no right whatever to question the decisions of God, however inscrutable they may be. The clay cannot talk back to the potter; the thing cannot talk back to the craftsman who made it. A craftsman may make two vessels, one for an honourable purpose and another for a menial purpose; the vessels have nothing whatever to do with it. That, said Paul, is what God has a right to do with men. He quotes the instance of Pharaoh (Romans 9: 17) and says that Pharaoh was brought on to the stage of history simply and solely to be the instrument through which God's avenging power was demonstrated. In any event the people of Israel had been forewarned of the election of the Gentiles and of their rejection, for, did not the prophet Hosea write: " I will call them my people which were not my people; and her beloved who was not beloved " (Hosea I: 10; Romans 9: 25).

But in any event this rejection of Israel was not callous and pointless and haphazard. It came about in order that the Gentiles might come in. The door was shut to the Jews that it might be opened to the Gentiles. The Jews were rejected that the Gentiles might be received. If God did harden the hearts of the Jews and blind their eyes, as He did, He did it with the ultimate purpose of opening a way for the Gentiles into the faith. Here is a strange and a terrible argument. Stripped of all its non-essentials, Paul's argument is that God can do what He likes with any man or nation, and that He deliberately darkened the minds and shut the eyes of the Jews in order that the Gentiles might come in.

What then was the fundamental mistake of the Jews? This may seem a curious question to ask in view of what we have just said. But, paradoxically, Paul holds that though the rejection of the Jews was the work of God, it need yet never have happened. Paul cannot get rid of the eternal paradox—nor does he desire to—that at one and the same time all is of God and man has free-will. The fundamental mistake of the Jews was that they tried to get into a right relationship with God through their own human efforts, through obedience to the law. They tried independently to earn salvation; whereas the Gentiles simply accepted the offer of God in perfect and total trust. Now the Jews should have known that the only way to God was the way of faith, and that human achievement leads nowhere. Did not Isaiah say: " Whosoever believeth on Him shall not be ashamed "? (Isaiah 28: 16; Romans 10: 11). Did not Joel say: " Whosoever shall call upon the name of the Lord shall be saved "? (Joel 2: 32; Romans 10: 13). True, no man can have faith until he hears the offer of God; but to the Jews that offer was made. They clung to the way of human achievement through obedience to the law; they staked everything on works; but they should have known that the way to God was the way of faith, for the prophets had told them so.

Now once again it is to be stressed that all this is God's arrangement; and that it was so arranged to allow the Gentiles to come in. Paul therefore turns to the Gentiles. He orders them to have no pride. They are in the position of wild olive shoots which have been grafted into a garden olive tree. They did not achieve their own salvation any more than the Jews did; in point of fact they are dependent on the Jews; they are only engrafted branches; the root and the stem is still the chosen people. The fact of their own election and the fact of the rejection of the Jews are not to combine to produce pride in the Gentile heart. If that happens, rejection can and will happen to them.

But is this the end? Far from it. It is God's purpose that the Jews will be moved to envy at the relationship of the Gentiles to God, and that they will come and ask to be admitted to it themselves. Did not Moses say: " I will provoke you to jealousy by them that are no people, and by a foolish nation I will anger you "? (Deuteronomy 32: 21; Romans 10: 19). In the end the Gentiles will be the very instrument by which the Jews are to be saved. "And so all Israel shall be saved " (Romans 11: 26).

So Paul comes to the end of the argument. We may summarily set out its steps, without all the ramifications.

(i) Israel is the chosen people.

(ii) To be a member of Israel means more than racial descent. There has always been election within the nation; and the best of the nation has always been the remnant who were faithful.

(iii) This selection by God is not unfair for God has the right to do what He likes.

(iv) God did harden the hearts of the Jews, but He did so only to open the door to the Gentiles.

(v) Israel's mistake was dependence on human achievement founded on the law; the necessary approach to God is that of the totally trusting heart.

(vi) The Gentiles must have no pride for they are only wild olives grafted into the true olive stock. They must remember that.

(vii) This is not the end; the Jews will be so moved to wondering envy at the privilege that the Gentiles have received that in the end they will be brought in by the Gentiles.

(viii) So in the very end all, Jew and Gentile, will be saved.

The glory is in the end of Paul's argument. He began by saying that some were elected to reception and some to rejection. In the end he comes to say that it is God's will that all men should be saved.

THE TRAGIC FAILURE

Romans 9: 1-6

> I tell you the truth as one who is united to Christ is
> bound to do. I do not lie. My conscience bears witness
> with me in the Holy Spirit when I say that my grief
> is great and there is unceasing anguish in my heart.
> I could pray that I myself might be accursed so that
> I was completely separated from Christ for the sake
> of my brothers, my kinsmen as far as human relation-
> ship goes. For my kinsmen are the Israelites, and
> theirs is the special sonship of God, and the glory and
> the covenants and the giving of the law and the worship
> of the Temple and the promises. To them the fathers
> belong. And from them, on His human side, came the
> Anointed One of God. Blessed for ever be the God
> who is over all! Amen.

WITH this passage Paul begins his attempt to explain the
Jewish rejection of Jesus Christ. He begins, not in anger,
but in sorrow. Here is no tempest of anger and no outbreak
of enraged condemnation; here is the poignant sorrow
of the broken heart. Paul was like the God whom he loved
and served—Paul hated the sin, but he loved the sinner.
No man will ever even begin to try to save men unless
he first loves them. Paul sees the Jews, not as people to
be lashed with anger, but as people to be yearned over with
longing love.

Willingly Paul would have laid down his life if he could
have won the Jews for Christ. It may be that his thoughts
were going back to one of the greatest episodes in Jewish
history. When Moses went up into the mountain top to
receive the law from the hands of God, the people who
had been left below sinned by making the golden calf
and by worshipping it. God was wrath with them; and
then Moses prayed the great prayer: " Yet now, if Thou
wilt forgive their sins—; and if not, blot me, I pray Thee,
out of Thy book which Thou hast written " (Exodus 32: 32).
Paul says that for the sake of his brethren he would consent
to be accursed if it would do any good. The word he uses

is *anathema* and it is a terrible word. A thing which was
anathema was *under the ban*. It was devoted to God for
utter destruction. When a heathen city was taken everything in it was devoted to utter destruction for everything
in it was polluted (Deuteronomy 3: 6; 2: 34; Joshua 6:
17; 7: 1-26). If a man tried to lure Israel away from the
worship of the true God then he was pitilessly and merci-
lessly condemned to utter destruction (Deuteronomy
13: 8-11). The dearest thing in all Paul's life was the fact
that nothing could separate him from the love of God in
Christ Jesus; but if it would do anything to save his
brethren he would even accept banishment from God.
Here again is the great truth; the man who would save the
sinner must love the sinner. When a son or a daughter
has done something wrong and incurred punishment,
many a father and a mother would gladly bear that punishment if only they could. As Myers makes Paul say in
his poem *Saint Paul*:

> " Then with a thrill the intolerable craving,
>   Shivers throughout me like a trumpet call;
> O to save these, to perish for their saving—
>   Die for their life, be offered for them all."

That is what God felt; that is what Paul felt; and that
is what we must feel.

Paul did not for a moment deny the place of the Jews
in the economy of God. He enumerates their privileges.

(i) In a special sense they were children of God, specially
chosen, specially adopted into the family of God. " You
are the children of the Lord your God " (Deuteronomy
14: 1). " Is not He thy father that hath bought thee? "
(Deuteronomy 32: 6). " Israel is my son, even my first-
born " (Exodus 4: 22). " When Israel was a child, then
I loved him, and called my son out of Egypt " (Hosea 11: 1).
The whole Bible is full of this idea of the special sonship
of Israel and of Israel's refusal to accept it in the fullest
sense. Boreham somewhere tells how he was visiting in a
friend's house when he was a boy. There was one room

131

into which it was forbidden to go. One day he was opposite
the room when the door opened and inside he saw a boy
of his own age, but in a dreadful state of animal idiocy. He
saw the boy's mother go to the boy's side. She must have
seen young Boreham in all his health and sanity and then
seen her own son and the comparison must have pierced
her heart. He saw her kneel by the idiot boy's bedside
and cry out in a kind of anguish: " I've fed you and clothed
you and loved you—and you've never known me." That
was what God might have said to Israel—only in this case
it was worse, for Israel's rejection was deliberate and open-
eyed. It is a terrible thing to break the heart of God.

(ii) Israel had the glory. The *shekinah* or *kaboth* occurs
again and again in Israel's history. It was the divine
splendour of light which descended when God was visiting
His people (Exodus 16: 10; 24: 16, 17; 29: 43; 33: 18-22)
Israel had seen the glory of God and had rejected God.
To us it has been given to see the glory of God's love and
God's mercy in the face of Jesus Christ. It is a terrible
thing to see the glory of God and then to choose the ways
of earth.

(iii) Israel had the covenants. A covenant is a relationship entered into between two people; it is a bargain for
mutual profit; an engagement for mutual friendship.
In the history of Israel again and again God had approached
the people of Israel and had entered into a special relationship with them. He did so with Abraham, with Isaac, with
Jacob and upon Mount Sinai when he gave the law.
Irenaeus distinguishes four great occasions when God
entered into this agreement with men. The first covenant
was the covenant with Noah after the flood, and the sign
of it was the rainbow in the heavens which stood for God's
promise that the floods would not come again. The second
covenant was the covenant with Abraham and its sign
was the sign of circumcision. The third covenant was the
covenant with the nation entered into on Mount Sinai
and its basis was the law. The fourth covenant is the new

covenant in Jesus Christ. It is an amazing thing to think of God approaching men and entering into a pledged relationship with them. It is the simple truth that God has never left men alone. God did not make one approach to men and then abandon them. God has made approach after approach to men; and He still makes approach after approach to the individual human soul. He stands at the door and knocks; and it is the awful responsibility of human will that man can refuse the approach of God.

(iv) They had the law. Israel could never plead ignorance of God's will; God had told them what He desired them to do. If they sinned they sinned in knowledge and not in ignorance, and the sin of knowledge is the sin against the light which is worst of all.

(v) They had the worship of the Temple. Worship is in essence the approach of the soul to God; and God in the Temple worship had given to the Jews a special road of approach to Himself. If the door to God was shut, they had shut it on themselves.

(vi) They had the promises. Israel could never say that it did not know its destiny. God had told them of the task and the privilege which was in store for them in His purpose. They knew that they were destined for great things in the economy of God.

(vii) They had the fathers. They had a tradition and a history; and it is a poor man who can dare to be false to his traditions and to shame the heritage into which he had entered.

(viii) Then comes the culmination. From them there came the Anointed One of God. All else had been a preparation for this. All had been leading up to this; and yet when He came they rejected Him. The biggest grief a man can have is to give his child every chance of success, to sacrifice and save and toil to give the child the opportunity, and then to find that the child, through his own disobedience or rebelliousness or self-indulgence, has failed to grasp it. Therein lies tragedy, for therein is the waste of love's labour and the defeat of love's dream. The tragedy of Israel was that God had prepared Israel for the day of the coming of His Son—and all the preparation was defeated and frustrated. It was not that God's law had been broken; it was that God's love had been spurned. It is not the anger, but the broken heart of God, which lies behind Paul's words.

THE CHOICE OF GOD

Romans 9: 7-13

But it is not as though the word of God had been completely frustrated. For not all who belong to the race of Israel are really Israel; nor are all really children because they can claim physical descent from Abraham. On the contrary, it is written: " In Isaac will your descendants be called." That is to say, it is not the children who can claim merely physical descent who are really the children of God. No! It is the children of the promise who are reckoned as the true descendants of Abraham, for the word of the promise runs like this: " I will come at this time and Sarah will have a son." Not only this, but when Rebecca too was brought to bed with child by one, I mean Isaac, our father—and note that the children were not yet born, and had done nothing either good or bad, so that God's purpose in choice should stand, not in consequence of any deeds, but simply because He called them—it was said to her: " The elder will be the servant of the younger." As it stands written: " Jacob I have loved, but Esau I have hated."

IF then the Jews have rejected and crucified Jesus, the Son of God, is that to say that God's purposes were frustrated and God's plan defeated? Paul produces a strange argument to prove that that is not so. In point of fact not all the Jews did reject Jesus; some of them accepted Him, for, of course, all the early followers were Jews, before the gospel went out to the Gentiles, and Paul himself was a Jew. Now, says Paul, if we go back through the history of Israel we will see again and again a process of selection at work. Again and again we see that it was not *all* Jews who were within the purpose and the design of God. Some were and some were not. The line of the nation through which God worked, and in which He carried out His plan, was not at any time composed of *all* those who could claim physical descent from Abraham. At the back of the whole plan there is not merely physical descent; there is the selection, the election of God. To prove his case, Paul cites two instances from Jewish history and buttresses them with proof texts. Abraham had two sons. There was Ishmael who was the son of the bondwoman Hagar, and there was Isaac who was the son of his wife Sarah. Both Ishmael and Isaac were true blood descendants of Abraham. Physically both were his children. It was late in life when Sarah had a son, so late that it was, humanly speaking, an impossibility. When Isaac was born, as he grew up, there came a day when Ishmael mocked at Isaac. Sarah resented it, and demanded that Hagar and her son Ishmael should be ejected and that Isaac alone should inherit. Abraham was very unwilling to eject Hagar and Ishmael, but God told him to do so, for it was in Isaac that his descendants would preserve his name (Genesis 21: 12). Now Ishmael had been the son of natural and normal human processes and human desires; but Isaac had been the son of God's promise, born when it was impossible, from the human point of view, that a son should be born at all (Genesis 18: 10-14). It was to the child of the promise that the real descent was given. Here then is the first proof that not all physical descendants of Abraham are to be ranked as Jews, as the chosen ones. Within the nation God's selection and election have gone on. Then Paul proceeds to cite another instance. When Rebecca, the wife of Isaac, was with child, she was told by God that in her womb there were two children who would be the fathers of two nations; but that in the days to come the elder would serve and be subject to the younger (Genesis 25: 23). So the twins Esau and Jacob were born,

and Esau was in point of fact the elder twin, and yet the
choice of God fell on Jacob; and it was through the line
of Jacob that God's will was to be done. To clinch the
argument Paul cites Malachi 1: 2, 3, where God is represented as saying to the prophet: " Jacob I have loved
and Esau I have hated." It is Paul's argument that there
is more to Jewishness than descent from Abraham, that
the chosen people were not simply the entire sum of all
the physical descendants of Abraham, that within that
family there was a process of election all through history.
A Jew would thoroughly understand and accept the argument so far. The Arabs were the descendants of Ishmael
who was a flesh and blood son of Abraham, but the Jews
would never have dreamed of saying that the Arabs
belonged to the chosen people. The Edomites were the
descendants of Esau—that in fact is what Malachi means—
and Esau was the true son of Isaac, even the twin brother
of Jacob, but no Jew would ever have said that the Edomites had any share in the chosen people. From the Jewish
point of view Paul has made his point; there *was* election
within the family of Abraham's physical descendants.
Paul makes the further point that that selection had nothing
to do with deeds and merit and human earning of it. The
proof of that is that Jacob was chosen and Esau was
rejected, *before either of them was born.* The choice was
made while they were still unborn babes in their mother's
womb.

Inevitably our minds stagger at this argument. It
presents us with the picture of a God who apparently
quite arbitrarily chooses one and rejects the other. To us
it is not a valid argument, because it makes God responsible
for an action which does not seem to us to be ethically
justified. But the fact remains that, strange as it seems to
us, and unacceptable as it seems to us, it would strike
home to a Jew. And even to us, at the heart of this argument, one great truth remains. Everything is of God;
behind everything is the action of God; even the things

which seem arbitrary and haphazard go back to God. There is nothing in this world which moves with aimless feet.

THE SOVEREIGN WILL OF GOD

Romans 9: 14-18

What shall we then say? Are you going to say that there is injustice with God? God forbid! For, He says to Moses: " I will have mercy on whomsoever I will have mercy and I will have pity on whomsoever I will have pity." So then the whole matter depends not on man's will and not on man's effort, but entirely on the mercy of God. For scripture says to Pharaoh: " For this one thing I assigned you a part in the drama of history—that I might demonstrate my power by what happens to you, and that my name might be broadcast throughout all the world." So then He has mercy on whom He will, but He hardens whom He will.

PAUL now begins to meet the very arguments and objections which rise in our own minds. He has stated that in all Israel's history the process of selection and election has gone on; he has further stressed the fact that this election was not based on any merit or deserving of the person elected; it was dependent on nothing else than the will of God Himself. The objector asks: " But, is that fair? Is that just? Is it just of God to pursue a policy of quite arbitrary selection, as it were, over the heads of men altogether? " Paul's answer, to put it bluntly, is that God can do what He chooses to do. In the terrible days of the Roman Empire, when no man's life was safe, and when any man might die at the whim of an irresponsible and suspicious Emperor, Galba, one of the Emperors, said, when he became Emperor, that now " he could do what he liked and do it to anyone." To be honest, that is what Paul is saying about God in this passage.

Again Paul cites two instances to prove his point and

buttresses them with scripture quotations. The first instance is from Exodus 33: 19. In that instance Moses is beseeching some real proof that God is really with the people of Israel. God's answer is that He will have mercy on those on whom He chooses to have mercy. The selection of the nation and God's attitude of loving mercy to the nation depends on God alone. The other instance is from Israel's battle for release from Egypt and from the power of Pharaoh. When Moses first went to ask for that release, he warned Pharaoh that God had simply brought Pharaoh on to the stage of history to demonstrate the divine power, and to make plain what that divine power did to a man who opposed it. Pharaoh had been brought into history to serve to all men as an example of what happens to the man who opposes God. (Exodus 9-16).

Once again, the mind staggers at this argument. It is, of course, in no sense true to say that God can do anything. God cannot do anything which contradicts His own nature. God cannot be responsible for any act which is unjust and which, in fact, breaks His own laws. We find it hard, and even impossible, to conceive of a God who irresponsibly gives mercy to one and not to another, and who raises up a king to be a mere puppet or lay figure through which God's avenging power may be demonstrated. Again, the argument would be valid and convincing to a Jew, because again it, in essence, means that God is behind everything.

And yet, when we get to the foot of this argument, it does conserve one great truth. It is impossible to think of the relationship between God and man in terms of justice. Man has no claim on God whatever. The created has no claim on the Creator. Whenever justice enters into it, the answer is that from God man deserves nothing and can claim nothing. The argument does make it clear that, in God's dealings with men, the essential thing can never be man's claim on God, but only God's will and God's mercy.

THE POTTER AND THE CLAY

Romans 9: 19-29

But, then, you may ask, " If this is so how can God go on blaming men if they do not take His way? Who can withstand God's purpose?" Fellow! Who are you to be arguing with God? Surely the thing that is moulded into shape cannot say to the man who moulds it, " Why did you make me like this?" Has not the potter complete authority over the clay, to make from the same lump one vessel for an honourable use and another for a menial service? What if God, although it was His will to demonstrate His wrath and to make known His power, did nonetheless treat with long patience the objects of His wrath, although they were ripe and ready for destruction? Yes, and what if He did it because it is His will to make known the wealth of His glory to the objects of His mercy, which He had prepared beforehand for glory—I mean us whom He called not only from among the Jews but also from among the Gentiles? Just as He says in Hosea: " A people which was not mine I will call my people; and her who was not beloved I will call beloved." And as He says in that same place where it was said to them: " You are not my people; there they shall be called the sons of the living God." And Isaiah cries about Israel: " Even though the number of the sons of Israel shall be as the sand of the sea, only the remnant will be saved, for the Lord will carry out His sentence on earth completely and summarily." And even as Isaiah foretold: " Unless the Lord of Hosts had left us some descendants, we would have become as Sodom, and we would have been like Gomorrah."

IN the previous passage Paul had been showing that all through the history of Israel there had been going on a process of election and selection by God. A very natural objection arises—if at the back of the whole process there is the selection and the rejection of God, how can God possibly blame the men who have rejected Him? The fault is not theirs at all; the fault is really God's. The responsibility lies not with them; the responsibility lies with God. Paul's answer is blunt almost to the point of crudity. His answer is that no man has any right to argue with God. When a potter makes a vessel, the vessel cannot talk back to the potter; the potter has absolute power over it; out of the one lump of clay he can make one vessel for an honourable purpose and another for a menial purpose, and the clay has nothing to do with it and has no right whatever to protest. In point of fact Paul took this picture from Jeremiah (Jeremiah 18: 1-6). There are two things to be said about this. (i) It is a bad analogy. One great New Testament commentator has said that this is one of the very few passages which we wish that Paul had not written. There is a difference between a human being and a lump of clay. A human being is a person and a lump of clay is a thing. Maybe you can do what you like with a *thing*, but you cannot do what you like with a *person*. Clay does not desire to answer back; clay does not desire to question. Clay cannot think and feel; clay cannot be anguished and bewildered and tortured. If someone had inexplicably suffered some tremendous, heart-breaking and soul-searing sorrow, it would not help much to tell them that he had no right to complain, because God can do what He likes. That is the mark of a tyrant and not of a loving Father. It is the basic fact of the gospel that God does *not* treat men as a potter treats a lump of clay; He treats them as a loving father treats his child. (ii) But when we have said that we must remember one thing—it was out of anguish of heart that Paul himself wrote this passage. He was faced with the bewildering fact that God's own people, his own kinsmen, had rejected and crucified God's own Son. It was not that Paul *wished* to say this; he was *driven* to say it. The only possible explanation that he could see was that, for His own purposes, God had somehow blinded His own people.

In any event, Paul does not leave the argument there. He goes on to say that this rejection by the Jews had happened in order that the door might be opened to the Gentiles. Now again, for once, Paul's argument is not good.

It is one thing to say that God *used* an evil situation to bring good out of it; it is quite another thing to say that God *created* an evil situation to bring good out of it. It is in fact to argue that God did evil that good might emerge. What Paul is saying is that God deliberately darkened the minds and blinded the eyes and hardened the hearts of the mass of the Jewish people in order that the way might open for the Gentiles to come in. Again, we must remember that this is not the argument of a theologian who was sitting quietly in a study thinking things out; it is the argument of a man whose heart was in despair to find some reason for a completely incomprehensible situation. In the end the only answer that Paul can find is that God did it.

Now Paul was arguing with Jews, and he knew that the only way he could buttress his argument was to support it with quotations from their own scriptures. So, then, he goes on to cite texts to prove that this rejection of the Jews and this acceptance of the Gentiles had actually been foretold in the prophets. Hosea had said that God would make a people His people who were not His people (Hosea 2: 23). He said that a people who were not God's people would be called the sons of God (Hosea 1: 10). He showed how Isaiah had foreseen a situation when Israel would have been obliterated had not a remnant been left (Isaiah 10: 22, 23; 13: 10). It is Paul's argument that Israel could have foreseen her doom had she only understood.

It is easy in this passage to criticize Paul; but the one thing that must be remembered is that Paul, in his despairing anguish for his own people, clung to the fact that somehow everything was God's work. For him there was nothing left to say but that.

THE JEWISH MISTAKE

Romans 9: 30-33

What shall we then say? The Gentiles who were not looking for a right relationship with God received

141

such a relationship, but it was a relationship which was the result of faith, while Israel which was looking for a law which would produce a right relationship with God never succeeded in finding such a law. Why? Because they tried to get into a right relationship with God, not by trusting God, but by depending on their own human achievements. They stumbled over the stone which makes men stumble, even as it stands written: " I have set in Zion a stone which makes men stumble, and a rock which makes them trip. And he who believes in Him will not be put to shame."

HERE Paul draws a contrast between two ways of feeling towards God. There was the Jewish way. The aim of the Jew was to set himself right with God. His view was that he could set himself right with God by strict obedience to the law. The Jew regarded a right relationship with God as something which could be earned. Now there is another way to put that which will show really what it means. Fundamentally, the Jewish idea was that a man, by strict obedience to the law, could in the end pile up a credit balance. When he had acquired this credit balance the result was that God was in his debt; God owed him salvation. Essentially, the Jew regarded the friendship of God as something which could be earned and won and achieved by human effort. It was obviously a losing battle, because man's imperfection can never satisfy God's perfection; man's sin can never earn the right to meet God's holiness; nothing that man can do can ever even begin to repay what God has done for him. That is precisely what Paul found. As he said, the Jew spent his life searching for a law, obedience to which would put him right with God, and he never found it because there is no such law to be found. The Gentile had never engaged upon this search. But when the Gentile, suddenly and all unexpectedly, was confronted with incredible love of God in Jesus Christ, he simply cast himself upon that love in total trust. It was as if the Gentile saw the Cross and said, " If God loves me like that I can trust Him with my life and with my

soul." The Jew sought to put God in his debt; the Gentile
was content to be in God's debt. The Jew believed he
could win salvation by doing things for God; the Gentile
was lost in amazement at what God had done for him.
The Jew sought to find the way to God by works; the
Gentile came by the way of trust. It was Paul's conviction
that no man can win God's favour.

> " Not the labours of my hands
> Can fulfil Thy law's demands;
> Could my zeal no respite know,
> Could my tears for ever flow,
> All for sin could not atone:
> Thou must save, and Thou alone."

Paul would have said " Amen " to that.

At the end of this passage we have the reference to
the stone. This is one of the characteristic references of the
early Christian writers. In the Old Testament there is a
series of rather mysterious references to *the stone*. In
Genesis 49: 24 God is described as the shepherd and *the
stone* of Israel. In Isaiah 8: 14 it is said that God shall be
for *a stone of stumbling* and a rock of offence to the houses
of Israel. In Isaiah 28: 10 God says, that he will lay in
Zion for a foundation *a stone, a precious corner stone*, a sure
foundation. In Daniel 2: 34, 35, 44, 45, there is a reference
to a mysterious *stone*. In Psalm 118: 22 the Psalmist
writes: " The *stone* which the builders refused is become
the headstone of the corner." Now when the Christian
began to search the Old Testament for forecasts of Christ
they came across these references to this wonderful stone.
And they identified Jesus with that stone. Their warrant
for so doing was that the gospel story shows Jesus Himself
making that identification and taking the verse in Psalm
118: 22 and applying it to Himself. He is depicted as
doing so at the end of the Parable of the Wicked Husbandmen (Matthew 21: 42). The Christians thought of the
wonderful stone which was the sure foundation, the stone
which was the corner stone which bound the whole building

together, the stone which had been rejected and had then become the chief of all the stones, as the picture of Christ Himself. The actual quotation which Paul uses here is a combination of Isaiah 8: 14 and 28: 16. The Christians and Paul took it to mean this—God had meant His Son to be the foundation of every man's life, but when He came the Jews had rejected Him, and because they had rejected Him that gift of God which had been meant for their salvation became the reason for their condemnation. This picture of the stone fascinated the Christians. We get it again and again in the New Testament (Acts 4: 11; Ephesians 2: 20; I Peter 2: 4-6).

The eternal truth behind this thought is this—Jesus Christ was sent into this world to be the Saviour of men. But Jesus Christ is also the touch-stone by which all men are judged. If a man's heart goes out in love and submission to Jesus, Jesus is for him salvation. If a man's heart is entirely unmoved or angrily rebellious, Jesus is for him condemnation. Jesus came into the world for our salvation, but by his attitude to Jesus a man can either gain salvation or merit condemnation.

THE MISTAKEN ZEAL

Romans 10: 1-13

Brothers, the desire of my heart for the Jews and my prayer to God for them is that they may be saved. I do say this for them—that they do have a zeal for God, but it is not a zeal which is based on a real knowledge. For they do not realize that a man can only achieve the status of righteousness by God's gift, and they seek to establish their own status, and so they have not submitted themselves to that power of God which alone can make them righteous in His sight. For Christ is the end of the whole system of law, for He came to bring everyone who believes and trusts into a right relationship with God. Moses writes that the man who works at the righteousness which comes from the law shall live by it. But the righteousness which stems from faith speaks like this—" Do not say in your heart, ' Who shall go up into heaven?' (that is, to bring Christ down), or, ' Who shall go down into the deep abyss?' (that is, to bring Christ again from among the dead)." But what does it say? "The word is near you. It is in your mouth and in your heart." And that word is the message of faith which we proclaim. This word of faith is our message, that, if you acknowledge with your mouth that *Jesus is Lord,* and if you believe in your heart that God raised Him from the dead, you will be saved. For belief with the heart is the way to a right relationship with God, and confession with the mouth is the way to salvation. For scripture says, "Every one who believes in Him will not be put to shame," for there is no distinction between Jew and Greek; for the same Lord is Lord over all, and He has ample resources for all who call upon Him. For "every one who calls on the name of the Lord will be saved."

PAUL has been saying some hard things about the Jews. He has been telling them truths which were difficult for them to hear and to bear. The whole passage from Romans 9 to 11 is a condemnation of the Jewish way and the Jewish attitude to religion. And yet we must note that from beginning to end there is no anger in it. There is nothing but wistful longing and heartfelt yearning. It is Paul's one desire that the Jews may be saved. If ever we are to bring men to the Christian faith our attitude must be the same. Great preachers have known this. "Don't scold," said one. "Always remember to keep your voice down," said another. A great present day preacher called preaching "pleading with men." Jesus wept over Jerusalem. There is a preaching which scarifies men; there is a preaching which blasts the sinner with tempestuously angry words; but always Paul speaks the truth, and speaks that truth in love.

Paul was entirely ready to admit that the Jews were zealous for God; but he also saw that that zeal was a misguided, misdirected thing. The whole of Jewish religion

was based on meticulous obedience to the law. Now it is
clear that that obedience to the law could only be given
by a man who was desperately in earnest about his religion.
It was not an easy thing; it must often have been extremely
inconvenient, and it must often have made life a very
uncomfortable thing. Take the Sabbath law. It was laid
down exactly how far a man could walk on the Sabbath.
It was laid down that he must lift no burden which weighed
more than two dried figs. It was laid down that no food
must be cooked on the Sabbath. It was laid down that,
in the event of sickness, measures might be taken to keep
the patient from becoming worse, but not to make him
better. To this day there are strict orthodox Jews in
this country who will not poke or mend a fire on the
Sabbath or switch on a light. If a fire has to be poked a
Gentile will be employed to do it. If a Jew is wealthy
enough he will sometimes instal a time switch to switch
on the lights at dusk on Sabbath without his doing so
himself. This is not something to smile at. It is something
to admire. The way of the law was not an easy way.
No one would undertake it at all unless he was supremely
in earnest about his religion. Zealous the Jews were and
are. Paul had no difficulty in granting that, but the zeal
was misdirected and misapplied. In the Fourth Book of
Maccabees there is the amazing incident of Eleazar the
priest. He was brought before Antiochus Epiphanes
whose aim was to stamp out Jewish religion. Antiochus
ordered him to eat pork, swine's flesh. The old man
refused. " We, O Antiochus," he said, " who live under a
divine law, consider no compulsion to be so forcible as
obedience to our law." He refused to touch pork. " No,
not if you pluck out my eyes, and consume my bowels
in the fire." If he had to die, his fathers would receive
him " holy and pure." He was ordered to be beaten.
" His flesh was torn off by the whips, and he streamed
down with blood, and his flanks were laid open by wounds."
He fell and a soldier kicked him. In the end the soldiers

so pitied him that they brought him dressed meat, which
was not pork, and told him to eat it and to say that he
had eaten pork. He refused. He was in the end killed.
" I am dying by fiery torments for Thy law's sake," he
prayed to God. " He resisted," says the writer, " even to
the agonies of death, for the law's sake." And what was
all this about? *It was about eating pork.* It seems incredible
that a man should die like that for a law like that. But
the Jews did so die. Truly they had a zeal for the law.
No man could deny that. They thought that by so doing
they were true to God. No man can say that they were
not desperately in earnest about their service to God.

The whole Jewish approach was that by this kind of
obedience to the law a man put himself into a right relationship with God; he earned credit and favour with God.
Nothing shows better the Jewish attitude than the three
classes into which they divided mankind. There were
those who were good, and whose balance was on the right
side; there were those who were bad, and whose balance
was on the debit side; there were those who were half
and between, and who, by doing one more good work,
could become good. The whole thing was a matter of
law and of achievement. To all this Paul answers: " Christ
is the end of the law." What he meant was: " Jesus Christ
is the end of legalism." The relationship between God and
man is no longer the relationship between a creditor and
a debtor, between an earner and an assessor, between a
judge and a man standing at the bar of judgment. Because
Jesus Christ lived and brought His message to men, man
is no longer faced with the task of satisfying God's justice;
he can only accept God's love. He has no longer to win
God's favour; he has to take the grace and love and mercy
which God freely offers to him.

To make his point Paul uses two Old Testament quotations. First, he quotes Leviticus 18: 5 where it says that
if a man meticulously obeys the commandments of the
law he will find life through them. That is true—*but no*

one ever has, for the simple reason that human imperfection can never satisfy divine perfection. Then Paul quotes Deuteronomy 30: 12, 13. In that passage Moses is saying that God's law is not distant and inaccessible and impossible; it is there in a man's mouth and life and heart. Paul allegorizes that passage. It is not our effort which brought Christ into the world or raised Him from the dead. It is not our effort which wins us goodness. The thing is done for us, and we have only to accept and to take.

Verses 9 and 10 are of prime importance. They give us the basis of the first Christian creed.

(i) A man must say *Jesus Christ is Lord.* The word for Lord is *kurios.* This is the key word of early Christianity. It has four stages of meaning. (*a*) It is the normal title of respect like the English *sir,* the French *monsieur,* or the German *herr.* (*b*) It was the normal title of the Roman Emperors. (*c*) It was the normal title of the Greek gods. It was prefaced before the god's name. *Kurios Serapis* is Lord Serapis. (*d*) In the Greek translation of the Hebrew scriptures it is the regular translation of the divine name, Jahveh or Jehovah. So, then, if a man called Jesus *kurios* he was ranking Him with the Emperor and with God; he was giving Him the supreme place in his life; he was giving Him implicit obedience and reverent worship. To call Jesus *kurios* was to call Him unique. First, then, a man to be a Christian must have a sense of the utter *uniqueness* of Jesus Christ.

(ii) A man must believe that Jesus is risen from the dead. The Resurrection was an essential of Christian belief. The Christian must believe not only that Jesus Christ *lived,* but also that Jesus Christ *lives.* He must not only know *about Christ*: he must *know Christ.* He is not studying an historical personage however great; he is living with a real presence. He must not only know the *sacrifice* of Christ; he must know the *conquest* of Christ. He must not only know Christ the *martyr*: he must know Christ the *victor* too.

(iii) But a man must not only believe in his heart; he must confess with his lips. Christianity is belief, plus confession. It involves witness before men. Not only God, but also our fellow men, must know that we are Christians. A man must declare to men what side he is on.

Now a Jew would find it hard to believe that the way to God was not through the law; this way of trust and of acceptance was shatteringly and incredibly new to him. Further, he would have real difficulty in believing that the way to God was open to *everybody*. The Gentiles did not seem to him to be in the same position as the Jews at all. So Paul concludes his argument by citing two Old Testament texts to prove his case. First, he cites Isaiah 29: 16: "Every one who *believes* in Him will not be put to shame." There is nothing about law there; it is all based on faith. Second, he cites Joel 2: 32: "*Every one* who calls on the name of the Lord will be saved." There is no limitation there; the promise is to *everyone*; therefore, there is no difference between Jew and Greek.

So, then, in essence this passage is an appeal to the Jews to abandon the way of legalism and to accept the way of grace. It is an appeal to them to see that all their zeal is futile and misplaced. It is an appeal to listen to the prophets who long ago declared that faith is the only way to God, and that that way is open to every man.

THE DESTRUCTION OF EXCUSES

Romans 10: 14-21

> How are they to call on Him on whom they have not believed? How are they to believe in Him of whom they have not heard? How are they to hear without someone to proclaim the good news to them? How are they to proclaim the good news unless they are sent to do so? But this is the very thing that has happened, as it stands written: "How beautiful are the feet of those who bring the good news of good things."

But all have not obeyed the good news. That is
quite true, because Isaiah says: " Lord, who has
believed what they heard from us?" So, then, faith comes
from hearing, and hearing comes from the word which
comes from Christ and which tells of Him. But,
suppose I still say: " Can it be that they have not
heard?" Indeed they have. " Their voice is gone
out to all the earth, and their words to the boundaries
of the inhabited world." Well, then, suppose I say:
" Did Israel not understand?" First, Moses says:
" I will make you jealous of a nation which is no
nation. I will make you angry with a nation that has
no understanding." Then Isaiah says, greatly daring:
" I was found by those who did not seek me. I appeared
plainly to those who did not enquire after me." And
he says to Israel: " All the day I have stretched out
my hands to a people who are disobedient and
contrary."

IT is agreed by all commentators that this is one of the
most difficult and obscure passages in the letter to the
Romans. It seems to us that what we have here is not
so much a finished passage as the notes for a passage.
There is a kind of telegraphic quality about the writing
here. It may well be that what we have here is the notes
of some address which Paul was in the habit of addressing
to the Jews to convince them of their mistake and error.

Basically the scheme of the passage is this—in the
previous passage Paul has been saying that the way to
God is not the way of works and of legalism; it is the way
of faith and trust. The objection is: But what if the Jews
never heard of that? It is with that objection that Paul
deals; and, as he deals with it in its various forms, on
each occasion he clinches his answer with a text from
scripture.

Let us take the objections and the answering scripture
texts one by one.

(i) The first objection is: " You cannot call on God
unless you believe in Him. You cannot believe in Him
unless you hear about Him. You cannot hear about Him
unless there is someone to proclaim the good news. There

can be no one to proclaim the good news unless God commissions and despatches someone to do so." Paul deals with that objection by quoting Isaiah 52: 7. There the prophet points out how welcome those are who bring the good news of good things. So Paul's first answer is: "You cannot say there was no messenger; Isaiah describes these very messengers; and Isaiah lived long enough ago."

(ii) The second objection is: "But, in point of fact, Israel did *not* obey the good news, even if your argument is true. What have you to say to that?" Paul's answer is: "Israel's disbelief was only to be expected, for, long ago, Isaiah was moved to say in despair: 'Lord, who has believed the things they heard from us?'" (Isaiah 53: 1). It is true that Israel did not accept and obey the good news from God, and in their refusal and their disobedience they were simply running true to form; history was repeating itself.

(iii) The third objection is a restatement of the first: "But, what if I do not accept the fact that they did in fact hear? What if I insist that they never got the chance to hear?" This time Paul quotes Psalm 19: 4: "Their voice is gone out to all the earth, and their words to the boundaries of the inhabited world." His answer in fact is: "You cannot say that Israel never got the chance to hear; for scripture plainly says that God's message has gone out to *all* the world. Nobody can say, in face of that, they did not get the chance to hear."

(iv) The fourth objection is: "But what if Israel did not understand?" Apparently the meaning is: "What if the message was so difficult to grasp, so obscure, so dark and unintelligible, that even when Israel did hear it they were unable to grasp its meaning and its significance?" Here is where the passage becomes really difficult. But Paul's answer is: "*Israel* may have failed to understand; but the *Gentiles* did not. They grasped the meaning of this offer all right, when it came to them all unexpectedly and all unsought." To prove this point Paul quotes two

passages. One is from Deuteronomy 32: 21 where God
says that, because of Israel's disobedience and rebellion,
He will transfer His favour to another people, and they
will be forced to become jealous of a nation which was no
nation; and to be angry with a people who had not the
chance to understand that they had. The second passage
is from Isaiah 65: 1 where God says that, in a strange
way, He has been found by a people who were not looking
for Him at all.

Finally, Paul insists that, all through history, God has
been stretching out hands of appeal to Israel, and Israel
has always been disobedient and contrary and perverse.

When we are reading a passage like this we must remember that it may seem strange to us; it may seem quite
unconvincing; it may seem to us, as is indeed the fact,
that some at least of the texts Paul quotes have been
wrenched out of their context and made to mean what they
were never intended to mean. Nevertheless there is in this
passage something which is of permanent meaning and
value. Beneath this passage there runs the conviction
that there are certain kinds of ignorance which are
inexcusable.

(i) There is the ignorance which comes from neglect of
knowledge. There is a legal maxim which says that genuine
ignorance may be a defence, but neglect of knowledge
never is. A man cannot be blamed for not knowing that
which he never had a chance to know; but he can be
blamed for neglecting to know that which was always
open to him to know. For instance, if a man signs a
contract without having read the conditions he cannot
complain if afterwards he finds out that the conditions
are very different from what he thought they were. If
we fail to equip ourselves for a task when every chance
was given to us to equip ourselves adequately for it, then
we must stand condemned. A man is responsible for failing
to know what he might have known.

(ii) There is the ignorance which comes from wilful blindness. Men have an infinite and a fatal capacity for shutting their minds to that which they do not wish to see, and stopping their ears to that which they do not wish to hear. A man may be well aware that some habit, some indulgence, some way of life, some friendship, some association must have fatal and disastrous results. He may be told so; he may see the fatal results in the lives of others; but he may simply refuse to look at the facts in his own case. To turn a blind eye to something may be in some few cases a virtue; in most cases it is folly.

(iii) There is the ignorance which is in essence a lie. The things about which we are in doubt are far fewer than we would like to think. There are in reality very few times when we can honestly say: " I never knew that things would turn out like this." God gave us conscience; God gave us the guidance of His Holy Spirit; and often we plead ignorance, when, if we were honest, we would have to admit that in our heart of hearts we knew the truth.

One thing remains to be said of this passage. If we have been following and remembering the argument so far as it has gone, one thing must have struck us. There is in it a contradiction and a paradox. All through this section Paul has been driving home the personal responsibility of the Jews. They ought to have known better; they had every chance to know better; he finishes this passage with a picture of God with outstretched hands of appeal to the Jewish nation, appeal which the nation rejected. Now he began the whole argument by saying that everything was of God, and that men had no more to do with it than the clay had to do with the work of the potter. Paul has set two things side by side; first, everything is of God, and, second, everything is of human choice. Paul makes no attempt to resolve this dilemma; and the fact is that there is no resolution to it. It is a dilemma of human experience. We know that God is behind everything; and yet, at the same time, we know that we have free will, and that we can accept or reject the offer of God. There is, in fact, no answer to this. It is the paradox of the human situation that God is in control, and yet the human will is free. It is not so much that Paul has contradicted himself as that he has approached the same problem first, from the divine, and second, from the human side.

THE CALLUS ON THE HEART

Romans 11: 1-12

So then, I ask, " Has God repudiated His people? " God forbid! I, too, am an Israelite, a descendant of Abraham, a member of the tribe of Benjamin. God has not repudiated His people whom long ago He marked out for His purposes. Do you not know what scripture says in the passage about Elijah? You remember how he talked to God in complaint against Israel: " Lord, they have killed your prophets; they have torn down your altars; and I alone am left and they are seeking my life." But what was the answer that came to him? " I have kept for myself seven thousand men, who have not bowed the knee to Baal." So, then, at this present time too, there is a remnant chosen by His grace. And if they were chosen by grace, their relationship to God is no longer dependent on works, for, if that were so, grace is no longer grace. What then? Israel has not obtained that for which she is searching; but the chosen remnant has obtained it, while the rest have been made so dull and insensitive in heart that they cannot see. As it stands written: " God gave them a spirit of lethargy—eyes not to see, ears not to hear—down to this day." And David says: " Let their table become a snare, and a trap, and a thing to trip them up, and a retribution for them, and let their backs be bent for ever." So, I say, " Have they stumbled that their fall might be complete?" God forbid! So far from that, salvation has become a gift for the Gentiles because of their fall, so as to move them to jealousy of the Gentiles. If their fall has brought wealth to the world, if their failure has brought wealth to the Gentiles, how much more shall the whole world be enriched, when they come in, and the whole process of salvation is completed?

THERE is a question which now has to be asked, a question which any Jew was bound to ask. Does all this mean that God has rejected and repudiated His people? That is a question that Paul's heart cannot bear. After all, he himself was a member of that people. So Paul falls back on an idea which runs through much of the Old Testament. In the days of Elijah, Elijah was in despair (I Kings 19: 10-14). He had come to the conclusion that he alone was left to be true to God. But God told him that, so far from that being true, there were still seven thousand in Israel who had not bowed the knee to Baal. So into Jewish thought there came the idea of *The Remnant*. The prophets began to see that there never was a time, and there never would be a time, when the whole nation was true to God; but, at the same time, always within the nation there was a remnant left who had never forsaken their loyalty or compromised their faith. Prophet after prophet came to see this. Amos (9: 8-10) thought of God sifting men as corn is sifted in a sieve until only the good is left. Micah (2: 12; 5: 3) had a vision of God gathering the remnant of Israel. Zephaniah (3: 12, 13) had the same idea. Jeremiah foresaw the remnant being gathered from all the countries throughout which they had been scattered (Jeremiah 23: 3). Ezekiel, the individualist, was convinced that a man could not be saved by either a national or an inherited righteousness; the righteous would deliver their own souls by their righteousness (Ezekiel 14: 14, 20, 22). Above all this idea dominated the thought of Isaiah. He called his son *Shear-Jashub*, which means *The Salvation of the Remnant*. Again and again he recurs to this idea of the faithful remnant who will be saved by God (Isaiah 7: 3; 8: 2, 18; 9: 12; 20: 21; 6: 9-13).

There is a tremendous truth beginning to dawn here. As one great scholar put it: " No Church or nation is saved *en masse*." The idea of a *Chosen People* will not hold water for this basic reason. The relationship with God is an individual relationship. A man must give his

own heart, make his own submission, surrender his own
life to God. God does not call men in crowds; God has
"His own secret stairway into every heart." A man is
not saved because he is a member of a nation, or because
he is a member of a family, or because he has inherited
righteousness and salvation from his ancestors; he is
saved because he has made an individual and personal
decision for God. It is not now the whole nation who are
lumped together *en masse* as the Chosen People. It is
those individual men and women who have given their
hearts to God, and who have obeyed Him, of whom the
remnant is composed. The remnant is the body of consecrated, dedicated men and women within the nation.

It is, then, Paul's argument that the Jewish nation has
not been rejected; but it is not the nation as a whole,
but the faithful remnant within it who are the true Jews.

And what of the others? It is here that Paul has a
terrible thought. He has the idea of God sending a kind
of torpor upon them, a drowsy sleep in which they cannot
and will not hear. He puts together the thought of a
series of Old Testament passages to prove this (Deuteronomy 29: 4; Isaiah 6: 9, 10; 29: 10). He quotes Psalm
69: 22, 23. "Let their table become a snare." The idea
is that men are sitting feasting comfortably at their banquet;
and their very ease, their very security, their very sense of
safety has become their ruin. They are so easy, so comfort-
able, so secure in their fancied safety that the enemy can
come upon them all unaware. That is what the Jews were
like. They were so secure, so self-satisfied, so at ease in
their confidence of being the Chosen People, that that
very idea of being the Chosen People had become the thing
that ruined them. The day will come when they cannot
see at all, and when they will grope with bent backs like
men stumbling blindly in the dark. In verse 7 the Authorised
Version says, "they have been blinded." More correctly,
it should be, "they have been hardened." The verb
is the verb *pōroun*. The noun *pōrōsis* will give us the meaning

better. It is a medical word, and it means a *callus*. It was specially used for the callus which forms round the fracture when a bone is broken, the hard bone formation which helps to mend the break. A callus has grown over the hearts of the people. When a callus grows on any part of the body that part loses feeling. It becomes insensitive. The minds of the mass of the people have become insensitive; they can no longer hear and feel the appeal of God. It can happen to any man. If a man takes his own way long enough, he will in the end become insensitive to the appeal of God. If he lives selfishly long enough, he will become insensitive to the appeal of the fine things. If he goes on sinning, he will in the end become insensitive to the horror of sin and the fascination of goodness. If a man lives long enough in ugly conditions he will in the end become insensitive to them. As Burns wrote:

> " I waive the quantum of the sin,
>   The hazard o' concealing;
> But och! it hardens a' within,
>   And petrifies the feeling! "

Just as a callus can grow on the hand, a callus can grow on the heart. That is what had happened to the mass of Israel. God save us from that!

But Paul has something more to say. That is tragedy, but out of that tragedy God has brought good, because it is that very insensitiveness of Israel which opened the way to the Gentiles to come in. Because Israel did not want the message of the good news, the message of the good news went out to people who were ready to welcome it and to accept it. Israel's refusal has enriched the world. And then Paul touches on the dream which is behind it all. If the refusal of Israel has enriched the world by opening a door to the Gentiles, what will the riches be like at the end of the day when God's plan is fully completed and Israel and the Gentiles come in?

And so, in the end, after the tragedy there comes the hope. Israel became insensitive, the nation with the callus on her heart; the Gentiles came by faith and trust into the love of God; but a day will come when the love of God will act like a solvent, even on the callus of the heart, and when Gentile and Jew will be gathered in. It is Paul's conviction that nothing in the end can defeat the love of God.

THE WILD OLIVE — PRIVILEGE AND WARNING
Romans 11: 13-24

Now I speak to you Gentiles. You well know that in so far as I am the apostle to the Gentiles, I magnify my office, for somehow I want to find a way to move my own flesh and blood to envy of the Gentiles, so that I may save some of them; for, if the fact that they are cast away has resulted in the reconciliation of the world to God, what will their reception mean? It can only be like life from the dead! If the first part of the dough is consecrated to God, so is the whole lump; if the root is consecrated to God, so are the branches. If some of the branches have been cut off, and if you like a wild olive have been grafted in among them, and if you have become a sharer in the rich root of the olive, do not allow yourself to look down boastfully upon the branches. If you are tempted to act like that, remember you do not bear the root but the root bears you. You will say: " Branches have been broken off that I may be grafted in." Well said! They were broken off because of their lack of faith; and you stand because of faith. Do not become proudly contemptuous, but keep yourself in godly fear; for if God did not spare the branches, which were natural branches, neither will He spare you. See, then, the kindness *and* the severity of God. On those who fell there comes the severity; on you there comes the kindness of God, if only you remain in that kindness. If you do not, you, too, will be cut away. But they, if they do not continue in their lack of faith, will be grafted in; for God is able to graft them in again. For, if you were cut from the olive, which is by nature a wild olive, and, if, contrary to nature, you were engrafted into the garden olive, how much more will the natural branches be engrafted into the olive to which they really belong?

I⊤ is to the Jews that Paul has been talking up to this time, and now he turns to the Gentiles. He is the apostle to the Gentiles, but he cannot ever forget his own people. In fact he goes the length of saying that one of his main objects is to move the Jews to envy when they see what Christianity has done for the Gentiles. One of the surest ways to make a man desire Christianity is to make him see in actual life what Christianity can do. There was a soldier who was wounded in battle. The padre crept out to him and did what he could for him. He stayed with him when the remainder of the troops retreated. In the heat of the day he gave him water from his own water-bottle, while he himself remained parched with thirst. In the night, when the chill frost came down, he covered the wounded man with his own coat, and finally wrapped him up in even more of his clothes to save him from the cold. In the end the wounded man looked up at the padre. " Padre," he said, " you're a Christian? " " I try to be," said the padre. " Then," said the wounded man, " if Christianity makes a man do for another man what you have done for me, tell me about it, because I want it." It was Christianity in action which moved him to envy a faith which could produce a life like that. It was Paul's hope, and prayer and ambition, that some day the Jews would see what Christianity had done for the Gentiles and would be moved to desire it.

To Paul it would be paradise if the Jews would come in. If the rejection of the Jews had done so much, if, through it the Gentile world has been reconciled to God, what superlative glory must come when the Jews come in. If the tragedy of rejection has had results so wonderful, what would the happy ending be like, when the tragedy of rejection had changed to the glory of reception? Paul can only say that it would be like life from the dead.

Then Paul uses two pictures to show that the Jews can never be totally and finally rejected. All food had to be made sacred to God. Before it was eaten it had to be offered to God. So the law laid it down (Numbers 15: 19, 20) that, if dough was being prepared, the first part of it must be offered to God; when that was done the whole lump of dough became sacred. It was not necessary, as it were, to offer every separate mouthful to God. The offering of the first part sanctified the whole. It was a very common thing to plant sacred trees in places which were sacred to the gods. When the little tree, the sapling, was planted it was dedicated to God; and thereafter every branch that came from it was sacred to God. It was not necessary to dedicate each branch separately; the dedication of the sapling made the whole tree sacred. What Paul deduces from that is this—the patriarchs were sacred to God; they had in a special way heard God's voice and obeyed God's word; in a special way they had been chosen and selected, and consecrated and dedicated by God. From them the whole nation sprang; and just as the first consecrated handful of dough made the whole lump sacred, and as the dedication of the sapling made the whole tree sacred, so the special consecration of the founders of the nation made the whole nation sacred in a special way to God. There is truth here. The remnant in Israel did not make themselves what they were; they inherited faith and belief from their forefathers before them. Every one of us lives to some extent on the spiritual capital of the past. None of us is a self-made man. We are what godly parents and ancestors have made us; and, even if we have strayed far away and shamed our heritage, we cannot totally part ourselves from the goodness and the fidelity that made us what we are.

Then Paul goes on to use a long allegory. More than once the prophets had pictured the nation of Israel as the olive tree of God. That was natural, because the olive tree was the commonest and the most useful tree in the Mediterranean world. " The Lord called thy name, a green olive tree, fair and of goodly fruit " (Jeremiah 11: 16). " His branches shall spread and his beauty shall be

as the olive tree" (Hosea 14: 6). So Paul thinks of the
Gentiles as branches of wild olive engrafted into the garden
olive tree which was Israel. It is quite true that from the
point of view of horticulture Paul's picture is impossible.
In horticulture it is the good olive that is grafted into the
stock of the wild olive that a fruit-bearing olive tree may
result. The process that Paul pictures was one that was
never used in actual practice, because it would have served
no useful purpose. But that is quite beside the point.
The point that Paul wishes to make is quite clear. The
Gentiles had been out in the deserts and the wildernesses,
and among the wild briars; and now, by the act of God's
grace, they are engrafted into the richness and the fertility
of the garden olive tree.

Out of this picture Paul has two words to speak.

(i) The first is *a word of warning*. It would have been
easy for the Gentiles to develop an attitude of contempt.
Had not the Jews been rejected that they might enter in?
In a world where the Jews were universally hated such
an attitude would have been all too easy. Paul's warning
is still necessary. In effect, what he says is this—*there
would have been no such thing as Christianity unless there
had been Judaism first*. Judaism is the root from which
Christianity has sprung. It will be a bad day when the
Christian Church forgets its debt to the root from which
it sprung. The Christian Church has a debt to Judaism
which it can never pay by any other means than by bringing
Christianity to the Jews. So Paul warns the Gentiles
against contempt. Grimly, he says that if the true branches
were lopped off because of their unbelief, still more can
that happen to the branches which are only grafted in.

(ii) The second is *a word of hope*. The Gentiles have
experienced the kindness of God; and the Jews have
experienced the severity of God. If the Gentiles remain
in faith they will remain in that kindness; but, if the Jews
come out of their unbelief and enter into belief, once
again they, too, will be engrafted in; for, says Paul,

if it was possible for an alien and a wild olive to be engrafted into the garden olive tree, how much more is it possible that the olive tree's own natural branches can be grafted in again? Once again Paul is dreaming of the day when the Jews will come in.

There is much in this passage which is recondite and hard to understand. It thinks in pictures which are out of our world altogether; but one thing is crystal clear—the connection between Judaism and Christianity, the connection betwęen the old and the new. Here is the answer to those who wish to discard the Old Testament as merely a Jewish book which is irrelevant for Christianity. He is a foolish man who kicks away the ladder which raised him to the height which he has reached. It would be a foolish branch which cut itself off from its stem. The new faith grew from the old. The Jewish faith is the root from which Christianity grew. The consummation will only come when the wild olive and the garden olive are altogether one, and when there are no branches at all left unengrafted on the parent stem.

THAT ALL MAY BE OF MERCY

Romans II: 25-32

> Brothers, I do want you to grasp this secret which only those who know God can understand, because I do not want you to become conceited about your own wisdom. I want you to understand that it is only a partial hardening which has happened to Israel, and it will only last until the full number of the Gentiles shall have come in. And then, in the end, all Israel will be saved, as it stands written: " A Saviour will come forth from Zion; and he will remove all kinds of wickedness from Jacob. This is the fulfilment of my covenant with them when I take away their sins." As far as the good news goes, they are enemies of God—but it is for your sake. But as far as God's choice goes, they are beloved of God, for their fathers' sakes, for the free gifts and the calling of God can

never be gone back upon. Once you disobeyed God,
but now you have found His mercy because of their
disobedience; just so, they have now disobeyed,
so that they now may enter into the same mercy
as you have now found. For God has shut up all men
to disobedience, that He may have mercy upon all.

PAUL is now coming to the end of his argument. He has
faced a bewildering, and, for a Jew, a heart-breaking
situation. Somehow he has had to find an explanation
of the fact that God's people rejected God's Son when He
came into the world. Paul never shut his eyes to that
tragic fact, but he found a way in which the whole tragic
situation could be fitted into the plan of God. It is true
that the Jews rejected Christ; but, as Paul saw it, that
rejection happened that Christ might be offered to the
Gentiles. To maintain the sovereignty of the purpose of
God, Paul even went the length of saying that it was God
Himself who hardened the hearts of the Jews in order to
open a way to the Gentiles; but, even then, however
contradictory it might sound, Paul still insisted on the
personal responsibility of the Jews for their failure to
accept the offer of God. Paul held fast at one and the same
time to divine sovereignty and human responsibility.
But now, at the end, there comes the note of hope. His
argument is a little complicated, and it will make it easier
if we try to identify and separate the various strands in it.

(i) Paul was sure that this hardening of the hearts of the
Jews was neither total nor permanent. It was to serve a
purpose, and when that purpose had been achieved then
it would be taken away. It was brought about to open
the way to the Gentiles, and when that way had been
opened it would be taken away.

(ii) Paul sets out the paradox of the Jewish place in the
plan of God. In order that the Gentiles might come in,
and that the universal purpose of the gospel might be
fulfilled, the Jews had arrived at a situation when they
were the enemies of God. The word that Paul uses is

echthroi. It is a difficult word to translate, and to give a meaning to, because it has both an active and a passive meaning. It can either mean *hostile to* or *hated by*. It can either mean *hating* or *hated*. It may well be that in this passage it has to be read in the two meanings at the one time. The Jews were hostile to God, and had refused the offer of God, and therefore they were under God's displeasure. That was the present fact about the Jews. But there was another fact about the Jews. Nothing could alter the fact that they were God's chosen people, and that they had a special place in the plan of God. No matter what they did, God can never go back upon His word and His promises. God's promise had been made to the fathers, and that promise must be fulfilled. It was therefore clear to Paul, and he quotes Isaiah 59: 20, 21 to prove it, that God's rejection of the Jews could not be permanent. He was clear that they, too, in the end must come in. At the moment, it was by their disobedience that the Gentiles had received the offer of Christ and had found mercy; but in the end they, too, would enter into that same mercy.

(iii) And then Paul has a strange thought. " God," he says, " shut up all men to disobedience that He may have mercy upon all." The one thing that Paul cannot conceive of is that any man of any nation could achieve, deserve, or merit his own salvation. Now, if the Jews had followed a process of complete obedience to God's will, it might well have been that they would have argued and reckoned that they had deserved, and merited, and earned, and were due the salvation of God, that they had earned that salvation as a right and a reward. So, what Paul is saying is, that God involved the Jews in disobedience so that when His salvation did come to them it might be unmistakably an act of His mercy and due in no way to their merit. The whole process was designed to show that neither Jew nor Gentile could ever be saved apart from the mercy of God.

When all is said and done there is one tremendous thing in this argument of Paul's. In many ways it may seem strange to us. In many cases the " proofs " he brings forward may seem quite unconvincing. At some times our minds and hearts may even shudder in repulsion at some of the things he says. But the argument is not irrelevant, for the one tremendous thing at the back of it is *a philosophy of history*. To Paul, *God was in control*. There was nothing which moved with aimless feet. Not even the most heart-breaking event or series of events was outside the will and purpose of God. Events can never run amok. The purposes of God can never be frustrated. It is told that once a child stood at the window on a night when the winds were raging on the face of the earth, and when the gale was terrifying in its savage velocity. " God," she said, " must have lost grip of His winds to-night." To Paul, that was precisely what never happened. Things and men, and processes and nations were never out of control, as he saw it. Everything was serving the purpose of God. And to that Paul would have added another tremendous conviction. He would have insisted that in it, and through it all, *God's purpose was a purpose of salvation, and not a purpose of destruction*. It may well be that Paul would even have gone the length of saying that God's arranging of things was designed to save men *even against their will*. In the last analysis it was not the wrath of God which was pursuing men, but the love of God which was tracking them down.

The situation of Israel was exactly that situation which Francis Thompson so movingly portrayed in *The Hound of Heaven*.

> " I fled Him down the nights and down the days;
>   I fled Him down the arches of the years;
> I fled Him down the labyrinthine ways
>   Of my own mind; and in the mist of tears
> I hid from Him, and under running laughter.

. . . . . .

> But with unhurrying chase,
> And unperturbed pace,
> Deliberate speed, majestic instancy,
> They beat—and a Voice beat
> More instant than the feet—
> ' All things betray thee, who betrayest Me.' "

And then there comes the time when the fugitive was beaten.

> " Naked I wait Thy love's uplifted stroke!
> My harness piece by piece Thou hast hewn from me,
> And smitten to my knee,
> I am defenceless utterly."

And then there comes the end:

> " Halts by me that footfall;
> Is my gloom, after all,
> Shade of His hand, outstretched caressingly?
> ' Ah, fondest, blindest, weakest,
> I am He Whom thou seekest!
> Thou dravest love from thee, who dravest Me! ' "

That was exactly the situation of Israel.   Israel fought their long battle against God.   They are still fighting it. But God's pursuing love is ever after them.   Whatever else Romans 9 to 11 may sometimes read like, it is in the last analysis the story of the still uncompleted pursuit of love.

THE CRY OF THE ADORING HEART

Romans 11: 33-36

> O the depth of the riches and the wisdom and the knowledge of God!   How His decisions are beyond the mind of man to trace!   How mysterious are His ways!   For who has known the mind of the Lord? Or, who has become His counsellor?   Who has first given anything to Him, so that he is due any repayment from God?   For all things come from Him, and exist through Him, and end in Him.   To Him be glory for ever!   Amen.

PAUL never wrote a more characteristic passage than this. Here theology turns to poetry. Here the seeking of the mind turns to the adoration of the heart. In the end all must pass out in a mystery that man cannot now understand, but it is a mystery at whose heart is love. If a man can say that all things come from God, that all things have their being through God, and that all things end in God, what more is left to say? There is a certain paradox in the human situation. God gave man a mind, and it is man's duty to use that mind to think to the very limits of human thought. But it is also true that there are times when that mind can only go so far, and, when that limit is reached, all that is left is to accept and to adore.

> " How could I praise,
> If such as I might understand? "

Paul had battled with a heart-breaking problem with every resource which his great mind possessed. He does not say that he has solved it, as one might neatly solve a geometrical problem; but he does say that, having done his best, he is content to leave it to the love and power of God. At many times in life there is nothing left to do but to say: " I have thought, and I cannot see the reason and the way. I cannot grasp Thy mind, but with my whole heart I trust Thy love. Thy will be done! "

THE TRUE WORSHIP AND THE ESSENTIAL CHANGE

Romans 12: 1, 2

> Brothers, I call upon you, by the mercies of God, to present your bodies to Him, a living, consecrated sacrifice, well-pleasing to God—for that is the only kind of worship which is truly spiritual. And do not shape your lives to meet the fleeting fashions of this world; but be transformed from it, by the renewal of your mind, until the very essence of your being is altered, so that, in your own life, you may prove that the will of God is good and well-pleasing and perfect.

HERE we have Paul following the pattern which he always followed when he wrote to his friends. He always ends his letters with a section of the most practical advice. The sweep of his mind may search through the infinities, but he never gets lost in them; he always finishes with his feet firmly planted upon the earth. He can, and does, wrestle with the deepest problems which theology has to offer, but he always ends with the ethical demands which govern the situation in life of every man.

" Present your bodies to God," he says. There is no more characteristically Christian demand. We have already seen that that is what a Greek would never say. To the Greek, what mattered was the spirit; the body was only a shackle and a prison-house; the body was something to be despised and even to be ashamed of. No real Christian ever believed that. The Christian believes that his body belongs to God just as much as his soul does, and that he can serve God just as well with his body as he can with his mind or his spirit. The body is the temple of the Holy Spirit, the place in which the Holy Spirit dwells, the instrument through which the Holy Spirit works. After all, the great fact of the incarnation basically means that God Himself did not grudge to take a human body upon Him, and to live in it and to work through it. Take the case of a church or a cathedral. It is built for the offering of worship of the spirit of man to God. But it has to be designed by the mind of some architect; it has to be built by the hands of craftsmen and of labouring men; only then does it become a shrine where men meet to worship. It is most literally a product of the mind and the body and the spirit of man.

" So," Paul says, " take your body; take all the tasks that you have to do every day; take the ordinary work of the shop, the factory, the shipyard, the mine; and offer all that as an act of worship to God." The word in verse 1 which the Authorised Version has translated *service* and which we have translated *worship* is a word

with an interesting history. It is the word *latreia* and it is
the noun of the verb *latreuein*. Originally the word *latreuein*
meant *to work for hire or pay*. It was the word which was
used of the labouring man who gave his strength to a
master and an employer in return for the pay the employer
would give him. It denotes, not slavery, but the voluntary
undertaking of work. It, then, came to mean quite generally
to serve; but it also came to mean *that to which a man gives
his whole life*. For instance, a man could be said *latreuein
kallei*, which means *to give his life to the service of beauty*.
In that sense, it comes very nearly to mean *to dedicate
one's life to*. Then, finally, this word came to be the word
which was characteristically and distinctively used of
the service of the gods. In the Bible it never means human
service; it is always used of service to and worship of God.

Now here we have a most significant thing. The true
worship, the really spiritual worship, is the offering of
one's body, and all that one does every day with it, to God.
Real worship is not the offering of elaborate prayers to
God; it is not the offering to God of a liturgy, however
noble, and a ritual, however magnificent. *Real worship
is the offering of everyday life to God*. Real worship is not
something which is transacted in a church; real worship
is something which sees the whole world as the temple
of the living God, and every common deed an act of worship.
As Whittier wrote:

> " For he whom Jesus loved hath truly spoken:
>   The holier worship which He deigns to bless,
> Restores the lost, and binds the spirit broken,
>   And feeds the widow and the fatherless."

A man may say, " I am going to church to worship God,"
but he should also be able to say, " I am going to the
factory, the shop, the office, the school, the garage, the
locomotive shed, the mine, the shipyard, the field, the
byre, the garden, to worship God."

This, Paul goes on to say, demands a radical change.
He says we must not be conformed to the world, but we

must be transformed from it. To express this idea he uses two almost untranslatable Greek words—words which, in our translation, we have taken almost sentences to express. The word he uses to be conformed to the world is *suschēmatizesthai*; the root of that word is *schēma*, and *schēma* means *the outward form*, which varies from year to year and from day to day. A man's *schēma* is not the same when he is seventeen as it is when he is seventy. A man's *schēma* is not the same when he goes out to work as when he is dressed for dinner. A man's *schēma* is continuously altering. So Paul says, " Don't try to match your life to all the fashions of this world; don't be like a chameleon which takes its colour from its surroundings; don't go with the world; don't let the world decide what you are going to be like." The word he uses for being *transformed* from the world is *metamorphousthai*; the root of that word is *morphē*, and *morphē* means the *essential unchanging* shape or element of anything. A man has not the same *schēma* at seventeen and seventy, but he has the same *morphē*; a man in dungarees has not the same *schēma* as a man in evening dress, but he has the same *morphē*; his outward form changes, but inwardly he is the same person. So, Paul is saying, that to worship and to serve God, we must undergo a change, not of our outward form, but of our inward personality, of the very essence of our being. What is that change? To put it in Pauline language—Paul would say that left to ourselves we live a life *kata sarka*, dominated by human nature at its lowest; in Christ we live a life *kata Christon* or *kata pneuma*, dominated by Christ or by the Spirit. An inward change has happened; the essential man has been changed; now he lives, not a self-centred, but a Christ-centred life.

This must happen, Paul says, by the renewal of your mind. The word that Paul uses for *renewal* is *anakainōsis*. In Greek there are two words for new—*neos* and *kainos*. *Neos* means new *in point of time*; *kainos* means new *in point of character and nature*. A newly manufactured pencil is *neos*; but a man who was once a sinner, and who is now on the way to being a saint, is *kainos*. When Christ comes into a man's life he is a *new* man; the centre of his being is different; the driving power of his life is different; his mind is different; for the mind of Christ is in him.

When Christ becomes the centre of life then we can offer the real worship, which is the offering of every moment and every action of life to God.

EACH FOR ALL AND ALL FOR EACH

Romans 12: 3-8

> For, through the grace that has been given to me, I say to everyone among you, not to have a mind proud beyond that which a mind should be, but to have a mind directed towards wisdom, as God has given the measure of faith to each one of you. For just as we have many members in one body, but all the members do not have the same function, so, although we are many, we are one body in Christ, and we are all members of each other. Since, then, we have different gifts, according to the grace that has been given to us, let us use them in mutual service. If we have received the gift of prophecy, let us prophesy according to the proportion of faith that we have received. If we have received the gift of practical service, let us use it in service. If our gift is in teaching, let us use it in teaching. If it lies in exhortation, let us use it in exhortation. If we are called upon to share, let us do it with simple kindliness. If we are called upon to supply leadership, let us do so with zeal. If the occasion arises when we must show mercy, let us do so with gracious cheerfulness.

ONE of Paul's favourite thoughts is to think of the Christian Church as a body (cp. 1 Corinthians 12: 12-27). The members of the body neither argue with each other or envy each other or dispute about their relative importance. Each part of the body carries out its own function, however prominent or however humbly unseen that function may be. It was Paul's conviction that the Christian Church should be like that. Each member of the Christian Church has a task to do; and it is only when each member contributes the help of his or her own task that the body of the Church functions as it ought to function.

Beneath this passage there lie very important rules for life.

(i) First of all, this passage urges us to know ourselves. One of the first basic commandments of the Greek wise men was: " Man, know thyself." We do not get very far in this world until we know what we can do and what we cannot do. An honest assessment of one's own capabilities, without conceit and without false modesty, is one of the first essentials of a useful life.

(ii) Second, this passage urges us to accept ourselves. It urges us to use the gift that God has given us. We are not to envy someone else's gift; we are not to complain and regret that some other gift has not been given to us. We are to accept ourselves as we are, and to use that gift which we have, That often means that we have to accept the fact that service for us may mean some humble sphere, and some almost unseen part to play. It was one of the great basic beliefs of the Stoics that there was a spark of God in every living creature. If anything in this world had life, the Stoic believed that, at least to some extent, it had God. Its life was God in it. The Sceptics laughed at this doctrine. " God in worms? " demanded the Sceptic. " God in dung-beetles?" Whereat the Stoic replied: " Why not? Cannot an earthworm serve God? Do you suppose that it is only a general who is a good soldier? Cannot the lowest private or camp attendant fight his best and give his life for the cause? Happy are you if you are serving God, and carrying out the great purpose as truly as an earthworm." The efficiency of the life of the universe depends on the humblest creatures. Paul is here saying that a man must accept himself; but even if he finds that the contribution he has to offer will be unseen and unknown, without praise and without prominence, he must make that contribution, certain that it is essential, and that without it life and the Church can never be what they were meant to be.

(iii) Third, Paul is really saying that whatever gift a man has that gift comes from God. He calls the gifts *charismata*. In the New Testament a *charisma* is something given to a man by God which the man himself could not have acquired or attained. It is a personal, individual gift given to him by God. In point of fact, life is like that. A man might practise for a lifetime and yet never play the piano like Kentner or Pouishnoff. These men have more than practice; they have the something plus, the *charisma* which is a gift of God. A man might toil for a lifetime and still be handless in the use of tools and wood and metals; another man can fashion wood and mould metal with a special skill, and tools become part of himself; he has the something plus, the *charisma*, which is a gift of God. One man might practise speaking for ever and a day, and still never acquire that magic something which moves an audience or a congregation; another man steps on to a platform or climbs into a pulpit, and the audience are in the hollow of his hand; he has that something plus, that *charisma*, which is a gift of God. A man might toil for a lifetime and never acquire the gift of putting his thoughts on paper in a vivid and intelligible way; another man without effort sees his thoughts grow on the sheet of paper in front of him; the second man has the something plus, the *charisma*, which is the gift of God. Every man has his own *charisma*. It may be for writing sermons, building houses, sowing seeds, fashioning wood, manipulating figures, playing the piano, singing songs, teaching children, playing football or golf. Whatever it is, every man has it; and it is a *charisma*, a something plus somewhere, given to him by God. His skill was not so much achieved as given. He owes it to God.

(iv) Fourthly, whatever gift a man has he must use that gift, and the motive of use must be, not his own personal prestige, but the conviction that it is at one and the same time his bounden duty and his God-given privilege to make his own contribution to the common good.

Let us look now at the gifts which Paul singles out here for special mention.

(i) There is the gift of *prophecy*. It is only rarely that prophecy in the New Testament has to do with foretelling the future; it usually has to do with *forthtelling the word of God*. The prophet is the man who can announce the Christian message with the authority of one who knows. To announce Christ to others a man must first know Christ himself. " What this parish needs," said Carlyle's father, " is a man who knows Christ other than at second-hand."

(ii) There is the gift of *practical service (diakonia)*. It is surely significant that practical service came to Paul's mind so high on the list. It may be that a man will never have the privilege of standing forth in public and proclaiming Christ; but there is no man who cannot every day in life show the love of Christ in deeds of service to his fellow men.

(iii) There is *teaching*. The message of Christ needs not only to be proclaimed; it needs also to be *explained*. It may well be that one of the great failures of the Church at this present time is that men are constantly urged and invited to become Christians, without ever being told what Christianity means. Exhortation and invitation without a background of teaching are empty things.

(iv) There is *exhortation*. Exhortation should have one dominating note, and that note should be *encouragement*. There is a naval regulation which says that no officer shall speak discouragingly to any other officer about any undertaking in which he may be engaged. There is a kind of exhortation which is a daunting and discouraging thing. Real exhortation aims not so much at dangling a man over the flames of hell as spurring him on to the joy of life in Christ.

(v) There is *sharing*. Sharing is to be carried out with

simple kindliness. The word that Paul uses is *haplotes*, and it is a difficult word to translate, because it has in it the meaning both of simplicity and of generosity. One great commentary quotes a passage from *The Testament of Issachar* which perfectly illustrates the meaning of *haplotēs*. " And my father blessed me, seeing that I walked in simplicity (*haplotēs*). And I was not inquisitive in my actions, nor wicked and envious towards my neighbour. I did not speak evil of anyone or attack a man's life, but I walked with a single eye (literally, with *haplotēs* of my eyes). To every poor and every afflicted man I provided the good things of earth in simplicity (*haplotēs*) of heart. The simple (*haplous*) man does not desire gold, doth not ravish his neighbour, doth not care for all kinds of dainty meats, doth not wish for diversity of clothing, doth not promise himself length of days, but receiveth only the will of God. He walketh in uprightness of life and beholdeth all things in simplicity (*haplotēs*)." There is a giving which pries into the circumstances of another as it gives, which gives, but which gives a moral lecture of criticism along with the gift, which gives not so much to relieve the need of the other as to pander to its own vanity and self-satisfaction, which gives with a grim sense of duty instead of radiant sense of joy, which gives always with some ulterior motive and never for the sheer joy of giving. Christian giving and sharing is in *haplotēs*, in the simple kindliness which delights in the sheer pleasure of giving for giving's sake.

(vi) There is *being called to occupy a leading place*. Paul says that if we are called to do so we must do so with zeal. One of the most difficult problems of the Church to-day is the getting of leaders in all the departments of its work. There are fewer and fewer people with a sense of service and of responsibility. There are fewer and fewer who are willing to give up their leisure and their pleasure to undertake leadership. In many cases unfitness and unworthiness is pleaded when the real reason is disinclination and laziness. Further, if such leadership is taken up, Paul says that it is to be taken up with *zeal*. There are two ways in which an elder may deliver a communion card; he may deliver it through the letter-box, or he may deliver it at the fireside. There are two ways in which a teacher may prepare a lesson. It may be prepared with heart and mind, or it may be prepared in the most perfunctory way. A man may dully and drably go through some task in the Church, or he may do it with the joy and thrill of zeal. The Church to-day needs leaders, and leaders who are men and women with zeal in their hearts.

(vii) There is *the time when mercy has to be shown*. It has to be shown with gracious kindliness, Paul says. It is possible to forgive a man in such a way that the very forgiveness is an insult. It is possible to forgive and at the same time to demonstrate an attitude of criticism and contempt. If ever we have to forgive a sinner we must remember that we are fellow sinners. " There but for the grace of God, go I," said George Whitefield as he saw the criminal walk to the gallows. There is a way of forgiving a man which pushes him further into the gutter; and there is a way of forgiving him which lifts him out of the mire. Real forgiveness is always based on love and never on superiority.

THE CHRISTIAN LIFE IN EVERYDAY ACTION

Romans 12: 9-13

> Your love must be completely sincere.
> Hate that which is evil and cling to that which is good.
> Be affectionate to one another in brotherly love.
> Give to each other priority in honour.
> Do not be sluggish in zeal.
> Keep your spirit at boiling point.
> Seize your opportunities.
> Rejoice in hope.
> Meet tribulation with triumphant fortitude.
> Be persevering in prayer.
> Share what you have to help the needs of God's dedicated people
> Be eager in giving hospitality.

HERE Paul presents his people with ten telegraphic rules for ordinary, everyday life. Let us look at them one by one.

(i) Love must be completely sincere. There must be no hypocrisy, no play-acting, no ulterior motive in Christian love. There is such a thing as cupboard love, which gives affection with one eye on the gain which may result. There is such a thing as a selfish love, whose aim is to get far more than it is to give. The Christian love is a love which is cleansed of self. It is a pure outgoing of the heart to others.

(ii) We must hate that which is evil and cling to that which is good. It has been said that our one security against sin lies in our being shocked by it. It was Carlyle who said that what we need is to see the infinite beauty of holiness, and the infinite damnability of sin. The words Paul uses are strong words. It has been said that no virtue is safe which is not passionate. A man is not safe when his life consists in a prudent avoidance of evil and a calculating adherence to that which is good. He must hate evil and love good. Of one thing we must be clear—what many people hate is not evil, but the consequences of evil. No man is really a good man when he is good simply because he fears the consequences of being bad. As Burns had it:

> " The fear o' Hell's a hangman's whip
> To haud the wretch in order;
> But where ye feel your honour grip,
> Let that ay be your border."

Not to fear the consequences of dishonour, but to love honour with a passionate love is the way to real goodness.

(iii) We must be affectionate to one another in brotherly love. The word that Paul uses for affectionate is *philostorgos*, and *storgē* is the Greek word for *family love*. We must love each other, because we are members of one family. We are not strangers to each other within the Christian Church; much less are we isolated units; we are brothers and sisters of each other, because we have the one father, even God. The Christian Church is not a collection of acquaintances; it is not even a gathering of friends; it is a family in God.

(iv) We must give each other priority in honour. More than half the trouble that arises in Churches concerns rights and privileges and places and prestige. Someone has not been given his or her place; someone has been neglected or unthanked; someone has been given a more prominent place on a platform than someone else—and there is trouble. The mark of the truly Christian man has always been humility. One of the humblest of men was that great saint and scholar Principal Cairns. Someone recollects an incident which showed Cairns as he was. He was a member of a platform party at a great gathering. As Cairns appeared there was a tremendous burst of applause. Cairns stood back and let the man next him pass, and began to applaud himself. He never dreamed that the applause was for him; he assumed it was for someone else. It is not easy to give each other priority in honour. There is enough of the natural man in most of us to like to get our rights; but the Christian man knows that he has no rights—that he has only duties.

(v) We must not be sluggish in zeal. There is a certain intensity in the Christian life. There is no room for lethargy in it. The Christian cannot take things in an easy-going way, for to him life is always a choice between life and death; the world is always a battle-ground between good and evil; the time is short; and life is a preparation ground for eternity. The Christian may burn out, but he cannot rust out.

(vi) We must keep our spirit at boiling point. The one man whom the Risen Christ could not stand was the man who was neither hot nor cold (Revelation 3: 15, 16). To-day people are apt to look askance upon enthusiasm; the modern battle-cry is " I couldn't care less." But the Christian man is a man desperately in earnest; he has a fire in his bones; and therefore he is aflame for Christ.

(vii) Paul's seventh injunction may be one of two things. The ancient manuscripts vary between two readings. Some read, " Serve the Lord," and some read, " Serve the time," that is, " Grasp your opportunities." The reason for the double reading is this. All the ancient scribes used contractions in their writing. In particular the commoner words were always abbreviated. One of the commonest ways of abbreviating was to miss out the vowels—as shorthand does—and to place a stroke along the top of the remaining letters. Now the word for *Lord* is *kurios* and the word for *time* is *kairos*, and the abbreviation for both of these words is *krs*. In a section so filled with practical advice it is more likely that Paul was saying to his people, " Seize your opportunities as they come." Life presents us with all kinds of opportunities—the opportunity to learn something new, or to cut out something old and wrong; the opportunity to speak a word of encouragement or of warning; the opportunity to help or to comfort. One of the tragedies of life is that we so often fail to grasp these opportunities when they come. " There are three things which come not back—the spent arrow, the spoken word, and the lost opportunity."

(viii) We are to rejoice in hope. When Alexander the Great was setting out upon one of his eastern campaigns, he was distributing all kinds of gifts to his friends. In his generosity he had given away nearly all his possessions. " Sir," said one of his friends, " you will have nothing left for yourself." " Oh yes I have," said Alexander, " I have still my hopes." The Christian must be essentially an optimist. Just because God is God, the Christian is always certain that " the best is yet to be." Just because he knows of the grace that is sufficient for all things, and the strength that is made perfect in weakness, the Christian knows that no task is too much for him. " There are no hopeless situations in life; there are only men who have grown hopeless about them." And there can never be any such thing as a hopeless Christian.

(ix) We are to meet tribulation with triumphant fortitude. Someone once said to a gallant sufferer: " Suffering colours all life, doesn't it? " " Yes," said the gallant one, " it does, but I propose to choose the colour." When the dreadful affliction of complete deafness began to descend on Beethoven, and when life seemed to be one unbroken disaster, he said: "I will take life by the throat." As William Cowper had it:

" Set free from present sorrow,
     We cheerfully can say,
'Even let the unknown to-morrow
     Bring with it what it may,
It can bring with it nothing
     But He will bear us through.' "

When Nebuchadnezzar cast Shadrach, Meshach and Abed-nego into the burning fiery furnace, in the old story, he was amazed that they took no harm. He asked if they had not cast three men into the flames. They told him it was so. "Lo," he said, "I see four men loose, walking in the midst of the fire, and they have no hurt; and the form of the fourth is like the Son of God" (Daniel 3: 24, 25). A man can meet anything when he meets it with Christ.

(x) We are to persevere in prayer. Is it not the case that there are times in life when we let day add itself to day and week to week, and when we never speak to God? When a man ceases to pray he despoils himself of the strength of Almighty God. No man can be surprised if life collapses if he insists on living life alone.

(xi) We are to share with those in need. In a world which is bent on getting, the Christian is bent on giving, because he knows that "what we keep we lose, and what we give we have."

(xii) The Christian is to be given to hospitality. Over and over again the New Testament insists on this duty of the open door (Hebrews 13: 2; I Timothy 3: 2; Titus I: 8; I Peter 4: 9). Tyndale used a magnificent word. He translated it that the Christian should have a *harborous* disposition. A home can never be a happy home when it is a selfish home. Christianity is the religion of the open hand, the open heart, and the open door.

THE CHRISTIAN AND HIS FELLOW MEN

Romans 12: 14-21

> Bless those who persecute you; bless them and do not curse them.
>
> Rejoice with those who rejoice, and weep with those who weep.
>
> Live in harmony with one another.
>
> Keep your thoughts from pride; and never refuse to be associated with humble people.
>
> Don't become conceitedly wise in your own estimation.
>
> Never return evil for evil.
>
> Take thought to make your conduct fair for all to see.
>
> If it is possible, as far as you can, live at peace with all men.
>
> Beloved, do not seek to revenge yourself on others; leave such vengeance to The Wrath, for it stands written: " Vengeance belongs to me; I will repay, says the Lord." Rather, if your enemy is hungry, give him food. If he is thirsty, give him drink. If you do this you will heap coals of fire on his head. Be not overcome by evil, but overcome evil with good.

HERE Paul offers a series of rules and principles wherewith to govern our relationships with our fellow men.

(i) The Christian must meet persecution with a prayer for those who persecute him. Long ago Plato had said that the good man will choose rather to suffer evil than to do evil, and it is always evil to hate. When the Christian is hurt, and insulted, and maltreated, he has the example of his Master before him, for He, upon His Cross, prayed for forgiveness for those who were killing Him. There has been no greater force to move men into Christianity than just this serene forgiveness which the martyrs in every age have showed. Stephen died praying for forgiveness for those who stoned him to death (Acts 7: 60). Among those who killed him was a young man named Saul, who afterwards became Paul, the apostle to the Gentiles, and the slave of Christ. There can be no doubt that that death scene of Stephen was one of the things that turned Paul to Christ. As Augustine said: " The Church owes Paul to the prayer of Stephen." Many a persecutor has become a follower of the faith he once sought to destroy, because he has seen how a Christian can forgive.

(ii) We have to rejoice with those who do rejoice, and to weep with those who weep. There are few bonds like the bond of a common sorrow. A writer tells of the saying of an American negro woman. A lady in Charleston met the negro servant of a neighbour. " I'm sorry to hear of your Aunt Lucy's death," she said. " You must miss her greatly. You were such friends." " Yes'm," said the servant, " I is sorry she died. But we wasn't no friends." " Why," said the lady, " I thought you were. I've seen you laughing and talking together lots of times." " Yes'm. That's so," came the reply. " We've laughed together, and we've talked together, but we is just 'quaintances. You see, Miss Ruth, we ain't never shed no tears. Folks got to cry together before dey is friends." The bond of tears is the strongest bond of all. And yet it is much easier to weep with those who weep than it is to rejoice with those who rejoice. Long ago Chrysostom wrote on this passage: " It requires more of a high Christian temper to rejoice with them that do rejoice than to weep with them that weep. For this nature itself fulfils perfectly; and there is none so hard-hearted as not to weep over him that is in calamity; but the other requires a very noble soul, so as not only to keep from envying, but even to feel pleasure with the person who is in esteem." It is, indeed, more difficult to congratulate another on his success, especially if his success involves disappointment to us, than it is to sympathize with his sorrow and his loss. It is only when self is dead that we can take as much joy in the success of others as in our own.

(iii) We are to live in harmony with one another. It was Nelson who, after one of his great victories, sent back a despatch in which he gave as the reason of it:

" I had the happiness to command a band of brothers."
It is a band of brothers that any Christian Church should
be. Leighton once wrote: " The mode of Church government is unconstrained; but peace and concord, kindness
and good will are indispensable." When strife enters
into any Christian society, the possibility and the hope
of doing any good work are gone.

(iv) We are to avoid all pride and all snobbishness.
We have always to remember that the standards by which
the world judges a man are not necessarily the standards
by which God judges him. Saintliness has nothing to do
with rank, or wealth, or birth. Dr. James Black in his
own vivid way described a scene in an early Christian
congregation. A notable convert has been made, and the
great man comes to his first Church service. He enters
the room where the service is being held. The Christian
leader points to a place. " Will you sit there please? "
" But," says the man, " I cannot sit there, for that would
be to sit beside my slave." " Will you sit there please? "
repeats the leader. " But," says the man, " surely not
beside my slave." " Will you sit there please? " repeats
the leader once again. And the man at last crosses the
room, sits beside his slave, and gives him the kiss of peace.
That is what Christianity did; and that is what Christianity
alone could do in the Roman Empire. The Christian
Church was the only place where master and slave sat
side by side. The Christian Church is still the place where
all earthly distinctions are gone, for with God there is
no respect of persons.

(v) We are to make our conduct fair for all to see.
Paul was well aware that Christian conduct must not
only be good; it must also look good. So-called Christianity
can be presented in the hardest and the most unlovely
way; but real Christianity is something which is fair for
all to see.

(vi) We are to live at peace with all men. But we must note that Paul adds two qualifications. (*a*) He says, *if it be possible*. There may come a time when the claims of courtesy have to submit to the claims of principle. Christianity is not an easy-going tolerance which will accept anything and shut its eyes to everything. There may come a time some battle has to be fought, and when that time comes the Christian will not shirk it. (*b*) He says, *as far as you can*. Paul knew very well that it is easier for some to live at peace than it is for others. He knew that one man can be compelled to control as much temper in an hour as another man in a lifetime. We would do well to remember that goodness is a great deal easier for some people than it is for others. If we remember that it will keep us alike from criticism and from discouragement.

(vii) We are to keep ourselves from all thought of taking revenge. Paul gives three reasons for that. (*a*) Vengeance does not belong to us; it belongs to God. In the last analysis no human being has a right to judge any other; only God can do that. (*b*) To treat a man with kindness rather than vengeance is the way to move his heart. Vengeance may break his spirit; but kindness will break his heart. "If we are kind to our enemies," says Paul, "it will heap coals of fire on their heads." That means, not that it will store up further punishment for them, but that it will, as we ourselves say, move them to burning shame. (*c*) To stoop to vengeance is to be ourselves conquered by evil. Evil can never be conquered by evil. If hatred is met with more hatred then hatred is only increased; but if hatred is met with love then an antidote for the poison is found. As Booker Washington said: "I will not allow any man to make me lower myself by hating him." The only real way to destroy an enemy is to make him a friend.

THE CHRISTIAN AND THE STATE

Romans 13: 1-7

> Let everyone render due obedience to those who
> occupy positions of outstanding authority, for there
> is no authority which is not allotted its place by God,
> for the authorities which exist have been set in their
> places by God. So he who sets himself up against
> authority has really set himself up against God's
> arrangement of things. Those who do set themselves
> against authority will receive condemnation upon
> themselves. For the man who does good has nothing
> to fear from rulers, but the man who does evil has.
> Do you wish to be free of fear of authority? Do
> good and you will enjoy praise from authority, for
> any servant of God exists for your good. If you do
> evil, then you must fear. For it is not for nothing
> that the man set in authority bears the sword, for
> he is the servant of God, and his function is to vent
> wrath and vengeance on the man who does evil.
> So, then, it is necessary for you to submit yourself,
> not because of the wrath, but for the sake of your
> own conscience.

> For this same reason you must pay your taxes too;
> for those set in authority are the servants of God,
> and continue to work for that very end. Give to all
> men what is due to them. Give tribute to those to
> whom tribute is due; pay taxes to those to whom
> taxes are due. Give fear to those to whom fear is due.
> Give honour to those to whom honour is due.

AT a first reading this is an extremely surprising passage,
for it seems to counsel absolute obedience on the part
of the Christian to the civil power. But, in point of fact,
this is a commandment which runs through the whole
New Testament. In I Timothy 2: I, 2, we read: " I
exhort, therefore, that first of all supplications, prayers,
intercessions, and giving of thanks be made for all men;
for kings and for all that are in authority; that we may
lead a quiet and peaceable life in all godliness and honesty."
In Titus 3: I the advice to the preacher is: " Put them in
mind to be subject to principalities and powers, to obey
magistrates, to be ready to every good work." In I Peter

2: 13-17 we read: " Submit yourselves to every ordinance of man for the Lord's sake; whether it be to the king, as supreme; or unto governors, as unto them that are sent by him, for the punishment of evil-doers, and the praise of them that do well. For so is the will of God, that with well-doing you may put to silence the ignorance of foolish men. . . . Honour all men. Love the brotherhood. Fear God. Honour the king." We might be tempted to argue that these passages come from a time when the Roman government had not begun to persecute and hunt the Christians. We know, for instance, in the Book of Acts that frequently, as Gibbon had it, the tribunal of the pagan magistrate was often the safest refuge against the fury of the Jewish mob. Time and again we see Paul receiving justice and protection at the hands of impartial Roman justice. But the interesting and the significant thing is that many years, and even centuries later, when persecution had begun to rage, and when the Christians were regarded as outlaws, the Christian leaders were saying exactly the same thing. Just Martyr (Apology 1: 17) writes, " Everywhere, we, more readily than all men, endeavour to pay to those appointed by you the taxes, both ordinary and extraordinary, as we have been taught by Jesus. We worship only God, but in other things we will gladly serve you, acknowledging you as kings and rulers of men, and praying that, with your kingly power, you may be found to possess also sound judgment." Athenagoras, pleading for peace for the Christians, writes (chapter 37): " We deserve favour because we pray for your government, that you may, as is most equitable, receive the kingdom, son from father, and that your empire may receive increase and addition, until all men become subject to your sway." Tertullian (Apology 30) writes at length: " We offer prayer for the safety of our princes to the eternal, the true, the living God, whose favour, beyond all other things, they must themselves desire. . . . Without ceasing, for all our emperors we offer prayer. We pray for life pro-

longed; for security to the empire; for protection for
the imperial house; for brave armies, a faithful senate, a
virtuous people, the world at rest—whatever, as man or
Caesar, an emperor would wish." He goes on to say that
the Christian cannot but look up to the emperor because
the Christian believes that the Emperor " is called by
our Lord to his office." And he ends by saying that " Caesar
is more ours than yours because our God appointed him."
Arnobius (4: 36) declares that in the Christian gatherings
" peace and pardon are asked for all in authority." It
was the consistent and official teaching of the Christian
Church that obedience must be given to, and prayers
must be made for, the civil power, even when the wielder
of that civil power was a Nero.

What is the thought and belief which is at the back of
this?

(i) In Paul's case there was one immediate cause of
his stressing of civil obedience. The Jews were notoriously
rebellious. Palestine, and especially Galilee, was constantly
seething with insurrection. Above all there were the
Zealots; they were convinced that there was no king for
the Jews but God; and that no tribute must be paid to
anyone except to God. Nor were they content with anything like a passive resistance. They believed that God
would not be helping them unless they embarked on violent
action to help themselves. They were sworn and pledged
to a career of murder and assassination. Their aim was
to make any civil government impossible. They were
known as the dagger-bearers. They were fanatical nation-
alists sworn to terrorist methods. Not only did they
use terrorism towards the Roman government; they also
wrecked the houses and burned the crops, and assassinated
the families of their own fellow-Jews who paid tribute
to the Roman government. In this Paul saw no point at all.
It was, in fact, the direct negation of all Christian conduct.
And yet, at least in one part of the nation, it was normal
Jewish conduct. It may well be that Paul writes here

with such inclusive definiteness because he wished to dissociate Christianity altogether from insurrectionist Judaism, and to make it clear that Christianity and good citizenship went essentially and necessarily hand in hand.

(ii) But there is more than a merely temporary situation in the relationship between the Christian and the state. It may well be true that the circumstances caused by the unrest of the Jews was in Paul's mind, but there were other things as well. First and foremost, there is this— no man can entirely dissociate himself from the society in which he lives and has a part. No man can, in conscience, opt out of the nation. As a part of the nation, he enjoys certain benefits which he could not have as an individual. He cannot reasonably claim all the privileges and then refuse all the duties. He is bound up in the bundle of life; as he is part of the body of the Church he is also part of the body of the nation. There is no such thing in this world as an isolated individual. A man has a duty to the state, and must discharge that duty even if a Nero is on the throne.

(iii) To the state a man owes protection. It was the Platonic idea of the state that the state existed for the sake of justice and safety; that it secured for a man security against wild beasts and savage men. "Men," as it has been put, "herded behind a wall that they might be safe." A state is essentially a body of men who have banded themselves together, who have covenanted together, to maintain certain relationships between each other by the observance of certain laws. Without the state, without these laws, and without the mutual agreement to observe them, the bad and selfish strong man would be supreme. The weaker would go to the wall. Life would become ruled by the law of the jungle. Every ordinary man owes his security to the state, and is therefore under a duty and a responsibility to the state.

(iv) To the state ordinary people owe a wide range of services which individually they could not enjoy. It would be impossible for every man to have his own water, light, sewage, transport system. It would be impossible for a man by himself to enjoy a system of municipal services and of social security. These things are only obtainable when men agree to live together. And it would be quite wrong for a man to enjoy everything wherewith the state provides him and to refuse all responsibility to the state. No man can take everything and give nothing. That, in fact, is one compelling reason why the Christian is bound in honour to be a good citizen, and to take his part in all the duties of citizenship.

(v) But Paul's main view of the state was that in his day, as he saw things, the Roman Empire was the divinely ordained instrument to save the world from chaos. Take away that Empire, as Paul saw it, and the world would disintegrate into flying fragments. It was in fact the *pax Romana*, the Roman peace, which gave the Christian missionary the chance to do his work. Ideally men should be bound together by Christian love; but they are not; and the cement which keeps them together is the state.

Paul saw in the state an instrument in the hand of God; the state preserved the world from chaos; those who administered the state were playing their part in that great task. Whether they knew it or not they were doing God's work, and it was the Christian's duty to help and not to hinder.

THE DEBTS WHICH MUST BE PAID AND THE DEBT WHICH NEVER CAN BE PAID

Romans 13: 8-10

> Owe no man anything, except to love each other; for he who loves the other man has fulfilled the law. The commandments, You must not commit adultery, You must not kill, You must not steal, You must not covet, and any other commandment there may be, are all summed up in this saying—You must love

your neighbour as yourself. Love does no harm to its neighbour. Love is, therefore, the complete fulfilment of the law.

THE previous passage dealt with what might be called a man's public debts. Verse 7 mentions two of these public debts. There is what Paul calls *tribute*, and what he calls *taxes*. By *tribute* he means the tribute that must be paid by those who are members of a subject nation. The standard tribute contributions that the Roman government levied on its subject nations were three. There was a *ground tax* by which a man had to pay, either in cash or in kind, one-tenth of all the grain, and one-fifth of the wine and fruit produced by his ground. There was *income tax*, which was one per cent of a man's income. There was a *poll tax*, which had to be paid by everyone between the ages of fourteen and sixty-five. By *taxes* Paul means the local taxes that had to be paid. There were customs duties, import and export taxes, taxes that must be paid for the use of main roads, for crossing bridges, for entry into markets and harbours, for the right to possess an animal, or to drive a cart or wagon. It is Paul's insistence that the Christian must pay his tribute and his taxes to state and to local authority, however galling these taxes may be.

Then Paul turns to *private* debts. He says, " Owe no man anything." It seems a thing almost unnecessary to say; but there were some who even twisted the petition of the Lord's Prayer, " Forgive us our debts, as we forgive our debtors," into a reason for claiming absolution from all debts and money obligations. Paul had to remind his people that Christianity does not mean an excuse for refusing our obligations to our fellow men; it means a reason for fulfilling them to the utmost.

Then Paul goes on to speak of the one debt that a man must pay every day, and yet, at the same time, must go on owing every day. That is the debt to love each other. Origen said: " The debt of love remains with us permanently

We endebuted to corps!

and never leaves us; this is a debt which we both discharge every day and for ever owe." It is Paul's claim that if a man honestly seeks to discharge this debt of love, he will automatically keep all the commandments. If he discharges the debt of love, he will not commit adultery. When two people allow their physical passions to sweep them away, the reason is, not that they love each other too much, but that they love each other too little. In real love there is at once respect and restraint which saves a man from sin. If he discharges the debt of love, he will not kill, for love never seeks to destroy, but always to build up. Love can never hate, for love is always kind. Love will never seek to destroy its enemy by killing him, but always by seeking to make him its friend. If he discharges the debt of love, he will never steal, for love is always more concerned with giving than with getting. If he discharges the debt of love, he will not covet. Covetousness (*epithumia*) is the inordinate and uncontrolled desire for the forbidden thing, for the thing that ought not to be desired, and love cleanses the heart, until that desire is gone.

There is a famous saying, " Love God—and do what you like." If love is the mainspring of a man's heart, if his whole life is dominated by love for God and love for his fellow men, he needs no other law, for the law of love makes all other laws unnecessary.

THE THREAT OF TIME

Romans 13: 11-14

> Further, there is this—realize what time it is, that it is now high time to be awakened from sleep; for now your salvation is nearer then when you believed. The night is far gone; the day is near. So, then, let us put away the works of darkness, and let us clothe ourselves with the weapons of light. Let us walk in loveliness of life, as those who walk in the day, and let us not walk in revelry or drunkenness, in immorality and in shamelessness, in contention and in strife.

> But put on the Lord Jesus Christ as a man puts on
> a garment, and stop living a life in which your first
> thought is to gratify the desires of Christless human
> nature.

LIKE so many great men, Paul was haunted by the shortness
of time. It was Andrew Marvell who could always hear
" time's winged chariot hurrying near." It was Keats
who was haunted by fears that he might cease to be before
his pen had gleaned his teaming brain. Robert Louis
Stevenson writes:

> " The morning drum-call on my eager ear
> Thrills unforgotten yet; the morning dew
> Lies yet undried along my fields of noon.
> But now I pause at whiles in what I do
> And count the bell, and tremble lest I hear
> (My work untrimmed) the sunset gun too soon."

But there was more in Paul's thought than simply the
shortness of time. It was the crisis of the world's history
which he expected, the Second Coming of Christ. The
Early Church expected it at any moment, and therefore
it had the urgency to be ready. It may be that that
expectancy has grown dim and faint; but one permanent
fact remains—no man knows when God will rise and bid
him go. The time grows ever shorter, for we are every
day one day nearer that time. Life is still lived in expectation of the crisis moment. We, too, must have all things
ready.

The last verses of this passage must be forever famous,
for they are the verses through which Augustine found
conversion. He tells the story in his _Confessions._ He was
walking in the garden. His heart was in distress, because
of his failure in his attempts to live the good life. He kept
exclaiming miserably, " How long? How long? To-morrow
and to-morrow—why not now? Why not this hour and
end to my depravity?" He was speaking and thinking
and weeping like this, when suddenly he heard a voice
saying, " Take and read; take and read." It sounded
like a child's voice; and he wracked his mind to try to

remember any child's game in which these words occurred, but could think of none. He hurried back to the seat where his friend Alypius was sitting, for he had left there a volume of Paul's writings. " I snatched it up and read silently the first passage my eyes fell upon: ' Let us not walk in revelry or drunkenness, in immorality and in shamelessness, in contention and in strife. But put on the Lord Jesus Christ, as a man puts on a garment, and stop living a life in which your first thought is to gratify the desires of Christless human nature.' I neither wished nor needed to read further. With the end of that sentence, as though the light of assurance had poured into my heart, all the shades of doubt were scattered. I put my finger in the page and closed the book: I turned to Alypius with a calm countenance and told him." (C. H. Dodd's translation). Out of God's word God had spoken to Augustine. It was Coleridge who said that he believed the Bible to be inspired because, as he put it, " It finds me." God's word can always find the human heart.

It is interesting to look at the six sins which Paul selects as being, as it were, typical of the Christless life.

(i) There is *revelry* (*kōmos*). This is an interesting word. Originally a *kōmos* was the band of friends who accompanied a victor home from the games, singing his praises and celebrating his triumph as they went. Later it came to mean a noisy band of revellers who swept their way through the city streets at night, a band of roysterers, what, in Regency England, would have been called a *rout*. It describes the kind of revelry which lowers a man's self and is a disturbance and nuisance to others.

(ii) There is *drunkenness* (*methē*). Especially to the Greeks, drunkenness was a particularly disgraceful thing. The Greeks were a wine-drinking people. Even children drank wine. Breakfast was called *akratisma*, and consisted of a slice of bread dipped in wine. But, for all that, drunkenness was considered a specially shameful thing, for the wine the Greek drank was much diluted, and was drunk because the water supply was inadequate and dangerous. This was a vice which not only a Christian but any respectable heathen would also have condemned.

(iii) There was *immorality* (*koitē*). The word *koitē* literally means a *bed*. The word has in it the meaning of the desire for the forbidden bed. This was the typical heathen sin. It is true to say that chastity was unknown; it is almost true to say that it had not begun to be thought of as a virtue. The word brings to mind the man who sets no value on fidelity, and who takes his pleasure when and where he will.

(iv) There is *shamelessness* (*aselgeia*). *Aselgeia* is one of the ugliest words in the Greek language. It does not describe only immorality; it describes the man who is lost to shame. Most people seek to conceal their evil deeds, and try to sin in secret; but the man in whose heart there is *aselgeia* is long past that. He does not care who sees him; he does not care how much of a public exhibition he makes of himself; he does not care what people think of him; reputation, and honour and decency, mean nothing to him. *Aselgeia* is the quality of the man who is so deeply in the grip of sheer lust that he dares publicly to do the things which are unbecoming for any man to do.

(v) There is *contention* (*eris*). *Eris* is the spirit that is born of unbridled and unholy competition. It comes from the desire for place and power and prestige, from the hatred of being surpassed, from the inability and unwillingness to take the second place. It is essentially the sin which places self in the foreground and the front of the picture. It is the entire negation of *agapē*, of Christian love.

(vi) There is *envy* (*ʒēlos*). *Zēlos* in Greek need not be a bad word. It can describe the noble emulation of a man who, when confronted with greatness of character, wishes to copy it and to attain to it. But it can also mean that grudging envy which grudges any man his nobility and his pre-eminence; it describes here the spirit which cannot be content with what it has, and which looks with jealous

eye on every blessing given to someone else and denied
to itself.

RESPECT FOR SCRUPLES

Romans 14: 1

> Welcome the man who is weak in the faith, but not
> with a view to passing judgment on his scruples.

IN this chapter Paul is dealing with a problem which may
have been a temporary and local problem in the Roman
Church, but which is also a problem which is continually
confronting the Church, and which is always demanding
a solution. In the Roman Church there were apparently
two lines of thought. There were some people who believed
that in Christian liberty the old *tabus* are gone; they
believed that it made no difference what a man eats or
drinks, that the old food laws are now irrelevant, and that
the lists of clean and unclean animals in which Leviticus
delights have nothing to do with the Christian. They
believed that Christianity does not consist in the special
observance of any one day or days; that the time of
meticulous Jewish Sabbath observance is gone. Now,
undoubtedly, Paul makes it clear that this in fact is the
standpoint of real and full Christian faith. But, on the
other hand, there were those who were full of scruples.
They believed that it was wrong to eat meat and that a
man must be a vegetarian; they believed in the strict
and rigid observance of one day, until the day became a
tyranny. Paul calls the ultra-scrupulous man the man who
is *weak in the faith*. What does Paul mean by that? And
why does he call such a man weak in the faith?

Such a man is weak in the faith for two reasons.

(i) He has not yet discovered the meaning of Christian
freedom; he is at heart still a legalist; he sees Christianity
as a thing of rules and regulations. His whole aim is to
govern his life by a series of laws and observances; he is
indeed frightened of Christian freedom and Christian liberty.

(ii) He has not yet liberated himself from a belief in the efficacy of works. In his heart he believes that he can gain God's favour by doing certain things and abstaining from doing others. Basically he is still trying to earn a right relationship with God, and has not yet accepted the way of grace. He is still thinking of what he can do for God more than of what God has done for him.

Paul bids the stronger brethren to welcome such a person, and not to besiege him and attack him with continual criticisms.

This problem is not a problem confined to the days of Paul. To this day in the Church there are two points of view. There is the broader and the more liberal point of view which sees no harm in many things, and which is well content that many an innocent pleasure—as it sees pleasure—should go on within the Church. And there is the narrower and the stricter point of view, which is shocked and offended at many things in which the liberal person sees no harm.

Paul's sympathies are all with the broader point of view; but, at the same time, he says that when one of these weaker and narrower brethren comes into the Church he must be received with brotherly sympathy. When we are confronted with someone who holds the narrower point of view there are three attitudes that we must avoid.

(i) We must avoid the attitude of *irritation*. An impatient annoyance with such a person gets us nowhere at all. However much we may disagree, and however much we may differ, we must first of all try to see the other person's point of view, to sympathize and to understand.

(ii) We must avoid the attitude of *ridicule*. No man remains unwounded when that which he thinks precious is laughed at. It is no small sin to laugh at another man's beliefs. To us they may seem to be prejudices rather than beliefs; that does not matter; no man has a right to laugh at that which some other man holds sacred. In any event, laughter will never woo the other man to a wider

view; it will only make him withdraw still more deter-
minedly into his rigidity.

(iii) We must avoid the attitude of *contempt*. It is very
wrong to regard the narrower person as an old-fashioned
fool whose views may be treated with contempt. A man's
views are his own and must be treated with respect. It is
not even possible to win a man over to our position unless
we have a genuine respect for his. Of all attitudes towards
our fellow man the most unchristian is contempt.

Before we leave this verse, it should be noted that there
is another perfectly possible translation. " Welcome the
man who is weak in the faith, but do not introduce him
straight away to the discussion of questions which can
only raise doubts." There are some people whose faith
is so strong that no amount of debate and questioning
will really shake it. There are some people whose approach
to religion is an intellectual approach and who actually
revel in the discussion of difficult things. But there are
others who have a simple faith which is only needlessly
disturbed by ingenious and clever discussion. It may well
be that our own age is overfond of discussion for discussion's
sake. It is always fatal to give the impression that Christianity consists of nothing but a series of questions under
debate. " We have found," said G. K. Chesterton, " all
the questions that can be found. It is time we stopped
looking for questions and started looking for answers."
" Tell me of your certainties," said Goethe, " I have doubts
enough of my own." There is one good rule which should
direct and guide the progress of any discussion—every
discussion, even if it has been a bewildered discussion,
and even if it has been discussing questions to which there
is no real answer, should always finish with an *affirmation*.
In a discussion group in a Church or in a society we should
never leave with nothing but a series of baffling questions.
There may be many questions left unanswered, but, at
the same time, there must be some certainty which is
left unshaken.

TOLERANCE FOR ANOTHER'S POINT OF VIEW

Romans 14: 2-4

> One man has enough faith to believe that he can eat any-
> thing; but he who is weak in the faith eats vegetables.
> Let not him who eats contemptuously despise him
> who does not eat; and let not him who does not eat
> pass censorious judgment on him who does eat, for
> God has received him. Who are you to judge another
> man's servant? It is in his own master's judgment
> that he stands or falls—and he will stand, for the
> Master is able to make him stand.

HERE emerges one of the definite points in debate in the
Roman Church. There were those who observed no special
food laws and *tabus* at all, and who ate anything; and
there were those who conscientiously abstained from meat,
and ate only vegetables. There were many sects and religions
in the ancient world which observed the strictest food
laws. The Jews themselves had their food laws. Leviticus 11
gives its lists of the creatures which may and which may
not be eaten. One of the strictest sects of the Jews was
the Essenes. They, in their communities, had communal
meals for which they bathed and wore special clothes.
The meals were specially prepared by priests, and unless
the meals were so prepared the Essenes would not eat them.
In the heathen world the Pythagoreans had their distinctive
food laws. Pythagoras taught that the soul of man was
a fallen deity confined to the body as to a tomb. He
believed in reincarnation through which the soul might
dwell in a man, an animal, or a plant in an endless chain
of being. Release from this chain of being was found through
absolute purity and discipline; and this discipline included
silence, study, self-examination and abstention from all
flesh. It is true to say that in almost any Christian congregation there would be those who observed special food
laws and tabus.

Here we have the same problem again. Within the
Church there was a stricter, narrower party, and a wider,
more liberal party. Paul unerringly pinpoints the danger

that was likely to arise. Almost certainly the more liberal
party would despise the scruples of the narrower party;
and, still more certainly, the narrower party would pass
censorious judgment on, what they believed to be, the
laxity of the more liberal party. That is a situation which
is just as real and perilous in the Church to-day as it was
in the time of Paul.

To meet it Paul lays down a great principle. No man has
any right to criticize another man's servant. The servant is
answerable and responsible to his master alone. Now all
men are the servants of God. It is not open to us to criticize
them, or to find fault with them, still less to condemn them.
That right belongs to God alone. It is not in our judgment
that a man stands or falls; it is in God's judgment. And,
Paul goes on, if a man is honestly living out his principles
as he sees them, God can make him able to stand.

There is many and many a congregation of the Church
torn in two because those who hold broader and more liberal
views are angrily contemptuous of those whom they regard
as stick-in-the-mud, die-hard conservatives and puritans;
and because those who are stricter in their outlook are
critical, censorious and condemning of those who wish the
right to do things which they think are wrong. It is not
open to us to criticize and to condemn each other. " I
beseech you by the bowels of Christ," said Cromwell to the
rigid Scots of his day, " think it possible that you may be
mistaken." We must banish both censoriousness and
contempt from the fellowship of the Church. We must
leave the judgment of others to God, and seek only to
sympathize and to understand.

DIFFERENT ROAD TO THE SAME GOAL

Romans 14: 5, 6

> One man rates one day beyond another; one regards
> all days alike. Let each man be fully convinced in his
> own mind. The man who observes a particular day
> observes it to the Lord. The man who eats, eats to the

Lord, for he says his grace. The man who does not eat, does not eat to the Lord, for he too says his grace to God.

HERE Paul introduces another point on which the narrower and the more liberal people may differ. The narrower people make a great deal of the observance of one special day. That was indeed a special characteristic of the Jews. More than once Paul was worried about people who made a fetish of observing days. He writes to the Galatians: " Ye observe days, and months, and times, and years: I am afraid of you, lest I have bestowed upon you labour in vain " (Galatians 4: 10, 11). He writes to the Colossians: " Let no man judge you in meat or drink, or in respect of an holy day, or of the new moon, or of the sabbath days: which are a shadow of things to come; but the body is of Christ " (Colossians 2: 16, 17). The Jews had made a tyranny of the sabbath, surrounding it with a jungle of rules and regulations and prohibitions. It was not that Paul wished to wipe out the Lord's Day—far from it; but he did fear an attitude which in effect believed that Christianity consisted in observing any particular day. There is far more to Christianity than Lord's Day observance. When the famous missionary Mary Slessor spent three lonely years in the bush she frequently got the days mixed up because she had no calendar. " Once she was found holding her services on a Monday, and again on Sunday she was discovered on the roof, hammering away, in the belief that it was Monday! " No one is going to argue that Mary Slessor's services were any less valid and valuable because they were held on Monday, or that she was in any sense breaking the commandment because she was working on the Sunday. Paul would never have denied that the Lord's Day is a precious day, and that, in fact, and in practice, it is the day which should be given to God, but he would have been equally insistent that not even the Lord's Day must become a tyranny: still less must it become a fetish; it is not the day that we ought to worship, but Him who is the Lord of all days.

And yet, in spite of all that, Paul pleads for sympathy between the narrower and the more liberal brethren. His point is that, however different their practice may be, their aim is the same. In their different attitude to days both of them believe that they are serving God; when they sit down to eat, the one eats meat and the other does not, but both say their grace to God. We would do well to remember that. If I am trying to get from Glasgow to London there are many routes that I may use. I am not confined to going by any one road. I could in fact get there without traversing one half mile of road that another man might use. It is Paul's plea that the common aim should unite us, and that the differing practice should not be allowed to divide us.

But Paul insists on one thing. Whatever course a man chooses, let him be fully convinced in his own mind. His actions should be dictated not by *convention*, still less by *superstition*, but altogether by *conviction*. He should not do things simply because other people do them, and simply because it is the " right " thing to do. He should not do them because in his heart of hearts he is governed by a system of semi-superstitious tabus. He should do them because he has thought them out, and has reached the conviction that for him at least it is the right thing to do.

And Paul would have added something else to that—no man should make his own practice the universal standard for all other people. This, in fact, is one of the curses of the Church. Men are so apt to think that their way of worship, their particular practice, is the only way of worship and the only practice. T. R. Glover somewhere quotes a Cambridge saying: " Whatsoever thy hand findeth to do, do it with thy might—but remember that someone thinks differently." We would do well to remember that, in a great many matters, it is a duty to have our own convictions, but it is an equal duty to allow others to have theirs without regarding them as sinners and outcasts.

THE IMPOSSIBILITY OF ISOLATION

Romans 14: **7-9**

> For none of us lives to himself, and none of us dies
> to himself. If we live, we live to the Lord; and if
> we die, we die to the Lord. Whether we live or die
> we belong to the Lord. It was for this purpose that
> Christ died and rose to life again—that He might
> be the Lord of the dead and of the living.

HERE Paul lays down the great fact that it is impossible
in the nature of things to live an isolated life. There is
no such thing in this world as a completely detached
individual. That, in fact, is doubly true. " Man," said
M'Neile Dixon, " has an affair with the gods and an
affair with the mortals." No man can disentangle himself
either from his fellow men or from God.

In three directions a man cannot disentangle himself
from his fellow men.

(i) He cannot isolate himself from *the past*. No man is a
self-made man. " I am a part," said Ulysses, " of all that
I have met." A man is a receiver of a tradition, of a heritage,
of an heredity. He is an amalgam of all that his ancestors
made him. True, he himself does something to that amalgam;
but he does not start from nothing. For weal or for woe,
he starts with that which all the past has made him. The
unseen cloud of witnesses do not only compass him about;
they dwell within him. A man cannot dissociate himself
from the stock from which he springs and from the rock
from which he is hewn.

(ii) He cannot isolate himself from *the present*. We live
in a civilization which is daily binding men more and
more closely together. There is nothing that a man can do
which can affect only himself. He has the terrible power
of making others happy or sad by his conduct; he has
the still more terrible power of making others good or
bad by his conduct. From every man there goes out an
influence which makes it easier for others to take the high
way or the low way. From every man's deeds there come

consequences which affect others more or less closely. A man is bound up in the bundle of life, and from that bundle he cannot escape.

(iii) He cannot isolate himself from *the future*. As a man receives life so he hands life on. He hands on to his children a heritage of physical life and of spiritual character. A man is not a self-contained individual unit; he is a link in a chain. Someone tells of a youth, who lived carelessly, and who began to study biology. Through a microscope he was watching certain of these living things whom you can actually see living and dying and begetting others in a moment of time. He rose from the microscope. " Now I see it," he said. " I am a link in the chain, and I will not be a weak link any more." It is our terrible responsibility that we leave something of ourselves in the world by leaving something of ourselves in others. Sin would be a far less terrible thing if it affected only a man himself. The terror of every sin is that it starts a new train of evil in the world.

But still less can a man disentangle himself from Jesus Christ.

(i) In this life Christ is forever a living presence. We do not need to speak of living as if Christ saw us; Christ does see us. All life is lived in His eye. A man can no more escape from the risen, ever-present Christ than he can from his shadow. There is no place where he can leave Christ behind, and there is nothing which he can do unseen.

(ii) Not even death breaks that presence. In this world we live in the unseen presence of Christ; in the next we shall see Him in His real and living presence. Death is not the chasm that ends in obliteration; it is the gateway that leads to Christ.

No human being can follow a policy of isolation. He is bound to his fellow men, and bound to Christ by ties that neither time nor eternity can break. He dare not live to himself and he cannot die to himself.

MEN UNDER JUDGMENT

Romans 14: 10-12

> Who are you to judge your brother in anything?
> Or, who are you contemptuously to despise your
> brother? For we shall all stand at God's judgment
> seat; for it stands written: " As I live, God says,
> every knee shall bow to me, and every tongue shall
> confess its faith to God." So, then, each of us shall
> render account to God for himself.

THERE is one fundamental and basic reason why we have
no right to judge anyone else; and that reason is that we
ourselves are each one of us men under judgment. It is
the very essence of humanity that we are not the judges
but the judged. To prove his point Paul quotes Isaiah
45: 23. This was indeed a thought with which any Jew
would agree. There was a rabbinic saying: " Let not thine
imagination assure thee that the grave is an asylum;
for perforce thou wast framed, and perforce thou wast
born, and perforce thou livest, and perforce thou diest,
and perforce thou art about to give account and reckoning
before the King of kings, the Holy One, blessed is He."
The only person who has any right to judge anyone is
God; and, least of all, has the man who will stand at the
bar of God's judgment any right to judge a fellow man who
also stands at that bar.

Just before this Paul has been thinking of the impossibility of the isolated life. But there is one situation
in which a man is isolated, and that is when he stands
before the judgment seat of God. In the old days of the
Roman Republic, in the corner of the Forum farthest
from the Capitol, there had stood the *tribunal*, the judgment
seat, where the Praetor Urbanus had sat dispensing justice.
When Paul wrote, Roman justice required more than one
judgment seat; and so in the great basilicas, the great
colonnaded porches around the Forum, the magistrates

sat dispensing justice. The Roman well knew the sight of a man standing before the judge's judgment seat. That is what happens to every man; and that is a judgment which he must face alone. Sometimes in this world he can make use of the merits of someone else. Many a young man has been spared some penalty and condemnation for the sake of his parents; many a husband has been given mercy for the sake of his wife or child; but in the judgment of God a man stands alone. Sometimes, when some great one dies, at the funeral service the coffin lies in front of the worshipping and mourning congregation, and, on the top of it, there lies arranged the gowns of the man's academic honours, or the insignia of his state dignities; but he cannot take them with him. Naked we come into the world, and naked we leave it. We stand before God in the awful loneliness of our own souls; to God we can take nothing but the self and the character which in life we have been building up.

And yet that is not the whole truth. We do not stand alone at the judgment seat of God, for we stand with Jesus Christ. We do not need to go stripped of everything; we may go clad in the merits that are his. Collin Brooks, the famous writer and journalist, writes in one of his books: " God may be kinder than we think. If He cannot say, ' Well done! good and faithful servant,' it may be that He will say at last, ' Don't worry, my bad and faithless servant: I don't altogether dislike you.' " That was a man's whimsical way of stating his faith; but there is more to it than that. It is not that God merely does not dislike us; it is that, sinners as we are, He loves us for the sake of Jesus Christ our Lord. True, we must stand before the judgment seat of God in the naked loneliness of our own souls; but, if we have lived with Christ in life, we shall stand with Him in death, and before God He will be the advocate to plead our cause.

A MAN AND HIS NEIGHBOUR'S CONSCIENCE

Romans 14: 13-16

> So, then, let us stop passing judgment on each other, and rather let this be our only judgment—the determination not to put any hindrance or stumbling-block in our brother's way. I know this, and I am firmly convinced of it in the Lord Jesus Christ, that there is nothing in itself which is unclean. All the same, if anyone thinks that anything is unclean, it is unclean to him. If your brother is grieved by something which you eat, you are no longer conducting yourself according to the principle that love lays down. Do not bring ruin by what you eat to that man for whom Christ died.

THE Stoics used to teach that there are a great many things which they called *adiaphora,* that is, *indifferent.* In themselves they were quite neutral; they were neither good nor bad. The Stoics put it this way—it all depends by what handle you pick them up. Now that is profoundly true. A picture to a student of art might be a work of art ; to someone else it might be an obscene drawing. A discussion to one group of people might be an interesting and a stimulating and a mind-kindling experience; to someone else the very same discussion might appear a succession of heresies, and even blasphemies. An activity, an amusement, a pleasure, a pastime might seem to one quite genuinely harmless, and to another a prohibited thing. More, there are pleasures which are quite harmless to one man, which can, in fact, be the ruin of another. The thing itself is neither clean or unclean; its character is determined by the person who sees it or does it.

That is what Paul is getting at here. There are certain things which a man who is strong in the faith may see no harm in doing; but, if a person with a more scrupulous and narrow outlook saw him doing them, his conscience would be hurt and shocked; and if such a person were persuaded to do them his conscience would be outraged and violated. We may take a very simple example. One man will genuinely see no harm in playing some outdoor game on the Sunday; and he may be right; but another man's whole conscience is shocked at such a thing, and, if he were persuaded to take part in it, all the time he would have the lurking and haunting feeling that he was doing wrong. There are many pleasures and pastimes which one man is genuinely and sincerely, and on principle, convinced are quite legitimate; but the more scrupulous and the narrower person regards them as sins, and, if he were persuaded to take part in them, he could not rid himself of the underlying feeling that he was participating in some forbidden thing.

Paul's advice is quite clear. *It is a Christian duty to think of everything, not as it affects ourselves only, but also as it affects others.* Now, note, that Paul is not saying that we must always allow our conduct to be dominated and dictated by the views, and even the prejudices, of others; there are matters which are essentially matters of principle, and in them a man must take his own way. But, there are a great many things which are neutral and indifferent; there are a great many things which are neither in themselves good or bad; there are a great many things which are really pleasures and pastimes, and habits and customs, which a man need not do unless he likes. They are not essential parts of life and conduct; they belong to what we might call the extras of life; and, it is Paul's conviction, that in such things we have no right to give offence to the more scrupulous brother. We have no right to distress and outrage his conscience by doing them ourselves, or by persuading him to do them. Life must be guided by the principle of love; and if we do so guide life we will think, not so much of our so-called rights to do as we like, as we will think of our responsibilities to others. We have no right to distress another man's conscience in the things which do not really matter. Christian freedom must never be used as an excuse for rough-riding over the genuine feelings of others. No pleasure is so important that it can justify bringing offence and grief, and even ruin, to others. Augustine used to say that the whole Christian ethic could be summed up in the saying: " Love God, and do what you like." In a sense it is true; but Christianity does not only consist in loving God; it also consists in loving our neighbour as ourselves.

THE PERIL OF CHRISTIAN FREEDOM

Romans 14: 17-20

> Do not allow that good gift of freedom which you possess to become a thing which gets you into disrepute. For the Kingdom of God does not consist of food and drink, but of righteousness and peace and joy, which are the gifts of the Holy Spirit. For the man who rules his life by this principle, and so becomes the slave of Christ, is well-pleasing to God and approved by men. So, then, let it be the things that make for peace that we pursue, and the things which build up one another. Do not destroy God's work for the sake of food. True, all things are pure; but it is wrong for a man to make life's road more difficult for someone else through what he eats.

IN essence, Paul is here dealing with the peril and the abuse of Christian freedom and Christian liberty. To a Jew, especially, Christian freedom had its dangers. All his life he had been compassed about by a multiplicity of rules and regulations. So many things were unclean and so many were clean. So many animals might not be eaten; so many purity laws must be observed. When the Jew came into Christianity he found that all the petty rules and regulations were abolished at one stroke, and the danger was that he might interpret Christianity as a new-found freedom to do exactly as he liked. Men must remember that Christian freedom and Christian charity must go hand in hand; men must hold fast to the truth that Christian freedom and brotherly-love, and mutual consideration, are all bound up together.

Paul reminds his people that Christianity, the Kingdom of Heaven, does not consist in eating and drinking what one likes. It consists in three great things, all of which are essentially *unselfish* things. There is *righteousness*, and righteousness consists in giving to men and to God what is their due. Now the very first thing that is due to a fellow man in the Christian life is sympathy and consideration; the moment we become a Christian the feelings of the other man become *more* important than our own; Christianity means putting others first and self last. We cannot give a man what is due to him and do what we like. There is *peace.* In the New Testament peace does not mean simply absence of trouble; peace is not a negative thing, it is intensely positive; it means everything that makes for a man's highest good. Now, the Jews themselves often thought of peace as meaning a state of right relationships between man and man. If we insist that Christian freedom means doing what we like, that is precisely the state we can never attain. Christianity consists entirely in *personal relationships* to man and to God. The untrammelled freedom of Christian liberty is conditioned by the Christian obligation to live in a right relationship, in *peace*, with our fellow men. There is *joy.* In Christianity joy can never be a selfish thing. Christian joy does not consist in making ourselves happy; it consists in making others happy. A so-called happiness which made someone else distressed and grieved is not a Christian happiness. If a man, in his own search for happiness, brings a hurt heart and a wounded conscience to someone else, the ultimate end of his search will be, not joy, but sorrow. Christian joy is not an individualistic thing; it is an interdependent thing. Christian freedom is never freedom to trample on the feelings of others. Joy comes to the Christian only when he brings joy to others, even if it costs him personal limitation.

When a man follows this principle he becomes the slave of Christ. Here is the very essence of the matter. Christian freedom means that we are free to do, not what we like, but what Christ likes. It means that we are free, not to do a thing, but to abstain from doing it. Without Christ a man is a slave to his habits, his pleasures, his indulgences. He is not really doing what he likes. He is doing what the things which have him in their grip make him do. Once the power of Christ enters into him he is master of himself, and then, and only then, real freedom enters into life. Then we are free not to treat men and not to live life as our own selfish and tempestuous human nature would have us to do; we are free to show to all men the same attitude of love as Jesus showed.

So Paul ends by setting out the Christian aim within the fellowship. (a) It is the aim of *peace*; it is the aim that the members of the fellowship should be in a right relationship with each other. A Church where there is strife and contention, a Church where there are quarrels and bitterness, a Church where there are divisions and breaches, has lost all right to the name of Church. It is not a fragment of the Kingdom of Heaven; it is simply an earthbound society. (b) It is the aim of *upbuilding*. The picture of the Church as a building runs through the New Testament. The members are stones within the building. Anything which loosens the fabric of the Church is against God; anything which makes that fabric stronger and more secure is of God. The tragedy is that in so many cases it is little unimportant things which disturb the peace of the brethren, matters of law and procedure and precedent and prestige. A new age would dawn in the Church if we remembered that our rights are far less important than our obligations, if we remembered that, while we possess Christian liberty and freedom, it is always an offence to use that freedom as if it conferred upon us the right to grieve and hurt the heart and conscience of someone else. Unless a Church is a body of people who, in love, consider one another it is not a Church at all.

RESPECT FOR THE WEAKER BROTHER

Romans 14: 21-23

It is the fine thing neither to eat meat, nor to drink wine, nor to do anything which makes the road more difficult for your brother to walk. As far as you yourselves are concerned you have enough faith to know that these things do not matter—well, then, let that be a matter between yourself and God. Happy is the man who never has cause to condemn himself for doing what he has come to the conclusion it was right to do. But he who has doubts about eating something stands condemned if he does eat it, because his decision to eat is not the result of faith.

ONCE again we are back at the point that what is right for one man may be the ruin of another man. Paul's advice is very practical.

(i) He has advice for the man who is strong in the faith. The man who is strong in the faith knows that food and drink make no difference. He has grasped the principle of Christian freedom. Well, then, let that freedom be something between him and God. He has reached this stage of faith; and God knows well that he has reached it. But that is no reason why he should flaunt this freedom in the face of the man who has not yet reached it. Many a man has insisted on the rights of his freedom, and then has had cause to regret that he ever did so when he sees the consequences of it. A man may come to the conclusion that his Christian freedom gives him a perfect right to make a reasonable use of alcohol; and, as far as he is concerned, it may be a perfectly safe pleasure, from which he runs no danger. But it may be that a younger man who admires him is watching him and taking him as an example. And it may also be that this younger man is one of these people to whom alcohol is a fatal thing, and whom a very little of it affects very adversely. Is the older man to use his Christian freedom to go on setting an example which may well be the ruin of the younger admirer? Or is he to limit himself, not for his own sake,

but for the sake of the one who follows in his footsteps?
Surely, the conscious limitation for the sake of others is
the Christian thing. If a man does not exercise it, he may
well find that something that he genuinely thought to
be permissible and right has brought ruin to someone else !
It is surely better to make this deliberate limitation than
to have the remorse of knowing that what one demanded
as a pleasure has become death to someone else. Again
and again, in every sphere of life, the Christian is confronted with the fact that he must examine things, not
only as they affect himself, but also as they affect other
people. A man is always in some sense his brother's keeper.
He is responsible, not only for himself, but for everyone
who comes into contact with him. " His friendship did
me a mischief," said Burns of the older man he met in
Irvine as he learned the art of flax-dressing. God grant
that none may say that of us because we misused the glory
of Christian freedom!

(ii) Paul has advice for the man who is weak in the
faith, the man with the scrupulous conscience. It may
be that this man may disobey or silence his scruples. He
may sometimes do something because everyone else is
doing it. He may do it because he does not wish to stand
in a minority of one. He may do it because he does not
wish to be different. He may do it because he does not
wish to court ridicule or unpopularity. Paul's answer is
that if, for any of these reasons, a man defies his conscience
he is guilty of sin. If a man in his heart of hearts believes
a thing to be wrong, if he cannot rid himself of the iner-
adicable feeling that it is forbidden, then, if he does it,
for him it is sin. A neutral thing only becomes a right thing
when it is done out of faith, out of the real, reasoned
conviction that it is the right thing to do. The only motive
for doing anything is that a man believes it to be right.
When a thing is done out of social convention, out of fear
of unpopularity, to please men then it is wrong. No man
is the keeper of another man's conscience, and each man's

conscience, in things indifferent, must be the arbiter for that man of what is right or wrong.

THE MARKS OF THE FELLOWSHIP

Romans 15: 1-6

It is the duty of us who are strong to bear the weaknesses of those who are not strong, and not to please ourselves. Let each one of us please our neighbour, but always for his good and always for his upbuilding in the faith. For the Anointed One of God did not please Himself, but, as it stands written, " The insults of those who were insulting you fell upon me." All the things that were written long ago were written to teach us, so that, through our fortitude, and through the encouragement which the scriptures give, we may hold fast to our hope. May the God who inspires us with fortitude, and gives us encouragement, grant to you to live in harmony with one another as Christ Jesus would have you to do, so that your praise to the God and Father of our Lord Jesus Christ may rise from a united heart and a united voice.

PAUL is still dealing with the duties of those within the Christian fellowship to one another, and especially with the duty of the stronger to the weaker brother. This passage gives us a wonderful summary of the marks which should characterize the Christian fellowship.

(i) The Christian fellowship should be marked by the *consideration* of its members for each other. Always their thoughts should be, not for themselves, but for each other. But it is to be noted that this consideration must not degenerate into an easy-going, sentimental, pliable laxity. It must always be designed for the other person's good, and for his upbuilding in the faith. It is not the toleration which tolerates because it is too lazy to do anything else. It is the toleration which knows that a man may be won much more easily to a fuller faith by surrounding him with an atmosphere of love than by attacking him with a battery of criticism.

(ii) The Christian fellowship should be marked by the
study of scripture; and from that study of scripture the
Christian draws *encouragement*. Scripture, from this point
of view, provides us with two things. (*a*) It gives us the
record of God's dealing with a nation, a record which is
the demonstration that it is always better to be right with
God and to suffer, than to be wrong with men and to avoid
trouble. The history of Israel is the demonstration in
the events of history that ultimately it is well with good
and evil with the wicked. Scripture demonstrates, not
that God's way is ever an easy way, but in the end it is
the only way to everything that makes life worth while
in time and in eternity. (*b*) It gives us the great and
precious promises of God. It is said that Alexander Whyte
sometimes had a habit of uttering one text when he left
some home during his pastoral visitation; and, as he
uttered it, he would say: " Put that under your tongue
and suck it like a sweetie." These promises are the promises
of a God who never breaks His word. They are tremendous
things to go out to meet life along with. In these ways
scripture gives to the man who studies it comfort in his
sorrow and encouragement in his struggle.

(iii) The Christian fellowship should be marked by
fortitude. Fortitude is an attitude of the heart to life.
Again, and in the New Testament, we meet this great
word *hupomonē*. It is far more than patience; it is the
triumphant adequacy which can cope with life, the strength
which does not only accept things, but which, in accepting
them, transmutes them into glory.

(iv) The Christian fellowship should be marked by
hope. A Christian is always a realist, but never a pessimist.
The Christian hope is not a cheap hope. The Christian
hope is not the immature hope which is optimistic because
it does not see the difficulties and has not encountered
the experiences of life. It might be thought that hope
is the prerogative of the young; but the great artists
did not think that. When Watts drew " Hope " he drew

her as a battered and bowed figure with one string left upon her lyre. The Christian hope is the hope which has seen everything and endured everything, and still has not despaired, because it believes in God. The Christian hope is not hope in the human spirit, in human goodness, in human endurance, in human achievement; the Christian hope is hope in the power of God.

(v) The Christian fellowship should be marked by *harmony*. However ornate a church may be, however perfect its worship and its music, however liberal its giving, it has lost the very first essential of a Christian fellowship if it has lost harmony. That is not to say that there will not be differences of opinion; it is not to say that there will be no argument and debate; but it will mean that those who are within the Christian fellowship will have solved the problem of living together. They will be quite sure that the Christ who unites them is greater by far than the differences which may divide them.

(vi) The Christian fellowship should be marked by *praise*. It is no bad test of a man to ask whether the main accent of his voice is that of grumbling discontent or cheerful thanksgiving. "What can I do, who am a little old lame man," said Epictetus, "except give praise to God?" The Christian should enjoy life because he enjoys God. He will carry his secret within him, for he will be sure that God is working all things together for good.

(vii) And the whole essence of the matter is that the Christian fellowship takes its pattern and its example, its inspiration and dynamic, from Jesus Christ. He did not please Himself. The quotation which Paul uses is from Psalm 69: 10. It is significant that when Paul speaks of *bearing* the weaknesses of others he uses the same word as is used of Christ bearing His Cross (*bastazein*). When the Lord of Glory chose to serve others instead of to please Himself, He set the pattern which every one who seeks to be His follower must accept.

THE INCLUSIVE CHURCH

Romans 15: 7-13

> So, then, welcome one another as Christ welcomed
> you, that God may be praised. What I mean is this—
> Christ became a servant of the Jewish race and way
> of life for the sake of God's truth, not only to guarantee
> the promises which the fathers received, but also
> that the Gentiles should praise God for His mercy.
> As it stands written: " Therefore I will offer praise
> to God among the Gentiles and I will sing to your
> name." And, again it says: " Rejoice, O Gentiles
> with His people." And, again: " Praise the Lord,
> all you Gentiles, and let all the peoples praise Him."
> And again Isaiah says: " There shall live the scion
> of Jesse, even He who rises up to rule the Gentiles;
> in Him the Gentiles set their hopes." May the God
> of hope fill you with all joy and peace in your faith,
> so that by the power of the Holy Spirit, you may
> overflow with hope.

HERE Paul makes one last appeal that all people within
the Church should be bound into one, that those who are
weak in the faith, and those who are strong in the faith,
should be one united body, that Jew and Gentile should
find a common fellowship in the family of the Church.
There may be many differences but there is only one Christ,
and the bond of unity is a common loyalty to Him. Christ's
work was for Jew and Gentile alike. He was born a Jew;
He was subject to the Jewish law; He came into the world
as a member of the Jewish race. He did that that all the
great promises which were given to the fathers of the Jewish
race might come true, and that salvation might come
first to the Jew. But He came, not only for the Jew, but
for the Gentile also. To prove that that is not his own novel
and heretical idea Paul cites four passages from the Old
Testament; he cites them from the Septuagint, which is
the Greek version of the Old Testament, and that is why
they vary from the translation of the Old Testament as
we know it. The passages which Paul cites are Psalm
18: 50; Deuteronomy 32: 43; Psalm 117: 1; Isaiah 11: 10.

In all these passages Paul finds ancient forecasts of the reception of the Gentiles into the faith. It is Paul's conviction that, just as Jesus Christ came into this world to save all men, so the Church must welcome all men, no matter what the differences may be. Christ was an inclusive Saviour, and therefore His Church must be an inclusive Church.

Then Paul once again goes on to sound the notes of the Christian faith. We must see how the great words of the Christian faith flash out one after another in this passage.

(i) There is *hope*. It is easy in the light of experience to despair of oneself. It is easy in the light of events to despair of the world. It is easy to drift into a cynical acceptance of a hopeless situation, or a defeated resignation that neither men nor the world will ever be better. Someone tells of a meeting in a certain church at a time of emergency. The meeting was constituted with prayer by the chairman. He addressed God as " Almighty and eternal God, whose grace is sufficient for all things." He used the usual phrases that all men use in prayer. Then when the prayer was finished the business part of the meeting began; and the chairman who had just prayed introduced the business by saying: "Gentlemen, the situation in this Church is completely hopeless, and nothing can be done." Either the prayer was composed of empty and meaningless words, or that statement was untrue. It has long ago been said that there are no hopeless situations; there are only men who have grown hopeless about them. It is told that there was a cabinet meeting in the darkest days of the war, just after France had capitulated. Mr. Churchill, as he then was, outlined the situation in its starkest colours. Quite literally, Britain stood alone. There was a silence when he had finished speaking, and on the faces of some there was written despair, and there were some who would have given up the struggle. Mr. Churchill was silent for a moment; then he looked round that dispirited company. "Gentlemen," he said, " I find it rather inspiring." There is something in Christian hope that nothing can kill, that not all the shadows can quench—and that something is the conviction that God is still alive. No man is hopeless so long as there is such a thing as the grace of Jesus Christ; and no situation is hopeless so long as there is such a thing as the power of God.

(ii) There is *joy*. There is all the difference in this world between pleasure and joy. The Cynic philosophers in the ancient days declared that pleasure was the unmitigated evil. Anthisthenes made the queer statement that he would "rather be mad than pleased." Their argument was that "pleasure is only the pause between two pains." You have some longing for something; that is the pain; you get it; the longing is satisfied and there is a pause in the pain; you enjoy it and the moment is gone; and the pain comes back again. And, in truth, that is the way that pleasure works. But the Christian joy is not dependent on things outside a man; its source is in the man, not in the circumstances. It comes from the consciousness of the living presence of the living Lord, the certainty that nothing can separate us from the love of God in Him.

(iii) There is *peace*. The ancient philosophers sought for what they called *ataraxia*, the untroubled life. They wanted above all serenity, that serenity which is proof alike against the shattering blows and the petty pinpricks of this life. One would almost say that to-day serenity is a lost possession. There are two things which make serenity impossible. (*a*) There is the *inner tension*. Men live a distracted life, for the word *distract* literally means *to pull apart*. So long as a man is a walking civil war, so long as he himself is a battleground, so long as he is a split personality, there can obviously be no such thing as serenity. There is only one way out of this, and that is for self to abdicate to Christ. When Christ controls the tension is gone. (*b*) There is *worry about external things*. There are many who are haunted by the chances and the changes of life. H. G. Wells tells how in New York harbour

he was once on a liner. It was foggy, and suddenly out
of the fog there loomed another liner, and the two ships
slid past each other with only yards to spare. He was
suddenly face to face with what he called the general
large dangerousness of life. It is hard not to worry, for
man is characteristically a creature who looks forward
to guess and fear. The only end to that worry is the utter
conviction that, whatever happens, God's hand will never
cause His child a needless tear. Things will happen that
we cannot understand, but if we are sure enough of love,
we can accept with serenity even those things which
wound the heart and baffle the mind.

(iv) There is *power*. Here is the supreme need of men.
It is not that we do not know the right thing; it is not
that we do not recognize the fine thing; the trouble is
to do it. The trouble is to cope with and to conquer things,
to make what Wells called " the secret splendour of our
intentions " into actual facts in life. That we can never
do alone. Only when the surge of the power of Christ
fills the weakness of man can we master life as we ought
to master it. By ourselves we can do nothing; but with
God all things are possible.

THE WORDS REVEAL THE MAN

Romans 15: 14-21

Brothers, I myself am quite sure that you, as you
are, are full of goodness and replete with all knowledge
and well able to give good advice to one another.
I write to you with a certain amount of boldness, as
it were, with the purpose of reminding you of what
you already know. My ground for doing so is the
God-given grace which made me the servant of Christ
Jesus to the Gentiles, and gave me the sacred task
of telling the good news, and my aim in doing so is
to make the Gentiles an offering acceptable to God,
an offering consecrated by the Holy Spirit. Now,
in Christ, I have good reason to take a legitimate
pride in my work in God's service. I can say this

for I will not venture to speak of anything other than
the things which Christ has wrought in me, by word
and deed, by the power of signs and wonders, and
by the power of the Holy Spirit, to bring the Gentiles
into obedience to Him. Thus from Jerusalem right
round to Illyricum, I have completed the announcing
of the good news of God's Anointed One. But it
has always been my ambition to announce the good
news, not where Christ's name has already been
preached, because I want to avoid building on another
man's foundation, but as it stands written: "Those
to whom the good news has not been told shall see;
and those who have not heard will understand."

THERE are few passages which reveal Paul's character
better than this. He is coming to the end of his letter,
and he is wishing to prepare the ground for the visit that
he hopes soon to pay to Rome. When we read this passage
we see something at least of Paul's secret in winning men.

(i) Paul reveals himself as *a man of tact*. There is no
angry rebuke here. He does not nag the brethren at Rome,
nor does he speak to them like some angry schoolmaster.
He tells them that he is only reminding them of what
they well knew, and he assures them that he is certain
that they have it in them to render outstanding service
to each other and to their Lord. Paul was much more
interested in what a man could be than in what a man was.
Paul saw faults with utter clarity; and he dealt with faults
with utter fidelity; but all the time he was thinking,
not of the wretched creature that a man was, but of the
splendid creature that he might be. It is told that once
when Michael Angelo began to carve a huge and shapeless
block of marble, he said that his aim was to release the
angel imprisoned in the stone. Out of the shapeless mass
he wrought the angel that his eye saw there. Paul was
like that. He did not want to knock a man down and
out; he did not criticize to cause hurt and pain; he spoke
with honesty and with severity, but he always spoke
because he wished to enable a man to be what he could be,
and had never yet attained to being.

(ii) The only glory that Paul claimed was that he was *the servant of Christ.* The word he uses (*leitourgos*) is a great word. In ancient Greece there were certain state duties called *liturgies* (*leitourgiai*) which were sometimes laid upon and sometimes voluntarily shouldered by men who loved their country. There were five of these voluntary services which patriotic citizens used to undertake. (*a*) There was *chorēgia,* which was the duty of supplying a chorus. When Aeschylus and Sophocles and Euripides were producing their immortal dramas, in each of them a verse-speaking chorus was necessary. There were great festivals like the City Dionysia when as many as eighteen new dramatic works would be performed. Men who loved their city would volunteer to collect, maintain, instruct and equip such a chorus at their own expense. (*b*) There was *gumnasiarchia.* The Athenians were divided into ten tribes; and they were great athletes. At certain of the great festivals there were the famous torch-races in which teams from the various tribes raced against each other. We still speak of *handing on the torch.* To win the torch-race was a great honour, and there were public-spirited men who at their own cost would select and support and train a team to represent their tribe. (*c*) There was *hestiasis.* There were occasions when the tribes met together to share in a common meal and a common rejoicing; and there were generous men who undertook the task of meeting the expense of such a gathering. (*d*) There was *archetheōria.* Sometimes the city of Athens sent an embassy to another city or to consult the oracle at Delphi or Dodona. On such an occasion everything had to be done in such a way that the honour of the city was maintained; and there were patriotic men who voluntarily defrayed the expenses of such an embassy. (*e*) There was *triērarchia.* The Athenians were the great naval power of the ancient world. And one of the most patriotic things that a man could do was voluntarily to undertake the expenses of maintaining a trireme or warship for a whole year. That the background of this word *leitourgos*. In later days such liturgies became compulsory and not voluntary as patriotism died. Later the word came to be used of any kind of service; and later still it came to be used especially of worship and service rendered in the temple of the gods. But the word always had this background of generous service to it. Just as a man in the ancient days laid his fortune on the altar of the service of his beloved Athens, and counted it his only glory, so Paul laid his everything on the altar of the service of Christ, and was proud to be the servant of his Master.

(iii) Paul saw himself, in the scheme of things, as *an instrument in the hands of Christ*. He did not talk of what he had done; but of what Christ had done with him. He never said of anything: " I did it." He always said: " Christ used me to do it." It is told that the change in the life of D. L. Moody came when he went to a meeting and heard a preacher say: " If only one man would give himself entirely and without reserve to the Holy Spirit, what that Spirit might do with him! " Moody said to himself: " Why should I not be that man? " And all the world knows what the Spirit of God did with D. L. Moody. It is when a man ceases to think what he can do and begins to think of what God can do with him that things begin to happen.

(iv) Paul's one ambition was to be *a pioneer*. It is told that when Livingstone volunteered as a missionary with the London Missionary Society they asked him where he would like to go. " Anywhere " he said, " so long as it is forward." And when he reached Africa he was haunted by the smoke of a thousand villages which he saw in the distance. It was Paul's one ambition to carry the good news of God to men who had never heard it. He takes a text from Isaiah 52: 15 to tell his aim.

> " Ye armies of the living God,
>   His sacramental host,
>   Where hallowed footsteps never trod,
>   Take your appointed post."

PLANS PRESENT AND FUTURE

Romans 15: 22-29

> And that is why on many occasions I found the way
> to come to you blocked. But now, since I have no
> longer a sphere for work in these areas, and since for
> many years back I have had a great desire to come to
> you, when I shall go to Spain, I hope to see you on
> my way through; and, I hope, after I have first
> enjoyed your company for a while, to be sped on
> my way by you. But at the moment I am on my way
> to Jerusalem, to render some service to God's dedicated
> people there. For Macedonia and Achaea resolved
> to make a contribution to the poor among God's
> dedicated people in Jerusalem. For that was their
> resolve and indeed they owe a debt to them. For if
> the Gentiles have received a share in spiritual blessings,
> they also owe a debt to render service to them in
> material things. When I have completed this business,
> and when I have duly delivered the gifts to them
> intact, I will leave for Spain by way of you. I know
> that when I do come to you, I will come bringing
> a full blessing from Christ.

HERE we have Paul telling of an immediate and of a future
plan.

(i) His future plan was to go to Spain. There were two
reasons why Paul should wish to go to Spain. First, Spain
was at the very western end of Europe. It was in one sense
the then limit of the civilized world, and the very fact
that it was such would lure Paul on to preach there. He
would characteristically wish to take the good news of
God so far that he could not take it farther.

(ii) At this time Spain was experiencing a kind of blaze
of genius. Many of the greatest men in the Empire were
Spaniards. Lucan, the epic poet, Martial, the master of the
epigram, Quintilian, the greatest teacher of oratory of
his day were all Spaniards. And, above all, Seneca, the
great Stoic philosopher, and, first, the guardian and,
afterwards, the prime minister of Nero, the Roman Emperor,
was a Spaniard. It may well be that Paul was saying to

himself that if only he could touch this land of Spain for Christ tremendous things might happen.

(iii) Paul's immediate plan was to go to Jerusalem. Paul had had a plan which was very dear to his heart. He had arranged for a collection to be taken from his young Churches for the poor in the Church of Jerusalem. There is no doubt that that collection would be necessary. In a city like Jerusalem much of the available employment must have been connected with the Temple and the needs of the Temple. All the priests and the Temple authorities were Sadducees, and the Sadducees were the supreme enemies of Jesus. It must therefore have happened that many a man, when he became a Christian in Jerusalem, lost his job and was in sore need. The help the younger Churches could give was much needed. But there were at least three other great reasons why Paul was so eager to take this gift to Jerusalem. (*a*) For him himself it was the payment of a debt and a duty. When it had been agreed that Paul should be the apostle to the Gentiles, one injunction had been laid upon him by the leaders of the Church—that he would remember the poor (Galatians 2: 10). " That," said Paul, " I was eager and willing to do," and Paul was not the man to break a promise or to forget a debt, and now that debt was about to be paid, at least in part. (*b*) There was no better way of demonstrating in the most practical way the unity of the Church. This was a way of teaching the young Churches that they were not isolated units, but members of a great Church throughout all the world. The great value of giving to others is that it makes us remember that we are not members of a congregation but of a Church which is as wide as the world. (*c*) There was no better way of putting Christianity into practical action. It was easy enough to talk about Christian generosity and to preach about it; here was a chance to turn Christian words into Christian deeds.

So Paul is on the way to Jerusalem, and he is planning a

journey to Spain. As far as we know Paul never got to
Spain, for in Jerusalem he encountered the trouble which
led to his long imprisonment and his death. It would
seem that this was one plan of the great pioneer which
never was worked out.

OPEN-EYED INTO DANGER

Romans 15: 30-33

> Brothers, I call upon you by the Lord Jesus Christ,
> and by the love of the Spirit, to strive along with me
> in prayer to God for me; for I need your prayers
> that I may be rescued from those in Jerusalem who
> do not believe, and that the help that I am bringing
> to Jerusalem may prove acceptable to God's dedicated
> people there. I want you to pray that by God's will
> I may come to you with joy, and enjoy a time of
> rest with you. The God of peace be with you all.
> Amen.

WE came to the end of the last passage by saying that as
far as we know Paul's plans to go to Spain were never
realized. We know for a certainty that when Paul did
go to Jerusalem he was arrested there and spent the next
four years in prison, two of them in Caesarea and two in
Rome. Here again Paul's great character comes out.

(i) When Paul went to Jerusalem he knew what he
was doing. He was well aware of the dangers that lay
ahead. He knew he was going into the lion's den and
putting himself into the power of those who hated him.
Just as his Master steadfastly set His face to go to Jerusalem (Luke 9: 51) so also did Paul. The highest courage
is to know that something perilous awaits us and still
to go on. That is the courage that Jesus showed; that
is the courage that Paul showed; and that is the courage
that all Christ's followers must show.

(ii) In such a situation Paul asked for the prayers of
the Christian Church at Rome. It is a great thing to go
on knowing that we are wrapped in the warmth of the

prayers of those who love us. However far we are separated from those we love, in whatever dangers they may be, we and they can meet around the mercy-seat of God.

(iii) Paul leaves them his blessing as he goes. It was no doubt all that Paul had to give. Even when we have nothing else we can still bear our friends and loved ones in prayer to God.

(iv) It was the blessing of the God of peace that Paul sent to Rome and it was with the presence of the God of peace he himself went to Jerusalem with all its threats. The man who has the peace of God in his heart can meet all life's perils unafraid.

A LETTER OF COMMENDATION

Romans 16: 1, 2

> I commend to you our sister Phoebe, who is a servant of the Church which is in Cenchreae. I want you to welcome her in the Lord in the way that God's people should welcome one another; and I want you to help her in whatever way she needs your help, for she had been a helper to many, and to me too.

WHEN a person is applying for a new job or a new position he usually gets a reference or a testimonial from someone who knows him well and who can pay tribute to his character and ability. When a person is going to live in some strange town he often takes with him a letter of introduction from someone who knows people in that town. In the ancient world such letters were very common. They were known as *sustatikai epistolai*, letters of commendation or introduction. We still possess many of these letters written on papyrus, and recovered from the rubbish heaps buried in the desert sands of Egypt. A certain Mystarion, an Egyptian olive-planter, sends his servant on an errand to Stotoetis, a chief priest, and gives him a letter of introduction to take with him.

Mystarion to his own Stotoetis, many greetings.

I have sent my Blastus to you for forked sticks for my olive-gardens.

See then that you do not detain him, for you know how I need him every hour.

To Stotoetis, chief priest at the island.

That is a letter of commendation to introduce the Blastus who has gone upon the errand. So Paul writes to introduce Phoebe to the Church at Rome.

Phoebe came from Cenchreae which was the port of Corinth. Sometimes she is called a *deaconess*, but it is not likely that she held what might be called an official position in the Church. There can have been no time in the Christian Church when the work of women was not of infinite value. It must have been specially so in the days of the early Church. In the case of baptism by total immersion, as it then was, in the visitation of the sick, in the distribution of food to the poor, women must have played a big part in the life and work of the Church, but they did not at that time hold any official position.

Paul bespeaks a welcome for Phoebe in the Roman Church. He asks the people at Rome to welcome her as God's dedicated people ought to welcome each other. There should be no strangers in the family of Christ; there should be no need for formal introductions between Christian people, for surely they are sons and daughters of the one father, and therefore brothers and sisters of each other. And yet a Church is not always the welcoming institution that it ought to be. It is possible for Churches, and still more possible for Church organizations, to become little cliques, almost little closed societies which are not really interested in welcoming the stranger. When a stranger comes amongst us, Paul's advice still holds good—welcome such a one as God's dedicated people ought to welcome each other.

A HOUSEHOLD WHICH WAS A CHURCH

Romans 16: 3, 4

> Give my greetings to Prisca and to Aquila, my fellow-workers in Christ Jesus, who risked their own necks to save my life. It is not only I who have cause to be thankful to them, but all the Churches of the Gentiles; and give my greetings to the Church that is in their house.

THERE is no more fascinating pair of people in the New Testament than Prisca and Aquila. Sometimes Prisca is also called Priscilla which is an affectionate diminutive form of her name. Let us begin with the facts about them of which we are sure.

They appear first in Acts 18: 2. From that passage we learn that they had previously been resident in Rome. Claudius had issued an edict in A.D. 52 banishing the Jews from Rome. Anti-semitism is no new thing, and the Jews were hated in the ancient world as they so often are to-day. When the Jews had been banished from Rome, Prisca and Aquila had settled in Corinth. They were tent-makers which was Paul's own trade, and he had found a home with them. When Paul left Corinth and went to Ephesus, Prisca and Aquila went with him and settled there (Acts 18: 18). The very first incident which is related of them is characteristic of them. There came to Ephesus that brilliant scholar Apollos; but Apollos had not at this time anything like a full grasp and appreciation of the Christian faith; so Aquila and Prisca took him into their house and gave him friendship and instruction in the Christian faith (Acts 18: 24-26). From the very beginning Prisca and Aquila were people who kept an open heart and an open door.

The next time we hear of them they are still in Ephesus. Paul wrote his first letter to the Corinthians from Ephesus and in it he sends greetings from Prisca and Aquila and from the Church that is in their house (I Corinthians 16: 19). This was long before the days when there was any such thing as a church building; and the home of Prisca and Aquila served as a meeting place for a group of Christian folk. The next time we hear of them they are here in Rome. The edict of Claudius which had banished the Jews had ceased to be effective and no doubt Prisca and Aquila and many another Jew drifted back to their old homes and their old business. And once again we discover that they are just the same—again there is a Church, a group of Christian people, meeting in their house. Once again, for the last time, they emerge in 2 Timothy 4: 19, and once again they are in Ephesus; and one of the last messages that Paul ever sent was a message of greeting to this pair of Christians who had come through so much with him.

Prisca and Aquila lived a curiously nomadic and unsettled life. Aquila himself had been born in Pontus in Asia Minor (Acts 18: 2). We find them resident first in Rome, then in Corinth, then in Ephesus, then back in Rome, and then finally back in Ephesus; but wherever we find them, we find that their home is a centre of Christian fellowship and service. Every home should be a Church, for a Church is a place where Jesus dwells. From the home of Prisca and Aquila, wherever they were, there radiated friendship and fellowship and love. If anyone is a stranger in a strange town or a strange land, one of the most valuable things in the world is to have a home from home into which to go. Such a home takes away loneliness and protects from temptation. Sometimes we think of a home as a place with a shut door, a place into which we can go and shut the door and keep the world out: but equally a home should be a place with an open door. The open door, the open hand, and the open heart are the characteristics of the Christian life.

So much is certain about Prisca and Aquila; but it may be that there is even a greater romance in their story. To this day in Rome there is a Church of St. Prisca on the Aventine. There is also a cemetery of Priscilla. Now this cemetery is the burying place of the ancient Roman family known as the Acilian family. In it there lies buried Acilius Glabrio. Acilius Glabrio was consul of Rome in A.D. 91 and that was the highest office which Rome could offer him; and it seems extremely likely that Acilius Glabrio died a martyr's death as a Christian. He must have been one of the first of the great Romans to become a Christian and to suffer for his faith. Now when people received their freedom in the Roman Empire they were enrolled in one of the great families and they took one of the family names as their name. One of the commonest female names in the Acilian family was Prisca; and Acilius is sometimes written Aquilius, which is very close to Aquila. Here we are faced with two fascinating possibilities.

(i) Perhaps Prisca and Aquila received their freedom from some member of the Acilian family, in which it may be that once they were slaves. Can it be that these two people sowed the seeds of Christianity into that family so that one day a member of it—Acilius Glabrio, no less a person than a Roman consul—became a Christian? Can it be that Christianity reached the highest person in the Roman state because Prisca and Aquila first brought it to the family from which he sprang?

(ii) There is an even more romantic possibility. It is an odd thing that in four out of the six mentions of this pair in the New Testament Prisca is named *before* her husband. Normally the husband's name would come first; we say " Mr. and Mrs." But in this case Prisca's name regularly comes before her husband's name. There is just the possibility that that is so because Prisca herself was not a freedwoman at all, but a great lady, actually a member by birth of the Acilian family. It may be that at some meeting of the Christians this great Roman lady met Aquila the humble Jewish tentmaker, that the two fell in love, that Christianity destroyed the barriers of race and rank and wealth and birth, and that these two, the

Roman aristocrat and the Jewish artisan, were joined for ever in Christian love and Christian service.

Of these speculations we can never be sure, but we can be sure that there were many in Corinth, in Ephesus and in Rome who owed their souls to Prisca and Aquila and to that home which was also a Church.

TO EVERY NAME A COMMENDATION

Romans 16: 5-11

> Give my greetings to my beloved Epaenetus, who was the first convert to Christ in Asia.
> Give my greetings to Mary who has toiled hard among you.
> Give my greetings to Andronicus and Junias, my kinsmen and my fellow-prisoners. They are of high mark among the apostles, and they were Christians before I was.
> Give my greetings to Ampliatus, my beloved in the Lord.
> Give my greetings to Urbanus, our fellow-worker in Christ, and to my beloved Stachys.
> Give my greetings to Apelles, a man of sterling worth in Christ.
> Give my greetings to those who are of the household of Aristobulus.
> Give my greetings to Herodion, my kinsman.
> Give my greetings to those of the household of Narcissus who are in the Lord.

No doubt behind every one of these names there is a story which is a romance in Christ. None of these stories do we know, but at some of them we can guess and speculate. In this chapter there are twenty-four individual names. There are two interesting things to note.

(i) Of the twenty-four, six are women. That is worth remembering, for often Paul is accused of belittling the status of women in the Church. If we really wish to see Paul's attitude to women in the Church it is a passage like this that we should read, where his appreciation of the work that they were doing in the Church shines and glows through his words.

(ii) Of the twenty-four names, thirteen occur in inscriptions or documents which have to do with the imperial household and Emperor's palace in Rome. Many of them are very common names, but nonetheless that is suggestive. In Philippians 4: 22 Paul speaks of the saints that are of Caesar's household. It may be that they were for the most part slaves, but it is still important that Christianity seems to have penetrated even thus early into the imperial palace and the imperial household.

Andronicus and Junias form an interesting pair of names, because it is most likely that Junias is a female name. That would mean that in the early Church a woman could be ranked and honoured as an apostle. The apostles in this sense were people whom the Church sent out to tell the story of the gospel of Jesus at large. Paul says that Andronicus and Junias were Christians before he was. That means that they must go right back to the time of Stephen; they must have been a direct link with the earliest Church at Jerusalem.

Behind the name of Ampliatus there may well lie an interesting story. Ampliatus is a quite common slave name. Now in the cemetery of Domatilla, which is the earliest of the Christian catacombs, there is a decorated tomb with the single name *Ampliatus* carved on it in bold and decorative lettering. Now the fact that the single name *Ampliatus* alone is carved on the tomb—Romans who were citizens would have three names, a nomen, a praenomen, and a cognomen—would indicate that this Ampliatus was a slave; but the elaborate tomb and the bold lettering would indicate that he was a man of high rank in the Church. And from that it is plain to see that in the early days of the Church the distinctions of rank and place were so completely wiped out that it was possible for a man at one and the same time to be a slave and a prince of the Church. Social distinctions did not exist.

We have no means of knowing that Paul's Ampliatus is the Ampliatus of the tomb in the cemetery of Domatilla, but it is not impossible that he is.

The household of Aristobulus may also be a phrase with an interesting history behind it. In Rome the word *household* did not describe only a man's family and personal relations; it included also his servants and slaves, as we would say, his whole establishment. Now in Rome for long there had lived a grandson of Herod the Great whose name was Aristobulus. This Aristobulus had lived always as a private individual and had inherited none of Herod's domains; but he was a close friend of the Emperor Claudius. When he died his servants and slaves would pass into the possession of and become the property of the Emperor, but they would still form a section of the Emperor's establishment known as *the household of Aristobulus*. So this phrase may well describe Jewish servants and slaves who had once belonged to Aristobulus, Herod's grandson, and who had now become the property of the Emperor. This is made the more probable by the name that is mentioned on each side of this phrase. *Apelles* may quite well be the Greek name that a Jew called *Abel* would take, and *Herodion* is a name which would obviously suit one who had some connection with the family of Herod.

The household of Narcissus may have still another interesting story behind it. Narcissus was a common name; but the most famous Narcissus was a freedman who had been secretary to the Emperor Claudius and who had exercised a notorious influence over the Emperor. He was said to have amassed a private fortune of almost £4,000,000. His power had lain in the fact that all correspondence addressed to the Emperor had to pass through his hands and never reached the Emperor unless he allowed it to do so. He made his fortune from the fact that people paid him large bribes to make sure that their petitions and requests did reach the Emperor. When Claudius was murdered and Nero came to the throne, Narcissus survived for a short time, but in the end he was compelled to commit suicide, and all his fortune and all his household of slaves passed into the possession of Nero. It may well be his one-time slaves which are referred to here. If Aristobulus really is the Aristobulus who was the grandson of Herod, and if Narcissus really is the Narcissus who was Claduius' secretary, then this means that many of the slaves at the imperial court were already Christians. The leaven of Christianity had reached the highest circles in the Empire.

HIDDEN ROMANCES

Romans 16: 12-16

> Give my greetings to Tryphaena and Tryphosa who toil in the Lord.
> Give my greetings to Persis, the beloved, who has toiled hard in the Lord.
> Give my greetings to Rufus, chosen in the Lord, and to his mother who was a mother to me too.
> Give my greetings to Asyncritus, to Phlegon, to Hermes, to Patrobas, to Hermas, and to the brothers who are with them.
> Give my greetings to Philologos and to Julias, to Nereus and to his sister, to Olympas, and to all God's dedicated people who are with them.
> Greet each other with the kiss that God's dedicated people use.
> All the Churches of Christ send you greetings.

No doubt behind all these names there lies a story; but it is only about a few of them that we can guess and reconstruct.

(i) When Paul wrote his greetings to Tryphaena and Tryphosa—who were very likely twin sisters—he wrote them with a smile, for the way in which he put it sounds like a complete contradiction in terms. Three times in this list of greetings Paul uses a certain Greek word for Christian work and toil. He uses it of Mary (verse 6), and of Tryphaena and Tryphosa and of Persis in this passage. It is the verb *kopian*, and kopian means *to toil to the point of exhaustion*; it means to give to the work all that one has got; it means to work to the stage of utter weariness. That is what Paul said that Tryphaena and Tryphosa were in the habit of doing; and the point of it all is that the names *Tryphaena* and *Tryphosa* means respectively *dainty* and *delicate*! It is as if Paul said: " You two may be called *dainty* and *delicate*; but you belie your names by working like trojans for the sake of the Church and for Christ." We can well imagine a twinkle in Paul's eye and a smile passing across his face as he dictated that greeting.

(ii) There is one of the great hidden romances of the New Testament behind the name of Rufus and of his mother, who was also a mother to Paul. It is obvious that Rufus is a choice spirit and a man well-known for work and saintliness in the Roman Church; and it is equally obvious that Paul felt that he owed a deep debt of gratitude to the mother of Rufus for the kindness that he had received from her. Who was this Rufus? Turn back to Mark 15: 21. There we read of one Simon a Cyrenian who was compelled to carry the Cross of Jesus on the road to Calvary; and this Simon is described as the *father of Alexander and Rufus*. Now if a man is identified by the names of his sons, it means that, although he himself may not be personally known to the community to whom the story is being told, the sons are. To what Church did Mark write his gospel? Almost certainly he wrote it for the Church of Rome, and he knew that that Church would know who Alexander and Rufus were. And again almost certainly here we find Rufus again. He was the son of that Simon who carried the Cross of Jesus. That must have been a terrible day for Simon. He was a Jew; he came from far off Cyrene in North Africa. No doubt he had scraped and saved for half a lifetime to celebrate one Passover in Jerusalem. He came and as he entered

the city on that day with his heart full of the greatness
of the Feast which he was going to attend, suddenly the
flat of a Roman spear touched him on the shoulder; he
was impressed into the Roman service; he found himself
carrying a criminal's cross. How the resentment must
have blazed in his heart! How angry and bitter he must
have been at this terrible indignity! All the way from
Cyrene for this! To have come so far to sit at the glory
of the Passover and for this dreadful and shameful thing
to have happened! No doubt he meant, as soon as he
reached Calvary, to fling the cross down and to stride
away with loathing in his heart. But something must
have happened. On the way to Calvary the spell of this
broken figure must have laid its tendrils round his heart.
He must have stayed to watch, and that figure on the
Cross drew Simon to Himself for ever and for ever. The
chance encounter on the road to Calvary changed Simon's
life for ever. He came to sit at the Jewish Passover and
he went away the slave of Christ. He must have gone
home and he must have brought his wife and sons into
the same experience as he had himself. We can weave
all kinds of speculations about this. It was men from
Cyprus and Cyrene who came to Antioch and who first
preached the gospel to the Gentile world (Acts II: 20).
Was Simon one of the men from Cyrene? Was Rufus
with him? Was it they who took the first tremendous
step to make Christianity the faith of a whole world?
Was it they who helped the Church to burst the bonds of
Judaism in which it might have been fettered? Can it
be that in some sense we to-day owe the fact that we are
Christians to the strange episode when a man from Cyrene
was compelled to carry a cross on the road to Calvary?
Turn to Ephesus when there is a riot raised by the people
who served Diana of the Ephesians and when the crowd
would have lynched Paul if they could have got at him
Who stands out to look that mob in the face? A man
called Alexander (Acts I9: 33). Is this the other brother

facing things out with Paul? And as for their mother—
surely she in some hour of need must have brought to
Paul the help and the comfort and the love which his own
family refused him when he became a Christian. It may
be guess-work, for the names Alexander and Rufus are
common names; but maybe it is true and maybe the most
amazing things happened from that chance encounter on
the way to Calvary.

(iii) There remains one other name which may have a
perhaps even more amazing story behind it—the name
of Nereus. In A.D. 95 there happened an event which
shocked Rome. Two of the most distinguished people
in Rome were condemned for being Christians. They
were husband and wife. The husband was Flavius Clemens.
He had been consul of Rome. The wife was Domatilla
and she was of royal blood. She was the granddaughter
of Vespasian, a former Emperor, and the niece of Domitian
the reigning Emperor. In fact the two sons of Flavius
Clemens and Domatilla had been designated Domitian's
successors in the imperial power. Flavius was executed
and Domatilla was banished to the island of Pontia where
years afterwards Paula saw the cave where " she drew
out a long martyrdom for the Christian name." And
now the point—the name of the chamberlain of Flavius
and Domatilla was Nereus. Is it possible that Nereus
the slave had something to do with the making into
Christians of Flavius Clemens the ex-consul and Domatilla
the princess of the royal blood? Again maybe it is an idle
speculation, for Nereus is a common name, but again,
maybe it is true. There is one other fact of interest to
add to this story. Flavius Clemens was the son of Flavius
Sabinus. Now Flavius Sabinus, the father, had been
Nero's city prefect in the days when Nero had sadistically
persecuted the Christians after he had charged them with
being responsible for the appalling fire which had devastated
Rome in A.D. 64. As city prefect Flavius Sabinus must
have been Nero's executive officer in that persecution.

It was then that Nero ordered the Christians to be rolled in pitch and to be set alight to form living torches for his gardens, to be sewed into the skins of wild beasts and to be flung to savage hunting dogs, to be shut up in ships which were sunk in the Tiber. Is it possible that thirty years before he died for Christ, the young Flavius Clemens, as he must then have been, had seen the dauntless courage and the heroism of the martyrs, and had wondered what made men able to die like that?

Five verses of names and of greetings—but they open vistas which thrill the heart!

A LAST LOVING APPEAL

Romans 16: 17-20

Brothers, I urge you to keep your eye on those who, contrary to the teaching which they have received, cause dissensions and put in your way things which would trip you up. Steer clear of them. Such men are not real servants of Christ, our Lord; they are the servants of their own greed. By their plausibility and their flattery they deceive the hearts of innocent folk. I know that you will deal with such people, for the story of your obedience has reached all men. So, then, I rejoice over you. I want you to be wise in what is good, and untainted with what is evil. The God of peace will soon overthrow Satan so that you may trample him under your feet. The grace of the Lord Jesus Christ be with you.

ROMANS was a letter which Paul found it very difficult to bring to an end. He has sent his greetings; but before he closes he makes one last appeal to the Christians in Rome to keep themselves from every evil influence. Paul picks out two characteristics of the men who are hurtful to the Church and to the Christian fellowship.

(i) They are men who cause dissensions among the brethren. Any man who does anything which disturbs the peace of a Church has much to answer for. A minister

was once talking to a man newly come to his congregation
from another town. The man had very obviously little
of the love of Christ upon him. The man said to the
minister: " You know such and such a congregation? "
And he named the congregation of which he had formerly
been a member. " Yes," said the minister. " Well,"
said the man with a certain evil relish, "I wrecked it! "
There are people who take a pride in making trouble, and
who like nothing better than to sow the poisonous seeds
of dissension and to await the coming strife. The man who
is a disturber of the peace, the man who has brought strife
to any band of brothers will answer for it some day to
Him who is the King and Head of the Church.

(ii) They are men who put hindrances in the way of
others. The man who makes it harder for someone else
to be a Christian also has much to answer for. The man
whose conduct is a bad example, whose influence is an
evil snare, whose teaching dilutes or emasculates the
Christian faith which he pretends to teach, will someday
bear his own punishment; and it will not be light, for
Jesus was stern to any man who caused one of His little
ones to stumble.

There are two interesting words in this passage. There
is the word we have translated *plausibility* (*chrēstologia*).
The Greeks themselves defined a *chrēstologos* as " a man
who speaks well and who acts ill." He is the kind of man
who, behind a facade of pious and religious words, is a
bad influence, the man who leads astray, not by direct
attack, but by subtlety, the man who pretends to serve
Christ, but who in reality is destroying the faith. There is
the word which we have translated *untainted* with what
is evil. It is the word *akeraios*, and it is used of metal which
has no suspicion of alloy, of wine and of milk which are
pure and not adulterated with water. It describes something which is absolutely pure of any kind of taint or
corruption. The Christian is a man whose utter sincerity
must be beyond all question and all doubt.

One thing is to be noted in this passage—it is clear that the latent trouble in the Church at Rome has not yet flared out into action. Paul, indeed, says that he believes that the Roman Church is well able to deal with it. Paul was a wise pastor, because he believed firmly that prevention was better than cure. Often in a Church or a society a bad situation is allowed to develop because no one has the courage to deal with it; and often, when the situation has fully developed, it is too late to deal with it. It is easy enough to extinguish a spark if steps to do so are taken at once, but it is almost impossible to extinguish a forest fire. Paul had the wisdom to deal with a threatening situation in time.

The passage closes with a most suggestive thing. Paul says that the *God of peace* will soon crush and overthrow Satan, the power of evil. We must note that the peace of God is the peace of action, of conquest and of victory. There is a kind of peace which can be had at the cost of evading all issues, refusing all decisions, shutting the eyes to things that are crying out to be dealt with, a peace which comes of a lethargic inactivity and an avoidance of all decisive action. The Christian must ever remember that the peace of God is not the peace which has submitted to the world, but the peace which has overcome the world.

GREETINGS

Romans 16: 21-23

> Timothy, my fellow-worker, sends you his greetings, as do Lucius, Jason and Sosipater, my kinsmen. I Tertius, who wrote this letter, send you my greetings in the Lord. Gaius, whose hospitality I and the whole Church enjoy, sends you his greetings, as does brother Quartus.

It is tempting to try to identify the group of friends who send their greetings with the greeting of Paul. Timothy was Paul's right hand man, the man whom Paul saw as his successor, the man of whom Paul later said that no one knew his mind so well (Philippians 2: 19, 20). Lucius may be the Lucius of Cyrene, who was one of the prophets and teachers of Antioch who first sent Paul and Barnabas out on their missionary journeys (Acts 13: 1). Jason may be the Jason who gave Paul hospitality at Thessalonica and who suffered for it at the hands of the mob (Acts 17: 5-9). Sosipater may be the Sopater of Berea who took his Church's share of the collection to Jerusalem with Paul (Acts 20: 2). Gaius may be the Gaius who was one of the two people whom Paul himself baptized at Corinth (I Corinthians 1: 14).

For the first and only time we know the name of the secretary and amanuensis who actually penned this letter to Paul's dictation, for Tertius slipped in his own greeting. No great man can do his work without the help that humble helpers give him. Paul's other scribes and secretaries are anonymous, so Tertius is the representative of those humble unknowns who were penmen for Paul.

One of the most interesting things in this whole chapter is the way in which again and again Paul characterizes people in one single sentence. He has no space to say more, but again and again a single sentence sums up the people about whom he is writing. Here there are two great summaries. Gaius is the man of hospitality; Quartus in one word is the brother. It is a great thing to go down to history as the man with the open house and the man with the brotherly heart. Some day people will sum us up in one sentence. What will that sentence be?

THE END IS PRAISE

Romans 16: 25-27

Now unto Him who is able to make you stand firm, in the way that the gospel I preach promises and the message Jesus brought offers, in the way which is now unveiled in that secret, which was for long ages wrapped in silence, but which is now full-disclosed, and made known to all the Gentiles—as the writings of the prophets said it would be, and as the command of God now orders it to be—that they might render to Him a submission born of faith, to the only wise God, through Jesus Christ, be glory for ever. Amen.

So the letter to the Romans comes to an end with a doxology which is also a summary of the gospel. Here there sound out the notes of the gospel which Paul preached and loved.

(i) It is a gospel which makes men able to stand firm. " Son of man," said God to Ezekiel, " stand upon thy feet and I will speak to thee " (Ezekiel 2: 1). The gospel is that power which makes a man able to stand erect, foursquare against the shocks of the world and the assaults of temptation. A journalist relates a great incident of the Spanish Civil War. There was a little garrison of beleaguered men. The end was near and there were some who wished to submit and to surrender and so to save their lives; but there were others who wished to fight on. At last the matter was settled when a gallant soul declared: " It is better to die upon our feet than to live upon our knees." Life can be difficult; sometimes a man is beaten to his knees by the battering that life can give to him. Life can be perilous; sometimes a man is like to fall in the slippery places of temptation. The gospel is God's power unto salvation; it is that power which keeps a man safe, which makes him able to meet life erect, even when life is at its worst and its most threatening.

(ii) It is a gospel which Paul preached and which was offered by Jesus Christ. That is to say, the gospel takes its source in Christ, and is transmitted by men. Without Jesus Christ there can be no gospel at all; but without men to transmit that gospel, other men can never hear of it. The Christian duty is that a man should himself be found of Christ and should straightway go and find others for Him. When Jesus had found Andrew, John says of him: " He first findeth his own brother Simon, and saith unto him, ' We have found the Messiah ' " (John I: 40, 41). Here is the Christian privilege and the Christian duty. The Christian privilege is to appropriate the good news for ourselves; the Christian duty is to transmit that good news to others. There is a famous story which tells how Jesus, after the Cross and the Resurrection, returned to His glory, still bearing the marks of His sufferings. One of the angels said to Him, " You must have suffered terribly for men down there." " I did," said Jesus. " Do they all know about what you did for them? " asked the angel. " No," said Jesus, " not yet. Only a few know about it in Palestine so far." " And," said the angel, " what have you done that they should all know about it? " " Well," said Jesus, " I asked Peter and James and John to make it their business to tell others, and the others still others, until the farthest man on the widest circle has heard the story." The angel looked doubtful, for he knew well what poor creatures men were. " Yes," he said, " but what if Peter and James and John forget? What if they grow weary of the telling? What if, away down in the twentieth century, men fail to tell the story of your love for them? What then? Haven't you made any other plans? " And back came the answer of Jesus, " I haven't made any other plans. *I'm counting on them.*" Jesus died to give us the gospel; and now He is counting on us to transmit it to all men.

(iii) It is a gospel which is the consummation of history. It is something which was there from all ages and which at the coming of Christ was revealed to the world. With the coming of Jesus something unique happened. With His coming eternity invaded time. With His coming God emerged on earth. His coming was the hinge of history. It was the event to which all history was working up; and it is the event from which all subsequent history flows. The plain fact is that after the coming of Christ the world could never be the same again. Something happened which cannot be disregarded. The coming of Jesus was the central fact of history, so that, indeed, men count all time from the time before Christ came, and the time after He came. It is as if with His coming life and the world began all over again.

(iv) It is a gospel which is meant for *all* men, and which was *always* meant for all men. It was not a gospel which was meant for the Jews; the going out of the gospel to the Gentiles was not an afterthought. The prophets, maybe scarce knowing what they were saying, had their hints and their forecasts of a time when all men of all nations would know God. That time is not yet; but it is the dream of God that some day the knowledge of God will cover the earth as the waters cover the sea, and it is the glory of man that he can help to make God's dream come true.

(v) It is a gospel which issues in an obedient world, a world where God is King. But that obedience is not an obedience which is founded on submission to an iron law, which breaks the man who opposes it; it is an obedience founded on faith, on utter trust, on complete yieldedness; it is founded on a surrender which is the result of love. It is the obedience which comes from the heart which can do no other than surrender itself in love to the love that loved it like that. For Paul the Christian is not a man who has surrendered to an ineluctable power; he is a man who has fallen in love with the God who is the lover of the souls of men, and whose love stands for ever full-displayed in Jesus Christ.

And so the long argument of the letter to the Romans comes to an end in a song of praise.